Genetic Algorithms with Python

Clinton Sheppard

First Printing: 2016

ISBN-13: 978-1540324009

ISBN-10: 1540324001

OCLC Number: 994749408

```
Clinton Sheppard <fluentcoder@gmail.com>
Austin, Texas, USA
www.cs.unm.edu/~sheppard
Twitter: @gar3t
Goodreads: https://www.goodreads.com/handcraftsman
```

The final code from each project is available in the appendix and at https://github.com/handcraftsman/GeneticAlgorithmsWithPython, licensed under the Apache License, Version 2.0 (https://www.apache.org/licenses/LICENSE-2.0).

The text of this book was written in AsciiDoc and converted to LaTeX using AsciiDoctor 1.5.8. The code was written and tested using JetBrains' PyCharm IDE for Python. Some images were produced using GraphViz and Paint.Net. The fonts are Liberation Serif v2.00.1, M+ MN Type-1, and FontAwesome icons included by AsciiDoc.

2019-06-21

Contents

A brief introduction to genetic algorithms

Genetic algorithms are one of the tools we can use to apply machine learning to finding good, sometimes even optimal, solutions to problems that have billions of potential solutions. They use biological processes in software to find answers to problems that have really large search spaces by continuously generating candidate solutions, evaluating how well the solutions fit the desired outcome, and refining the best solutions.

When solving a problem with a genetic algorithm, instead of asking for a specific solution, you provide characteristics that the solution must have or rules its solution must pass to be accepted. For example, when filling a moving truck you provide a set of rules like: load big things first, distribute the weight to both sides, put light things on top but not loose, and interlock things with odd shapes so they don't move around. The more constraints you add the more potential solutions are blocked. Suppose you say: put the refrigerator, washer and dryer along the front left wall, load boxes of books along the front right wall, mattresses down the middle, and clothes on top of the mattresses. These more specific rules do not work if you are loading packages, or Christmas trees, but the previous goal oriented ones still do.

Goal oriented problem solving

Imagine you are given 10 chances to guess a number between 1 and 1000 and the only feedback you get is whether your guess is right or wrong. Could you reliably guess the number? With only *right* or *wrong* as feedback, you have no way to improve your guesses so you have at best a 1 in 100 chance of guessing the number. A fundamental aspect of solving problems using genetic algorithms is that they must provide feedback that helps the engine select the better of two guesses. That feedback is called the fitness, for how closely the guess fits the desired result. More importantly it implies a general progression.

If instead of *right* or *wrong* as feedback you receive *higher* or *lower* indicating that the number is higher or lower than your guess, you can always find the number because

10 guesses are sufficient to binary search your way to any number in the 1 to 1000 range.

Now imagine multiplying the size of this problem so that instead of trying to find 1 number you are simultaneously trying to find a set of 100 numbers, all in the range 1 to 1000, you only receive back a fitness value indicating how closely that set of numbers matches the desired outcome. Your goal would be to maximize or minimize that fitness. Could you find the right set of 100 numbers? You might be able to do better than random guessing if you have problem-specific knowledge that helps you eliminate certain number combinations. Using problem-specific knowledge to guide the genetic algorithm's creation and modification of potential solutions can help them find a solution orders of magnitude faster.

Genetic algorithms and genetic programming are very good at finding solutions to very large problems. They do it by taking millions of samples from the search space, making small changes, possibly recombining parts of the best solutions, comparing the resultant fitness against that of the current best solution, and keeping the better of the two. This process repeats until a stop condition like one of the following occurs: the known solution is found, a solution meeting all requirements is found, a certain number of generations has passed, a specific amount of time has passed, etc.

First project

Imagine you are asked to guess a 3-letter password; what kind of feedback would you want? If the password is aaa and you guess abc what should the fitness value be? Would something simple like how many of the letters in your guess are correct be sufficient? Should bab, which has one correct letter, get a better fitness value than zap, also one correct letter but the wrong letters are alphabetically farther away, or should the fitness be the same? These are some of the first decisions you have to make when planning to implement a genetic algorithm to find a solution to your problem. Genetic algorithms are good at finding good solutions to problems with large search spaces because they can quickly find the parts of the guesses that improve fitness values or lead to better solutions.

In the project above, let's say the fitness function returns a count of the number of letters that match the password. That means abc, bab and zba all get a fitness value of one, because they each have one letter correct. The genetic algorithm might then combine the first two letters of abc with the last letter of zba through crossover, to create the guess aba. The fitness for that guess would be two because two letters match the password. The algorithm might also mutate the last letter of zba to get zbc and a fitness value of zero. Depending on how the engine is configured it might throw out zbc immediately, it might keep it in order to maintain genetic diversity, or perhaps it would only keep it if it is better than some cutoff fitness value when compared with all the other guesses tried by the engine.

We will look more at the password project in the first project, and go on to explore a variety of projects to learn different ways of solving problems with genetic algorithms. However, this book is not about showing you a hand-picked set of problems you can solve with genetic algorithms. It is about giving you experience making genetic algorithms work for you using sample projects that you understand and can fall back upon when learning to use other machine learning tools and techniques, or applying genetic algorithms in your own field of expertise.

Genetic programming with Python

This book uses the Python programming language to provide a working implementation for you to study. Python is a low ceremony, powerful and easy-to-read language whose code can be understood by entry-level programmers. If you have experience with another programming language then you should have no difficulty learning Python by induction while also exploring genetic algorithms. You do not, however, have to learn to write Python. I explain the occasional Python-specific feature, and try not to use 3rd-party modules, so you should be able to follow along in your favorite programming language as well. That being said, if you encounter a programming construct you've never seen before and can't intuit, Python.org and StackOverflow.com are great places to find explanations.

example Python syntax

```
# this is a comment
import math  # imports make code from other modules available

# code blocks are initiated by a trailing colon followed by indented lines
class Circle:                      # define a class
    def __init__(self, radius):    # constructor with parameter radius
        self.radius = radius       # store the parameter in a class variable

    def get_area(self):            # function that belongs to the class
        return math.pi \
            * self.radius \
            * self.radius          # trailing \ continues the expression
                                   # on the next line
# code that is not in a class is executed immediately
for i in range(1, 10):
    if (i & 1) == 0:
        continue
    circle = Circle(i)             # create an instance
    print("A circle with radius {0} has area {1:0.2f}".format(
        i, circle.get_area()       # `print` writes output to the console
    ))
```

You can run the code above in your browser at: https://repl.it/EWUh

Like blacksmiths, programmers create their own tools. We frequently prototype a solution by using tools we already have available, not unlike using a pair of pliers to pull a nail. Once we get a good understanding of the problem, however, we usually restart with a better combination of tools or build a problem-specific one. In this book we will co-evolve a genetic engine while examining increasingly difficult projects with the engine. Why not just use one of the genetic programming packages already available for Python like Pyvolution, DEAP, Pyevolve, pySTEP, etc? Because they all have different interfaces and options, some of which may not be applicable to a problem, and we're trying to learn about genetic algorithms not specific engines. By co-evolving the engine you'll know exactly how it works so you'll be able to use its features effectively to solve the next problem with a genetic algorithm of your own design. The engine will be a by-product of applying genetic algorithms to the different projects in this book. If you were to co-evolve an engine with a different set of projects, or even the projects in this book in a different order, you would end up with a different engine. But, by co-evolving an engine you will gain experience with some of the features available in commonly used packages, and see how they can affect the performance of your code.

About the author

I am a polyglot programmer with more than 15 years of professional programming experience. Occasionally I step out of my comfort zone and learn a new language to see what that development experience is like and to keep my skills sharp. This book grew out of my experiences while learning Python, but it isn't about Python.

When learning a new programming language, I start with a familiar project and try to learn enough of the new language to solve it. For me, writing a genetic engine is that familiar project. Why a genetic engine? For one thing, it is a project where I can explore interesting puzzles, and where even a child's game like Tic-tac-toe can be viewed on a whole new level. Also, I can select increasingly complex puzzles to drive evolution in the capabilities of the engine. This allows me to discover the expressiveness of the language, the power of its tool chain, and the size of its development community as I work through the idiosyncrasies of the language.

About the text

The code snippets in this book were programmatically extracted from working code files using the tags feature of AsciiDoctor's include directive.

Hello World!

Guess my number

Let's begin by learning a little bit about genetic algorithms. Reach way back in your memories to a game we played as kids. It is a simple game for two people where one picks a secret number between 1 and 10 and the other has to guess that number.

```
Is it 2?  No
Is it 3?  No
Is it 7?  No
Is it 1?  Yes
```

That works reasonably well for 1..10 but quickly becomes frustrating or boring as we increase the range to 1..100 or 1..1000. Why? Because we have no way to improve our guesses. There's no challenge. The guess is either right or wrong, so it quickly becomes a mechanical process.

```
Is it 1?  No
Is it 2?  No
Is it 3?  No
Is it 4?  No
Is it 5?  No
...
```

So, to make it more interesting, instead of *no* let's say *higher* or *lower*.

```
1?  Higher
7?  Lower
6?  Lower
5?  Lower
4?  Correct
```

That might be reasonably interesting for a while for numbers in the range 1..10 but soon you'll increase the range to 1..100. Because people are competitive, the next revision is to see who is a better guesser by trying to find the number in the fewest guesses. At this point the person who evolves the most efficient guessing strategy wins.

However, one thing we automatically do when playing the game is make use of domain knowledge. For example, after this sequence:

```
1?  Higher
7?  Lower
```

Why wouldn't we guess 8, 9, or 10? The reason is, of course, because we know that those numbers are not *lower* than 7. Why wouldn't we guess 1? Because we already tried it. We use our memory of what we've tried, our successes and failures, and our *knowledge of the domain*, number relationships, to improve our guesses.

When playing a card game inexperienced players build a mental map using the cards in their hand and those on the table. More experienced players also take advantage of their knowledge of the problem space, the entire set of cards in the deck. This means they may also keep track of cards that have not yet been played, and may know they can win the rest of the rounds without having to play them out. Highly experienced card players also know the probabilities of various winning combinations. Professionals, who earn their living playing the game, also pay attention to the way their competitors play... whether they bluff in certain situations, play with their chips when they think they have a good hand, etc.

A genetic algorithm does not know what *lower* means. It has no intelligence. It does not learn. It will make the same mistakes every time. It will only be as good at solving a problem as the person who writes the code. And yet, it can be used to find solutions to problems that humans would struggle to solve or could not solve at all. How is that possible?

Genetic algorithms use random exploration of the problem space combined with evolutionary processes like mutation and crossover (exchange of genetic information) to improve guesses. But also, because they have no experience in the problem domain, they *try things a human would never think to try*. Thus, a person using a genetic algorithm may learn more about the problem space and potential solutions. This gives them the ability to make improvements to the algorithm, in a virtuous cycle.

What can we learn from this?

> Technique: The genetic algorithm should make informed guesses.

Guess the Password

Now let's see how this applies to guessing a password. Start with a randomly generated initial sequence of letters, then mutate or change one random letter at a time until the sequence of letters is "Hello World!". Conceptually:

pseudo code

```
_
letters = [a..zA..Z !]
target = "Hello World!"
guess = get 12 random letters from _letters
while guess != target:
    index = get a random value from [0..length of target]
    guess[index] = get 1 random letter from _letters
```

If you try this in your favorite programming language you'll find that it performs worse than playing the number guessing game with only *yes* and *no* answers because it cannot tell when one guess is better than another.

One solution is to help it make an informed guess by telling it how many of the letters from the guess are in the correct locations. For example "World!Hello?" would get 2 because only the 4th letter of each word is correct. The 2 indicates how close the answer is to correct. This is called the fitness value. "hello world?" would get a fitness value of 9 because 9 letters are correct. Only the h, w, and question mark are wrong.

First Program

It is time for some code. By the way, if you do not already have a favorite Python development environment, I highly recommend JetBrains' PyCharm IDE.

Genes

To begin with, the genetic algorithm needs a gene set to use for building guesses. For this project that will be a generic set of letters. It also needs a target password to guess:

guessPassword.py

```
1  geneSet = " abcdefghijklmnopqrstuvwxyzABCDEFGHIJKLMNOPQRSTUVWXYZ!."
2  target = "Hello World!"
```

ⓘYou can run the code for this section in your browser at https:// repl.it/EUX2

Generate a guess

Next the algorithm needs a way to generate a random `string` from the gene set.

```
1 import random                                                    <==
2
3
4 geneSet = " abcdefghijklmnopqrstuvwxyzABCDEFGHIJKLMNOPQRSTUVWXYZ!."
```

```
  target = "Hello World!"
6
8 def generate_parent(length):
      genes = []
10    while len(genes) < length:
          sampleSize = min(length - len(genes), len(geneSet))
12        genes.extend(random.sample(geneSet, sampleSize))
      return ''.join(genes)
```

ⓘ list.extend() appends multiple items to a list. string.join() uses
the given string as a separator to create a new string with the values
being joined, for example: 'x'.join(['a','b','c']) gets "axbxc".

ⓘ random.sample() takes sample-size values from the input without
replacement. This means there will be no duplicates in the generated parent unless the gene set contains duplicates, or the requested
length is greater than the number of items in the gene set. The implementation above can generate a long string with a small set of genes
and uses as many unique genes as possible.

Fitness

The *fitness* value the genetic algorithm provides is the *only* feedback the engine receives to guide it toward a solution. In this project the *fitness* value is the total number
of letters in the guess that match the letter in the same position of the password.

```
16 def get_fitness(guess):
17     return sum(1 for expected, actual in zip(target, guess)
18             if expected == actual)
```

ⓘ zip() is a built-in function that makes it possible to iterate over two
lists (or iterables) simultaneously.

Mutation

Next, the engine needs a way to produce a new guess by mutating the current one.

```python
def mutate(parent):
    index = random.randrange(0, len(parent))
    childGenes = list(parent)
    newGene, alternate = random.sample(geneSet, 2)
    childGenes[index] = alternate if newGene == childGenes[index] else newGene
    return ''.join(childGenes)
```

This implementation converts the parent `string` to an array with `list()`, then replaces 1 letter in the array with a randomly selected one from the gene set, and finally recombines the result into a `string` with `.join()`. It uses an alternate replacement if the randomly selected new gene is the same as the one it is supposed to replace, which can prevent a significant number of wasted guesses.

Display

Next, it is important to monitor what is happening so that the engine can be stopped if it gets stuck. Having a visual representation of the gene sequence, which may not be the literal gene sequence, is often critical to identifying what works and what does not so that the algorithm can be improved.

Normally the display function also outputs the fitness value and how much time has elapsed.

```python
import datetime                                                          <==
import random
```

```python
def display(guess):
    timeDiff = datetime.datetime.now() - startTime
    fitness = get_fitness(guess)
    print("{}\t{}\t{}".format(guess, fitness, timeDiff))
```

Main

The main program begins by initializing *bestParent* to a random sequence of letters and calling the display function.

```python
random.seed()
startTime = datetime.datetime.now()
bestParent = generate_parent(len(target))
bestFitness = get_fitness(bestParent)
display(bestParent)
```

The final piece is the heart of the genetic engine. It is a loop that:

- generates a guess,

- requests the *fitness* for that guess, then

- compares the *fitness* to that of the previous best guess, and

- keeps the guess with the better fitness.

This cycle repeats until a stop condition occurs, in this case when all the letters in the guess match those in the target.

```
     while True:
44       child = mutate(bestParent)
         childFitness = get_fitness(child)
46       if bestFitness >= childFitness:
             continue
48       display(child)
         if childFitness >= len(bestParent):
50           break
         bestFitness = childFitness
52       bestParent = child
```

Run the code and you'll see output similar to the following:

```
ftljCDPvhasn    1    0:00:00
ftljC Pvhasn    2    0:00:00
ftljC Pohasn    3    0:00:00.001000
HtljC Pohasn    4    0:00:00.002000
HtljC Wohasn    5    0:00:00.004000
Htljo Wohasn    6    0:00:00.005000
Htljo Wohas!    7    0:00:00.008000
Htljo Wohls!    8    0:00:00.010000
Heljo Wohls!    9    0:00:00.013000
Hello Wohls!   10    0:00:00.013000
Hello Wohld!   11    0:00:00.013000
Hello World!   12    0:00:00.015000
```

Extract a reusable engine

We have a working engine but it is currently tightly coupled to the Password project, so the next task is to extract the genetic engine code from that specific to guessing the password so it can be reused for other projects. Start by creating a new file named genetic.py.

Next move the *mutate* and *generate_parent* functions to the new file and rename them to _mutate and _generate_parent. This is how protected functions are named in Python. Protected functions are only accessible to other functions in the same module.

Generation and Mutation

Future projects will need to be able to customize the gene set, so that needs to become a parameter to _generate_parent and _mutate.

genetic.py

```
import random


def _generate_parent(length, geneSet):                          <==
    genes = []
    while len(genes) < length:
        sampleSize = min(length - len(genes), len(geneSet))
        genes.extend(random.sample(geneSet, sampleSize))
    return ''.join(genes)


def _mutate(parent, geneSet):                                   <==
    index = random.randrange(0, len(parent))
    childGenes = list(parent)
    newGene, alternate = random.sample(geneSet, 2)
    childGenes[index] = alternate if newGene == childGenes[index] else newGene
    return ''.join(childGenes)
```

`get_best`

The next step is to move the main loop into a new public function named *get_best* in the `genetic` module. Its parameters are:

- the function it calls to request the fitness for a guess,

- the number of genes to use when creating a new gene sequence,

- the optimal fitness value,

- the set of genes to use for creating and mutating gene sequences, and

- the function it should call to display, or report, each improvement found.

```
20  def get_best(get_fitness, targetLen, optimalFitness, geneSet, display):   <==
        random.seed()
22      bestParent = _generate_parent(targetLen, geneSet)                      <==
        bestFitness = get_fitness(bestParent)
24      display(bestParent)
        if bestFitness >= optimalFitness:
26          return bestParent

28      while True:
            child = _mutate(bestParent, geneSet)                               <==
30          childFitness = get_fitness(child)
            if bestFitness >= childFitness:
32              continue
            display(child)
34          if childFitness >= optimalFitness:
                return child
36          bestFitness = childFitness
            bestParent = child
```

Notice that the *display* and *get_fitness* functions are called with only one parameter - the child gene sequence. This is because a generic engine does not need access to the target value, and it does not care about how much time has passed, so those are not passed to it.

The result is a reusable module named genetic that can be used in other programs via import genetic.

Use the genetic module

The code remaining in guessPassword.py is specific to the password guessing project. To get it working again first import the genetic module.

guessPassword.py

```
1  import datetime
2
3  import genetic                                                              <==
```

Fitness

Now change the fitness function to receive the target password as a parameter. We could implement it as a global variable in the algorithm file but this change facilitates trying different passwords without side effects.

```python
import genetic


def get_fitness(genes, target):                                    <==
    return sum(1 for expected, actual in zip(target, genes)
               if expected == actual)
```

Display

The display function also needs to take the target password as a parameter.

```python
def display(genes, target, startTime):                             <==
    timeDiff = datetime.datetime.now() - startTime
    fitness = get_fitness(genes, target)
    print("{}\t{}\t{}".format(genes, fitness, timeDiff))
```

Next, helper functions that take only one parameter must be defined so they are compatible with what the engine expects. Each helper function will take the candidate gene sequence it receives and call the local functions with additional required parameters as necessary. Note that the helper functions are nested inside the *guess_password* function so that they have access to the target and start time variables.

```python
geneset = " abcdefghijklmnopqrstuvwxyzABCDEFGHIJKLMNOPQRSTUVWXYZ!."   <==


def test_Hello_World():
    target = "Hello World!"
    guess_password(target)


def guess_password(target):
    startTime = datetime.datetime.now()

    def fnGetFitness(genes):                                       <==
        return get_fitness(genes, target)

    def fnDisplay(genes):                                          <==
        display(genes, target, startTime)

    optimalFitness = len(target)
    best = genetic.get_best(fnGetFitness, len(target), optimalFitness,   <==
                            geneset, fnDisplay)
```

Main

There are many ways to structure the main code, the most flexible is as a unit test. To start that transition first rename guessPassword.py to guessPasswordTests.py. Next, to make it possible to execute the code from the command line add:

guessPasswordTests.py

```
39 if __name__ == '__main__':
40     test_Hello_World()                                        <==
```

If you are following along in an editor be sure to run your code to verify it works at this point.

Use Python's unittest framework

The next step is to make the code work with Python's built-in test framework.

```
1 import datetime
2 import unittest                                                <==
```

To do that the main test function must be moved into a *class* that inherits from unittest .TestCase. The other functions can be moved into the *class* as well if you want, but if they are then self must be added as the first parameter to each because they will then belong to the test *class*.

```
   class GuessPasswordTests(unittest.TestCase):                  <==
20     geneset = " abcdefghijklmnopqrstuvwxyzABCDEFGHIJKLMNOPQRSTUVWXYZ!.,"

22     def test_Hello_World(self):                               <==
           target = "Hello World!"
24         self.guess_password(target)

26     def guess_password(self, target):                         <==
           startTime = datetime.datetime.now()
28
           def fnGetFitness(genes):
30             return get_fitness(genes, target)

32         def fnDisplay(genes):
               display(genes, target, startTime)
34
           optimalFitness = len(target)
36         best = genetic.get_best(fnGetFitness, len(target), optimalFitness,
                           self.geneset, fnDisplay)               <==
38         self.assertEqual(best, target)                        <==
```

When the `unittest` module's `main` function is called, it automatically executes each function whose name starts with `test`.

```
41  if __name__ == '__main__':
42      unittest.main()                                                    <==
```

This allows the test to be run from the command line and, incidentally, without the output from its display function.

```
python -m unittest -b guessPasswordTests
.
----------------------------------------
Ran 1 test in 0.020s

OK
```

> ⚠️ If you get an error like `'module' object has no attribute 'py'` then you used the filename `guessPasswordTests.py` instead of the module name `guessPasswordTests`.

A longer password

"Hello World!" doesn't sufficiently demonstrate the power of the genetic engine so try a longer password:

```
26      def test_For_I_am_fearfully_and_wonderfully_made(self):
            target = "For I am fearfully and wonderfully made."
28          self.guess_password(target)

30      def guess_password(self, target):
```

Run

```
. . .
ForMI am feabaully and wWndNyfulll made.    33   0:00:00.047094
For I am feabaully and wWndNyfulll made.    34   0:00:00.047094
For I am feabfully and wWndNyfulll made.    35   0:00:00.053111
For I am feabfully and wondNyfulll made.    36   0:00:00.064140
For I am feabfully and wondNyfully made.    37   0:00:00.067148
For I am feabfully and wondeyfully made.    38   0:00:00.095228
For I am feabfully and wonderfully made.    39   0:00:00.100236
For I am fearfully and wonderfully made.    40   0:00:00.195524
```

Nice!

Introduce a Chromosome *class*

The next change is to introduce a Chromosome *class* that has *Genes* and *Fitness* attributes. This will make the genetic engine more flexible by making it possible to pass those values around as a unit.

genetic.py

```
40  class Chromosome:
41      def __init__(self, genes, fitness):
42          self.Genes = genes
43          self.Fitness = fitness
```

Then use Chromosome in the other functions as necessary.

```
 4  def _generate_parent(length, geneSet, get_fitness):
        genes = []
 6      while len(genes) < length:
            sampleSize = min(length - len(genes), len(geneSet))
 8          genes.extend(random.sample(geneSet, sampleSize))
        genes = ''.join(genes)
10      fitness = get_fitness(genes)
        return Chromosome(genes, fitness)                      <==
```

```
14  def _mutate(parent, geneSet, get_fitness):
        index = random.randrange(0, len(parent.Genes))         <==
16      childGenes = list(parent.Genes)                        <==
        newGene, alternate = random.sample(geneSet, 2)
18      childGenes[index] = alternate if newGene == childGenes[index] else newGene
        genes = ''.join(childGenes)
20      fitness = get_fitness(genes)
        return Chromosome(genes, fitness)                      <==
```

```
24  def get_best(get_fitness, targetLen, optimalFitness, geneSet, display):
        random.seed()
26      bestParent = _generate_parent(targetLen, geneSet, get_fitness)
        display(bestParent)
28      if bestParent.Fitness >= optimalFitness:               <==
            return bestParent
30
        while True:
32          child = _mutate(bestParent, geneSet, get_fitness)
            if bestParent.Fitness >= child.Fitness:            <==
34              continue
            display(child)
36          if child.Fitness >= optimalFitness:                <==
                return child
38          bestParent = child
```

It requires compensating changes to the algorithm file functions but those changes also eliminate some double work (i.e. recalculating the fitness).

guessPasswordTests.py

```
12  def display(candidate, startTime):                              <==
13      timeDiff = datetime.datetime.now() - startTime
14      print("{}\t{}\t{}".format(
15          candidate.Genes, candidate.Fitness, timeDiff))          <==
```

```
        def fnDisplay(candidate):                                   <==
32          display(candidate, startTime)                           <==

34      optimalFitness = len(target)
        best = genetic.get_best(fnGetFitness, len(target), optimalFitness,
36                          self.geneset, fnDisplay)
        self.assertEqual(best.Genes, target)                        <==
```

Benchmarking

The next improvement is to add support for benchmarking because it is useful to know how long the engine takes to find a solution on average and the standard deviation. That can be done with another *class* as follows:

genetic.py

```
46  class Benchmark:
        @staticmethod
48      def run(function):
            timings = []
50          for i in range(100):
                startTime = time.time()
52              function()
                seconds = time.time() - startTime
54              timings.append(seconds)
                mean = statistics.mean(timings)
56              print("{} {:3.2f} {:3.2f}".format(
                    1 + i, mean,
58                  statistics.stdev(timings, mean) if i > 1 else 0))
```

This function runs the provided function 100 times and reports how long each run takes, the mean, and standard deviation. To calculate the standard deviation we'll use a 3rd-party module named statistics:

genetic.py

```
1  import random
2  import statistics                                                <==
3  import time                                                      <==
```

⚠You may need to install the `statistics` module on your system. This can be accomplished from the command line with `python -m pip install statistics`

Now, to use the benchmarking capability simply add a test and pass the function to be benchmarked.

guessPasswordTests.py

```
42      self.assertEqual(best.Genes, target)
43
44  def test_benchmark(self):
45      genetic.Benchmark.run(self.test_For_I_am_fearfully_and_wonderfully_made)
```

When run, this function works great but is a bit chatty because it also shows the output from the display function for all 100 runs. That can be fixed in the benchmark function by temporarily redirecting the standard output to nowhere.

genetic.py

```
3  import sys                                                          <==
4  import time
```

```
       timings = []
52     stdout = sys.stdout                                             <==
       for i in range(100):
54         sys.stdout = None                                           <==
           startTime = time.time()
56         function()
           seconds = time.time() - startTime
58         sys.stdout = stdout                                         <==
           timings.append(seconds)
```

If you get an error like the following when you run the benchmark test:

```
AttributeError: 'NoneType' object has no attribute 'write'
```

Then you are probably using Python 2.7. It does not support redirecting `stdout` to `None`. It must have someplace to write the data. One solution to that problem is to add the following *class*:

genetic.py

```
class NullWriter():
    def write(self, s):
        pass
```

Then replace the following in *Benchmark.run*:

```
for i in range(100):
    sys.stdout = None
```

with:

```
for i in range(100):
    sys.stdout = NullWriter()
```

That change allows you work around the difference between Python 2.7 and 3.5 this time. However, code in future projects uses other features of Python 3.5, so I suggest switching to Python 3.5 so that you can focus on learning about genetic algorithms without these additional issues. If you want to use machine learning tools that are tied to Python 2.7, wait until you have a solid understanding of genetic algorithms then switch to Python 2.7.

The output can also be improved by only displaying statistics for the first ten runs and then every 10th run after that.

genetic.py

```
        timings.append(seconds)
60      mean = statistics.mean(timings)
        if i < 10 or i % 10 == 9:                              <==
62          print("{} {:3.2f} {:3.2f}".format(
                1 + i, mean,
64              statistics.stdev(timings, mean) if i > 1 else 0))
```

Now the benchmark test output looks like the following.
sample output

```
1 0.19 0.00
2 0.17 0.00
3 0.18 0.02
. . .
9 0.17 0.03
10 0.17 0.03
20 0.18 0.04
. . .
90 0.16 0.05
100 0.16 0.05
```

This means that, averaging 100 runs, it takes .16 seconds to guess the password, and 68 percent of the time (one standard deviation) it takes between .11 (.16 - .05) and .21 (.16 + .05) seconds. Unfortunately that is probably too fast to determine if a change is due to a code improvement or due to something else running on the computer at the same time. That problem can be solved by making the genetic algorithm guess a random sequence that takes 1-2 seconds to run.

guessPasswordTests.py

```
2 import random                                                    <==
3 import unittest
```

```
44    def test_Random(self):                                       <==
          length = 150
46        target = ''.join(random.choice(self.geneset) for _ in range(length))
          self.guess_password(target)
48
      def test_benchmark(self):
50        genetic.Benchmark.run(self.test_Random)                  <==
```

Your cpu is probably different from mine so adjust the length as necessary.

Benchmarks

average (seconds)	standard deviation
1.46	0.35

Summary

In this project we built a simple genetic engine that makes use of random mutation to produce better results. This engine was able to guess a secret password given only its length, a set of characters that might be in the password, and a fitness function that returns a count of the number characters in the guess that match the secret. This is a good benchmark project for the engine because as the target string gets longer the engine wastes more and more guesses trying to change positions that are already correct. As the engine evolves in later projects, we'll try to keep this benchmark fast. Also, as you work your way through more projects you'll learn ways to improve the performance of the code in this project.

Final Code

The final code for all projects is available online from:

https://github.com/handcraftsman/GeneticAlgorithmsWithPython

One Max Problem

At a high level the next project involves getting the engine to produce 100 1's when the genes can only be 0 or 1. You should be able to do that with our current engine. Go try it. Note: you can repeat a string 3 times with "1'' * 3, if that is useful.

Solution

```python
def test_onemax(self):
    target = "1" * 100
    self.geneset = "01"
    self.guess_password(target)
```

That's easy enough right? However, most real world genetic algorithm problems would be much more complex to solve if we were limited to using a `string` for the DNA. So we're going to use this problem to make our engine more flexible.

Make password code work with a `list` of genes

Let's start by changing the password related code to be compatible with an engine that provides a `list` of genes instead of a `string` of genes.

We can use the `join` function (without a separator) to combine the `list` of characters into a `string` in the display function

guessPasswordTests.py

```python
   def display(candidate, startTime):
14     timeDiff = datetime.datetime.now() - startTime
       print("{}\t{}\t{}".format(
16         ''.join(candidate.Genes),                              <==
           candidate.Fitness,
18         timeDiff))
```

and in the assertion in `guess_password`.

```
41        optimalFitness = len(target)
42        best = genetic.get_best(fnGetFitness, len(target), optimalFitness,
43                          self.geneset, fnDisplay)
44        self.assertEqual(''.join(best.Genes), target)              <==
```

Change genetic to work with a list

To make the `genetic` module work with a list we can start by using Python's array slicing feature to simply make a copy of the genes in the mutation function, instead of using the `list` constructor to convert from a `string` to a `list`.

```
16  def _mutate(parent, geneSet, get_fitness):
17      childGenes = parent.Genes[:]
```

Then remove the following line from _mutate and _generate_parent since we no longer need to convert the `list` back to a `string` in the engine:

```
genes = ''.join(childGenes)
```

Next, update those functions to use the `list`, as follows:

```
16  def _mutate(parent, geneSet, get_fitness):
        childGenes = parent.Genes[:]
18      index = random.randrange(0, len(parent.Genes))
        newGene, alternate = random.sample(geneSet, 2)
20      childGenes[index] = alternate \                                <==
            if newGene == childGenes[index] \                         <==
22          else newGene
        fitness = get_fitness(childGenes)                             <==
24      return Chromosome(childGenes, fitness)                        <==
```

```
    def _generate_parent(length, geneSet, get_fitness):
 8      genes = []
        while len(genes) < length:
10          sampleSize = min(length - len(genes), len(geneSet))
            genes.extend(random.sample(geneSet, sampleSize))
12      fitness = get_fitness(genes)                                  <==
        return Chromosome(genes, fitness)                            <==
```

That's it for the engine modifications. You should now be able to run the tests again.

Build the OneMax test class

In real world genetic algorithm problems we are unlikely to have a solution to compare against. Instead we know the features we want the solution to have. So let's restate the OneMax problem as: maximize the number of genes that are the integer 1. Now create a new file called oneMaxTests.py using the stub below to get you started, and see if you can write the code to solve this problem using integer genes.

oneMaxTests.py

```
import datetime
import unittest

import genetic


def get_fitness(genes):
    # return a count the number of 1's in the genes


def display(candidate, startTime):
    # display the current genes, their fitness, and elapsed time


class OneMaxTests(unittest.TestCase):
    def test(self, length=100):
        geneset = [0, 1]
        # create the helper functions and optimal fitness
        # then call genetic.get_best()
        # finally, assert that the fitness of the result is optimal
```

Solution

My implementation is below. Yours is probably different, and that's OK!

Fitness

In the fitness function we can simply count the number of 1's in the list of genes.

oneMaxTests.py

```
def get_fitness(genes):
    return genes.count(1)
```

Display

Since 100 numbers would be a lot to display, just show the first and last 15 along with the fitness and elapsed time.

```
def display(candidate, startTime):
    timeDiff = datetime.datetime.now() - startTime
    print("{}...{}\t{:3.2f}\t{}".format(
        ''.join(map(str, candidate.Genes[:15])),
        ''.join(map(str, candidate.Genes[-15:])),
        candidate.Fitness,
        timeDiff))
```

This uses `str` to convert the integers in *candidate.Genes* to a string. Without `map` the code would need a loop like the following to convert the candidate genes to a `string`:

```
result = []
for i in candidate.Genes
    result += str(candidate[i])
return result
```

Test

And here's the full test harness.

```
def test(self, length=100):
    geneset = [0, 1]
    startTime = datetime.datetime.now()

    def fnDisplay(candidate):
        display(candidate, startTime)

    def fnGetFitness(genes):
        return get_fitness(genes)

    optimalFitness = length
    best = genetic.get_best(fnGetFitness, length, optimalFitness,
                            geneset, fnDisplay)
    self.assertEqual(best.Fitness, optimalFitness)
```

Run

It can find the solution very quickly.

sample output

```
010101101010010...101010110100101    50.00    0:00:00.001000
010101101010010...101010110100101    51.00    0:00:00.001000
...
110111101111111...111111110111111    95.00    0:00:00.008000
110111111111111...111111110111111    96.00    0:00:00.008000
110111111111111...111111110111111    97.00    0:00:00.009000
110111111111111...111111111111111    98.00    0:00:00.009000
111111111111111...111111111111111    99.00    0:00:00.010000
111111111111111...111111111111111   100.00    0:00:00.011000
```

Benchmarks

Since the engine can solve this problem so fast we'll benchmark this project with a longer array. As with the Guess Password benchmark I'm choosing a length that takes between 1 and 2 seconds on average on my computer. You should use a length appropriate for your computer.

```
34          self.assertEqual(best.Fitness, optimalFitness)
35
36      def test_benchmark(self):
37          genetic.Benchmark.run(lambda: self.test(4000))
```

> ⓘ `genetic.Benchmark.run` expects a parameterless function that it can call. If we try to pass it `self.test(4000)` we end up sending the result of calling the `test` function. That's not what we want. `lambda` is a Python language feature that lets us create a function inline without calling it. We're creating a parameterless function and passing it to the `run` function. When called, that function calls `self.text(4000)`.

Updated Benchmarks

project	average (seconds)	standard deviation
Guess Password	1.21	0.25
One Max	1.25	0.17

We can see in the updated benchmarks that eliminating the string conversion may also have given us a tiny performance improvement in the password guessing project.

Aside

In this project the genetic engine randomly chooses an array index to change, even if the array already contains a 1 at that index, because the engine doesn't know the change it is making is useless until after it has called the fitness function. A physical equivalent is to take 100 coins and put green sticky dots on one side and yellow sticky dots on the other. Then have a partner blindfold you and drop the coins on a table top. Your goal is to turn all the coins yellow-side up. If you turn one yellow-side up they tell you it was a success. Otherwise, they undo the change and tell you it was a failure. To keep you from building a mental map they could optionally move the coin somewhere else afterward. Tough game right?

Now think about possible changes to the coin game that would make it solvable. For example, what if they were to remove the coin from the table when you turn it yellow-side up. That would be extremely useful right? Assuming every coin started yellow-side up, you would at most turn each coin twice, meaning you could turn all coins yellow-side up in at most 200 turns no matter which way they started. If the genetic algorithm, instead of the engine, had control of choosing the next index, then the equivalent would be for it to record the index it changes. Then, if the display function is called next by the engine instead of `get_index`, the algorithm would know that the array contains a 1 at that index. It could then simply add the index to a list of indexes it ignores when guessing. A side benefit of this solution is that, like the human player in the coin game, the genetic algorithm does not need to know the state of the entire array. It can begin with zero knowledge and start tracking indexes that improve the fitness, just like the classic Battleship game.

Summary

In this project the flexibility of the `genetic` module was increased by allowing the genes to be any type instead of only characters in a `string`. This is a critical feature, as before long we will want to use something other than just keyboard characters for genes.

Sorted Numbers

In this project we will make a genetic algorithm that produces a sorted `list` of numbers. This project is slightly more difficult than the previous two because even though there are many potential solutions instead of just one, now each of the genes has a constraint based on another gene's value; specifically, it must have a value greater than the gene to its left in the array. Just as we did in the previous project we'll start with a stub that you should be able to use to solve this problem.

Test class stub

```python
import datetime
import unittest

import genetic


def get_fitness(genes)
    # return a count of the number of genes that are in ascending order


def display(candidate, startTime):
    # display the current genes, their fitness, and elapsed time
    # example: 53, 74, 95    => 3 0:00:00.001004


class SortedNumbersTests(unittest.TestCase):
    def test_sort_3_numbers(self):
        self.sort_numbers(3)

    def sort_numbers(self, totalNumbers):
        geneset = [i for i in range(100)]
            # start a timer
            # create the helper functions and optimal fitness
            # then call genetic.get_best()
            # finally, assert that the fitness of the result is optimal
```

For this project the gene set is integers in the range 0 to 99, created above with the `list` comprehension `[i for i in range(100)]`.

List comprehensions enable us to build a `list` by saying what we want instead of how to get it. This is equivalent to:

```
geneset = []
for i in range(100):
    geneset.append(i)
```

The Python compiler may be able to write faster code for list comprehensions in some cases. You may recall that we sometimes use a variant of this in the display function to convert a `list` of numbers to a `string` using `map`.

Go fill in the details in the test stub and see if you can implement a solution before you read further. Working through the problem on your own first will help you better understand my implementation.

Solution

This should not have been difficult for you. If it was, review my solution then do it one more time from scratch to help the patterns stick in your mind.

Fitness

The fitness function will return a count of the adjacent numbers that are in ascending order with 1 freebie because the initial position doesn't have a gene to its left.

```
def get_fitness(genes):
    fitness = 1
    for i in range(1, len(genes)):
        if genes[i] > genes[i - 1]:
            fitness += 1
    return fitness
```

Display

The display function will output the array values separated by a comma.

```
def display(candidate, startTime):
    timeDiff = datetime.datetime.now() - startTime
    print("{}\t=> {}\t{}".format(
        ', '.join(map(str, candidate.Genes)),
        candidate.Fitness,
        timeDiff))
```

sort_numbers

```python
    def sort_numbers(self, totalNumbers):
        geneset = [i for i in range(100)]
        startTime = datetime.datetime.now()

        def fnDisplay(candidate):
            display(candidate, startTime)

        def fnGetFitness(genes):
            return get_fitness(genes)

        optimalFitness = totalNumbers
        best = genetic.get_best(fnGetFitness, totalNumbers, optimalFitness,
                                geneset, fnDisplay)
        self.assertTrue(not optimalFitness > best.Fitness)


if __name__ == '__main__':
    unittest.main()
```

Run

```
23, 99, 43  => 2 0:00:00.001004
53, 74, 95  => 3 0:00:00.001004
```

Great!

Get 10 sorted digits

Let's increase it from 3 to 10 sorted numbers.

```python
class SortedNumbersTests(unittest.TestCase):
    def test_sort_10_numbers(self):
        self.sort_numbers(10)

    def sort_numbers(self, totalNumbers):
```

Run

Now when we run the test it stalls.

```
54, 59, 7, 69, 73, 76, 42, 46, 39, 87   => 7 0:00:00.001000
54, 59, 7, 69, 73, 76, 42, 46, 63, 87   => 8 0:00:00.001000
54, 59, 66, 69, 73, 76, 42, 46, 63, 87  => 9 0:00:00.003000
```

Our first stall

When a genetic algorithm stalls it is often a clue to a pattern in the result or that there is something you know that the algorithm does not. For example, in the final output above the numbers form a pattern of runs that our current fitness function did not anticipate. The easiest way for the algorithm to make progress would be to change the values of the 7th-9th indexes from [42, 46, 63] to values in the range 77-86. The problem is it has no way to do that. So we will look at a simpler version of the issue to see why. For example, in the following sequence

```
3, 1, 6
```

the engine can change 1 to 4 or 5 to get a higher fitness. But in the following sequence

```
3, 1, 2, 6
```

the engine has to change 2 values to get a higher fitness. The problem is *get_best* is coded to only keep a change if the fitness is higher. So changing 2 to 5 or 1 to 4 in the above sequence does not improve the fitness and those changes will be abandoned. One solution would be to change the engine somehow, perhaps to keep changes that don't make the fitness worse, instead of keeping only those that increase it. We could do that but there's a better way that shows us something important.

Engineer a solution

Consider this sequence.

```
9, 30, 1, 20, 60
```

Would the following be an improvement?

```
9, 30, 15, 20, 60
```

Or this?

```
9, 16, 1, 20, 60
```

Both changes would be improvements because they smooth the point where the two runs meet from a gap of 29 to a gap of 15. Either could then be followed by another similar change that further reduces the gap, or even converts the two sorted runs into a single one. The way to help the engine keep this kind of change is to give partial credit in the fitness.

Fitness Technique: Give partial credit in the fitness if possible.

Use a *Fitness* object

We need to somehow prefer sequences with small gaps between the runs to those with large gaps. There are a couple of ways to do that. One way that is often seen when the engine has constraints on the type of the fitness value is to scale up the fitness value, multiplying by a large value like 1000 for example, and then subtracting the amount of the gap. Another way would be to make the fitness score a floating point value with the gap value in the decimal portion and subtracted from 1. These would both work but we would then have to decode them either mentally or actually if we want to break out each part of the fitness value for display.

Lucky for us our engine doesn't have a type limitation so we're going to keep the values separate but encapsulated in a problem-specific fitness object that can be compared to its own type. This allows us to determine the better of two gene sequences based on their fitness, while making the fitness object responsible for how it is displayed.

We start with the constructor.

sortedNumbersTests.py

```
51 class Fitness:
52     def __init__(self, numbersInSequenceCount, totalGap):
53         self.NumbersInSequenceCount = numbersInSequenceCount
54         self.TotalGap = totalGap
```

Next we need to be able to compare two fitness values.

```
56     def __gt__(self, other):
57         if self.NumbersInSequenceCount != other.NumbersInSequenceCount:
58             return self.NumbersInSequenceCount > other.NumbersInSequenceCount
59         return self.TotalGap < other.TotalGap
```

ⓘ __gt__ is name of the function that the built-in greater-than comparer looks for. If we provide an implementation, the comparer will use it. We could implement other comparison functions, such as less-than, equal, etc., but we only need to know if the fitness of the new gene sequence is better than the previous one. If we're careful with the comparisons we make in *get_best* then we can be lazy in implementing fitness objects in the future.

Lastly, the *Fitness* object needs to know how to convert itself to a `string` for display:

```
61  def __str__(self):
62      return "{} Sequential, {} Total Gap".format(
63          self.NumbersInSequenceCount,
64          self.TotalGap)
```

Use only > for fitness comparison

We need to be able to compare a *Chromosome*'s fitness with the optimal fitness in the engine and only use greater-than comparisons in the implementation.

genetic.py

```
    if not optimalFitness > bestParent.Fitness:
30      return bestParent

32  while True:
        child = _mutate(bestParent, geneSet, get_fitness)
34      if not child.Fitness > bestParent.Fitness:
            continue
36      display(child)
        if not optimalFitness > child.Fitness:
38          return child
        bestParent = child
```

Then we need to pass an instance of *Fitness* to *get_best* as the optimal value.

sortedNumbersTests.py

```
37      optimalFitness = Fitness(totalNumbers, 0)
38      best = genetic.get_best(fnGetFitness, totalNumbers, optimalFitness,
39                              geneset, fnDisplay)
40      self.assertTrue(not optimalFitness > best.Fitness)
```

Finally, we need to calculate the gap value and return an instance of *Fitness*.

```
def get_fitness(genes):
8    fitness = 1
    gap = 0
10   for i in range(1, len(genes)):
        if genes[i] > genes[i - 1]:
12          fitness += 1
        else:
14          gap += genes[i - 1] - genes[i]

16   return Fitness(fitness, gap)
```

Run 2

Now when we run the test it can find a solution about 70 percent of the time. When it can't the result looks like this:

```
. . .
10, 16, 18, 28, 30, 33, 7, 8, 9, 11  => 9 Sequential, 26 Total Gap    0:00:00.008001
10, 16, 18, 28, 30, 6, 7, 8, 9, 11   => 9 Sequential, 24 Total Gap    0:00:00.012001
10, 16, 18, 28, 29, 6, 7, 8, 9, 11   => 9 Sequential, 23 Total Gap    0:00:00.021002
```

Study the results

By studying the last line of output we see that we can to get partial fitness improvements by moving 29 and 6 closer to each other. However, they are both prevented from moving by a neighbor - 6 can't be replaced by a higher number, and 29 can't be replaced by a lower number, without reducing the fitness. This means considering only the gap at the discontinuity is insufficient. What would let us move forward is if 28 was reduced or 9 was increased, or if one of the neighbors changed so that we could have room to reduce the gap.

Engineer a solution

Now we will implement a change mentioned earlier. Instead of keeping only changes that have a better fitness than the parent, we're going to allow the engine to keep any change that results in a fitness equivalent to or better than the parent, like this:

genetic.py

```
32    while True:
          child = _mutate(bestParent, geneSet, get_fitness)
34        if bestParent.Fitness > child.Fitness:            <==
              continue                                        <==
36        if not child.Fitness > bestParent.Fitness:
              bestParent = child                              <==
38            continue
          display(child)
40        if not optimalFitness > child.Fitness:
              return child
42        bestParent = child
```

Run 3

Now when we run the test it can find a sorted sequence every time.

```
. . .
11, 3, 9, 27, 55, 69, 71, 76, 89, 86 => 8 Sequential, 11 Total Gap    0:00:00.001000
11, 3, 9, 41, 45, 47, 71, 76, 83, 86 => 9 Sequential, 8 Total Gap     0:00:00.001000
9, 3, 6, 18, 45, 47, 52, 76, 83, 86 => 9 Sequential, 6 Total Gap 0:00:00.002000
2, 3, 6, 36, 45, 47, 52, 76, 83, 86 => 10 Sequential, 0 Total Gap`    0:00:00.002000
```

We can tell that it kept equivalent genetic lines to get 9 items sorted and again to get
10 sorted because more than one number changed to get each of those improvements.
We can also see it switching genetic lines when multiple characters change at the same
time in the output from the password problem.

```
C!pDrdy!QtDq     0    0:00:00
ULzEoMJmzF!a     1    0:00:00.001000
HXoSocjYQtZb     2    0:00:00.005000
HxiKoIWeVj!x     3    0:00:00.007000
HxiKoIWerj!x     4    0:00:00.007000
HxEKoIWYrl!x     5    0:00:00.007000
HovlobWJrlUX     6    0:00:00.010000
HovlobWJrldv     7    0:00:00.010000
HuTlo WRrldp     8    0:00:00.016001
HeUlo WirldK     9    0:00:00.017001
HeUlo WUrld!    10    0:00:00.017001
Hello WNrld!    11    0:00:00.024001
Hello World!    12    0:00:00.034002
```

Split *get_best*

The loop code in *get_best* is becoming complex. One way to fix that is to extract a gener-
ator function. *get_best* will be responsible for displaying improvements and breaking
the loop.

```
   def get_best(get_fitness, targetLen, optimalFitness, geneSet, display):
28     random.seed()

30     def fnMutate(parent):
           return _mutate(parent, geneSet, get_fitness)
32
       def fnGenerateParent():
34         return _generate_parent(targetLen, geneSet, get_fitness)

36     for improvement in _get_improvement(fnMutate, fnGenerateParent):    <==
           display(improvement)                                           <==
38         if not optimalFitness > improvement.Fitness:                   <==
               return improvement                                         <==
```

And the `_get_improvement` will be responsible for generating successively better gene sequences which it will send to *get_best* via `yield`.

genetic.py

```
42 def _get_improvement(new_child, generate_parent):          <==
       bestParent = generate_parent()
44     yield bestParent                                        <==
       while True:
46         child = new_child(bestParent)
           if bestParent.Fitness > child.Fitness:
48             continue
           if not child.Fitness > bestParent.Fitness:
50             bestParent = child
               continue
52         yield child                                         <==
           bestParent = child
```

Benchmarks

Benchmark this project by having it produce a sequence of sorted numbers that takes 1-2 seconds to run on average.

sortedNumbersTests.py

```
44         self.assertTrue(not optimalFitness > best.Fitness)
45
46     def test_benchmark(self):
47         genetic.Benchmark.run(lambda: self.sort_numbers(40))
```

Since we modified the `genetic` module the previous benchmarks may have changed, so here are the updated benchmarks for all of the projects we've done so far:

project	average (seconds)	standard deviation
Guess Password	1.25	0.31
One Max	1.19	0.15
Sorted Numbers	1.27	0.75

Summary

In this project we considered a couple of ways to encode multiple goals into the fitness value, and how to use a comparable class instead of a number for fitness values. We also improved the engine by making it switch to new, equally good genetic.

The 8 Queens Puzzle

In this project we will solve the 8 Queens Puzzle.

In the game of chess, the queen can attack across any number of unoccupied squares on the board horizontally, vertically, or diagonally.

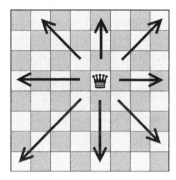

The 8 Queens Puzzle involves putting 8 queens on a standard chessboard such that none are under attack.

Take a couple of minutes to try to solve this with something physical like coins on a paper chessboard to get a feel for how it might work.

It turns out that getting 7 queens into safe positions on a chessboard isn't too difficult.

```
Q . . . . . . .
. . . . Q . . .
. . . . . . Q .
. Q . . . . . .
. . . Q . . . .
. . . . . . . Q
. . . . . . . .
. . Q . . . . .
```

Getting 8 takes a bit more work. According to WikiPedia (see: http://en.wikipedia.org/wiki/Eight_queens_puzzle) there are only 92 solutions to this puzzle and once we remove mirrors and rotations there are only 12 unique solutions.

There are 64 x 63 x 62 x 61 x 60 x 59 x 58 x 57 potential locations for the queens assuming we don't apply some logic to reduce the search space. That's a very large number, so clearly a straight iterative method is impractical.

This puzzle is like the sorted numbers project in that there are constraints on the genes, but instead of one or two constraints per gene we now have many because of the relationships between the genes that the engine knows nothing about.

Also, in the projects we've done so far the genes *were* the solution, so we were able to display them without transformation and our fitness code could simply compare them to each other or the known answer.

At a high level, the community calls the genetic encoding the *genotype* and the genes' ultimate form or behavior in the solution the *phenotype*.

The *genotype* is the way the parts of the problem are encoded so they can be manipulated by the genetic algorithm.
Example: potential genotypes for this project include:
- 64 bits, one for each of the 64 squares on the board
- 48 bits, 6 for each of the queen locations, because we can count to 64 with 6 bits
- 8 integers in the range 0..63 or 1..64
- 16 integers representing the row and column location of each queen

The *phenotype* is how the decoded genes are used in solving the problem. In each of the examples above the phenotype is locations of 8 queens on the board.
The fitness function then evaluates the phenotype in the context of the problem being solved to return a fitness value to the engine.

Also, like in the sorted numbers project, we have multiple potential solutions, and we're not going to hard-code them. So, we will have to calculate fitness based on characteristics.

At this point you should have enough information to attempt an implementation. Use whatever programming language you prefer, it does not have to be Python. Come back here once you are ready to step through my implementation process. This should be your pattern for the rest of the projects so that you approach each solution implementation having at least thought about what genes you would use, and how you might evaluate fitness.

Test class

```
1  import datetime
2  import unittest
3
4  import genetic
```

To start with we need to define the genotype. We will use two genes for the position of each queen – one each for the row and column. The chessboard conveniently has the same number of rows as columns (8) so we'll use the digits 0-7.

```
7  class EightQueensTests(unittest.TestCase):
8      def test(self, size=8):
9          geneset = [i for i in range(size)]
```

Board

We will use the genes as row and column indexes to plot queen locations on a board.

```
12  class Board:
        def __init__(self, genes, size):
14          board = [['.'] * size for _ in range(size)]
            for index in range(0, len(genes), 2):
16              row = genes[index]
                column = genes[index + 1]
18              board[column][row] = 'Q'
            self._board = board
```

We could have introduced a *Location* class to convert and encapsulate pairs of genes as Row and Column locations but since there is a direct correlation we don't need it. If we had chosen one of the other genotypes described above, it would have been an important step.

Display

The display function will let us visualize the queen locations

```python
def display(candidate, startTime, size):
    timeDiff = datetime.datetime.now() - startTime
    board = Board(candidate.Genes, size)
    board.print()
    print("{}\t- {}\t{}".format(
        ' '.join(map(str, candidate.Genes)),
        candidate.Fitness,
        timeDiff))


class EightQueensTests(unittest.TestCase):
```

but first we need to add a print function to *Board* class:

```python
        self._board = board

    def print(self):
        # 0,0 prints in bottom left corner
        for i in reversed(range(len(self._board))):
            print(' '.join(self._board[i]))
```

This produces output like the following:

```
Q . . . . . . .
. . . . Q . Q .
. . Q . . . . .
. . . . . . . Q
. . . . . . . .
. Q . . . . . .
. . . Q . . . .
. . . . . . Q .
1 2 7 4 6 6 4 6 3 1 6 0 2 5 0 7 - 3 0:00:00.005012
```

> ⓘ Printing comma separated values without a format `string` automatically separates them with a space.

The row of digits under the board is the set of genes that created that board layout. The number to the right is the fitness, and the elapsed time is on the end.

Fitness

To drive improvement we'll need to increase the fitness value whenever more queens can coexist on the board.

We'll start with considering the number of columns that do not have a queen. Here's a layout that gets an optimal score but is undesirable:

```
Q Q Q Q Q Q Q Q
. . . . . . . .
. . . . . . . .
. . . . . . . .
. . . . . . . .
. . . . . . . .
. . . . . . . .
. . . . . . . .
```

We'll also consider the number of rows that do not have queens. Here's a revised board where both situations are optimal but the layout still allows queens to attack one another:

```
Q . . . . . . .
. Q . . . . . .
. . Q . . . . .
. . . Q . . . .
. . . . Q . . .
. . . . . Q . .
. . . . . . Q .
. . . . . . . Q
```

To fix this problem we'll include the number of southeast diagonals that do not have a queen. Again we can find a corner case as follows:

```
. . . . . . . Q
. . . . . . Q .
. . . . . Q . .
. . . . Q . . .
. . . Q . . . .
. . Q . . . . .
. Q . . . . . .
Q . . . . . . .
```

To resolve this final issue we'll include the number of northeast diagonals that do not have a queen.

We can calculate indexes for the northeast diagonals in Excel using the formula =$A2+
B$1 which results in a grid as follows

```
      0    1    2    3    4    5    6    7
0     0    1    2    3    4    5    6    7
1     1    2    3    4    5    6    7    8
2     2    3    4    5    6    7    8    9
3     3    4    5    6    7    8    9    10
4     4    5    6    7    8    9    10   11
5     5    6    7    8    9    10   11   12
6     6    7    8    9    10   11   12   13
7     7    8    9    10   11   12   13   14
```

The indexes of the southeast diagonals can be calculated using =(8-1-$A2)+B$1 which
we can visualize as follows:

```
      0    1    2    3    4    5    6    7
0     7    8    9    10   11   12   13   14
1     6    7    8    9    10   11   12   13
2     5    6    7    8    9    10   11   12
3     4    5    6    7    8    9    10   11
4     3    4    5    6    7    8    9    10
5     2    3    4    5    6    7    8    9
6     1    2    3    4    5    6    7    8
7     0    1    2    3    4    5    6    7
```

Using the 2 formulas above along with the row and column values we can write a
fitness function that touches each board position exactly once, which makes it run
fast.

> Fitness Rule: The fitness function should run as fast as possible be-
> cause we're going to call it potentially millions of times.

The fitness value will be the sum of those four counts, subtracted from the maximum
value (8+8+8+8, or 32). This means the optimal value will be zero and higher values
will be worse. In all previous projects, higher fitnesses were better. How do we make
this work? The same way we did in the Sorted Numbers problem. We add a problem-
specific *Fitness* class where __gt__ is coded to prefer fewer queens under attack.

```
   class Fitness:
38     def __init__(self, total):
           self.Total = total
40
       def __gt__(self, other):
42         return self.Total < other.Total

44     def __str__(self):
           return "{}".format(self.Total)
46

48 if __name__ == '__main__':
```

Then we count the number of rows, columns, and diagonals that have queens to determine how many are under attack:

```
   def get_fitness(genes, size):
8      board = Board(genes, size)
       rowsWithQueens = set()
10     colsWithQueens = set()
       northEastDiagonalsWithQueens = set()
12     southEastDiagonalsWithQueens = set()
       for row in range(size):
14         for col in range(size):
               if board.get(row, col) == 'Q':
16                 rowsWithQueens.add(row)
                   colsWithQueens.add(col)
18                 northEastDiagonalsWithQueens.add(row + col)
                   southEastDiagonalsWithQueens.add(size - 1 - row + col)
20
       total = size - len(rowsWithQueens) \
22             + size - len(colsWithQueens) \
               + size - len(northEastDiagonalsWithQueens) \
24             + size - len(southEastDiagonalsWithQueens)

26     return Fitness(total)

28
   def display(candidate, startTime, size):
```

This requires the addition of a *get* function to the *Board* class:

```
           self._board = board
52
       def get(self, row, column):
54         return self._board[column][row]

56     def print(self):
```

Test

Finally our test harness brings all the parts together.

```
40  def test(self, size=8):
        geneset = [i for i in range(size)]
42      startTime = datetime.datetime.now()

44      def fnDisplay(candidate):
            display(candidate, startTime, size)
46
        def fnGetFitness(genes):
48          return get_fitness(genes, size)

50      optimalFitness = Fitness(0)
        best = genetic.get_best(fnGetFitness, 2 * size, optimalFitness,
52                              geneset, fnDisplay)
        self.assertTrue(not optimalFitness > best.Fitness)
```

Run

Now we can run the test to see if the engine can find a solution.

```
. . . . . Q . .
. . . Q Q . . .
. . . . Q . . .
. . . . . . . .
. . . . . . . .
. Q . . . . . .
. . Q . . . . .
. . . Q . . . Q
3 6 7 0 1 2 4 5 4 6 3 0 2 1 5 7 - 9 0:00:00
```

```
Q . . . . Q . .
. . Q . . . . .
. . . . Q . . .
. . . . . . . Q
. . . . . . . .
. . . . . . Q .
. . Q . . . . .
. . Q . . . . .
0 7 7 4 6 2 4 5 2 6 2 0 2 1 5 7 - 4 0:00:00.001003
```

```
. . . . Q . . .
. . Q . . . . .
Q . . . . . . .
. . . . . Q . .
. Q . . . . . .
. . . . . . . Q
. . . . . Q . .
. . . Q . . . .
7 2 1 3 0 5 4 7 3 0 6 4 2 6 5 1 - 0 0:00:00.098260
```

Some generations are left out for brevity but you can see that the engine can easily find optimal solutions to this puzzle. The solution above is particularly pleasing. We'll see it again in another project.

Benchmarks

The cool thing about our implementation is it works for N queens on an NxN chessboard too, so we can benchmark it with a more difficult problem, like 20 queens.

```
    def test_benchmark(self):
        genetic.Benchmark.run(lambda: self.test(20))


class Board:
```

```
. . . . . . . . . . . . Q . . . . . . .
. . . . . . . . . . . . . . . . . . . Q
. Q . . . . . . . . . . . . . . . . . .
. . . . . . . Q . . . . . . . . . . . .
. . . . . . . . . . . . . . . . Q . . .
. . . . . Q . . . . . . . . . . . . . .
. . . . . . Q . . . . . . . . . . . . .
. . . . . . . . Q . . . . . . . . . . .
Q . . . . . . . . . . . . . . . . . . .
. . . . . . . . . . . . . . Q . . . . .
. . . . . . . Q . . . . . . . . . . . .
. . . Q . . . . . . . . . . . . . . . .
. . . . . . . . . . . Q . . . . . . . .
. . . Q . . . . . . . . . . . . . . . .
. . . . . . . . . . . . . . Q . . . . .
. . . . . . . Q . . . . . . . . . . . .
. . . . . . . . . Q . . . . . . . . . .
. . . . . . Q . . . . . . . . . . . . .
. . . . . . . . . . . Q . . . . . . . .
. . Q . . . . . . . . . . . . . . . . .
10 4 11 19 5 14 6 2 17 10 14 1 8 9 18 15 3 6 4 8 13 3 2 0 1 17 15 7 9 16 7 13 12 12
    19 18 0 11 16 5 - 0 0:00:00.639702
```

We didn't change any code in the `genetic` module, so we can just run the N queens benchmark.

Benchmark

average (seconds)	standard deviation
1.38	1.17

Aside

If you think about it you should be able to see the queens problem as a variant of a scheduling or resource allocation problem, with the rows and columns representing resources, and the queens being people or things that require or consume resources, possibly with additional constraints (i.e. the diagonal attacks). With a different test class and genes you could solve a number of scheduling or resource allocation problems with the current engine. For example: baking pizzas in ovens, one pizza per oven. The rows could become ovens - possibly with special features like cooks-faster or -slower or only small pizzas. The columns become time slots, and the queens become pizzas with features like size, required cooking time, value, bonus for faster delivery, etc. Then you try to maximize the number of pizzas, or the amount of money earned. You get the idea.

Exercise

Change the 8 queens code to produce all 92 solutions.

Summary

In this project we learned the difference between genotype and phenotype. This was the first project we've had where the genotype was different from the phenotype. We also learned that we can easily make the engine select for gene sequences with lower fitness values instead of higher ones, should that be useful in solving a problem.

Graph Coloring

In this project we will try a type of problem known as graph coloring. Variations involve using the fewest number of colors while making each node a unique color, trying to use an equal number of each color, etc. By experimenting we can see that a shape surrounded by an even number of neighbors can generally be filled with only 3 colors.

While a shape surrounded by an odd number of neighbors requires 4 colors.

We will to try to use only 4 colors to color a map of the United States with the constraint that no adjacent states have the same color. To do this by hand, color any state then use alternating colors on its neighboring states, and only introduce a new color when necessary.

Now when we do this in code we don't care about the visual representation, just the physical relationships between the states, which we can encode as a graph, or more simply as a set of rules indicating which states cannot have the same color.

Data

We'll start off with a file containing a list of states and the set of states that are adjacent to each. Each row of the file contains the information for one state. There are 2 fields on each line, separated by a comma. The first field contains a unique code for the state. The second field contains a semicolon-separated list of the codes for its neighboring states. I used 2 columns in the table below to keep the list together.

AK,	MT,ID;ND;SD;WY
AL,FL;GA;MS;TN	NC,GA;SC;TN;VA
AR,LA;MO;MS;OK;TN;TX	ND,MN;MT;SD
AZ,CA;NM;NV;UT	NE,CO;IA;KS;MO;SD;WY
CA,AZ;NV;OR	NH,MA;ME;VT
CO,KS;NE;NM;OK;UT;WY	NJ,DE;NY;PA
CT,MA;NY;RI	NM,AZ;CO;OK;TX
DC,MD;VA	NV,AZ;CA;ID;OR;UT
DE,MD;NJ;PA	NY,CT;MA;NJ;PA;VT
FL,AL;GA	OH,IN;KY;MI;PA;WV
GA,AL;FL;NC;SC;TN	OK,AR;CO;KS;MO;NM;TX
HI,	OR,CA;ID;NV;WA
IA,IL;MN;MO;NE;SD;WI	PA,DE;MD;NJ;NY;OH;WV
ID,MT;NV;OR;UT;WA;WY	RI,CT;MA
IL,IA;IN;KY;MO;WI	SC,GA;NC
IN,IL;KY;MI;OH	SD,IA;MN;MT;ND;NE;WY
KS,CO;MO;NE;OK	TN,AL;AR;GA;KY;MO;MS;NC;VA
KY,IL;IN;MO;OH;TN;VA;WV	TX,AR;LA;NM;OK
LA,AR;MS;TX	UT,AZ;CO;ID;NV;WY
MA,CT;NH;NY;RI;VT	VA,DC;KY;MD;NC;TN;WV
MD,DC;DE;PA;VA;WV	VT,MA;NH;NY
ME,NH	WA,ID;OR
MI,IN;OH;WI	WI,IA;IL;MI;MN
MN,IA;ND;SD;WI	WV,KY;MD;OH;PA;VA
MO,AR;IA;IL;KS;KY;NE;OK;TN	WY,CO;ID;MT;NE;SD;UT
MS,AL;AR;LA;TN	

Take a break here and at least think about what genes you would use, and how you would evaluate fitness.

Reading the file

We'll use the `csv` module to read the file and split the lines on commas. Then we'll manually split the adjacent state list on semicolon and link the state and its list of adjacent states in a key-value table (`dict`).

graphColoringTests.py

```python
import csv

def load_data(localFileName):
    """ expects: AA,BB;CC where BB and CC are the
        initial column values in other rows
    """
    with open(localFileName, mode='r') as infile:
        reader = csv.reader(infile)
        lookup = {row[0]: row[1].split(';') for row in reader if row}
    return lookup
```

Rule

Now that we've read the data we need to build the rules. A *Rule* connects two states indicating that they are adjacent. When we create the rule we always sort the *state* and *adjacent* codes alphabetically. This makes it possible to eliminate duplicates.

```python
class Rule:
    def __init__(self, node, adjacent):
        if node < adjacent:
            node, adjacent = adjacent, node
        self.Node = node
        self.Adjacent = adjacent
```

Hashing and Uniqueness: Since we want to be able to put rules in a key-value table and uniquely identify them in a `list` we need to define `__hash__` and `__eq__`. The important feature of the `__hash__` function is that no combination of state and adjacent codes should get the same hash value. The implementation below multiplies the hash of the state code by a prime number then exclusive-ORs it with the hash of the adjacent state code.

```
22     def __eq__(self, other):
           return self.Node == other.Node and self.Adjacent == other.Adjacent

24     def __hash__(self):
           return hash(self.Node) * 397 ^ hash(self.Adjacent)
```

ⓘ The number 397 is only significant in that it is a prime number and thus useful in preventing hash collisions.

We may also want to be able to display a rule so we'll add a `__str__` implementation.

```
27     def __str__(self):
28         return self.Node + " -> " + self.Adjacent
```

State adjacency Rules

Next we will build the set of *Rule* objects. While we're doing so we will perform a sanity check on the data as follows: Whenever a key state says it is adjacent to another state, the adjacent state's rules should also say it is adjacent to the key state. We do that by keeping a count of the number of times we've seen each state pair. We should see each twice, so if we see it only once we know we have a data problem.

```
14 def build_rules(items):
       rulesAdded = {}
16     for state, adjacent in items.items():
           for adjacentState in adjacent:
18             if adjacentState == '':
                   continue
20             rule = Rule(state, adjacentState)
               if rule in rulesAdded:
22                 rulesAdded[rule] += 1
               else:
24                 rulesAdded[rule] = 1
       for k, v in rulesAdded.items():
26         if v != 2:
               print("rule {} is not bidirectional".format(k))
28     return rulesAdded.keys()

30
   class Rule:
```

We now have the ability to convert a file of node relationships to a set of adjacency *Rule* objects.

Test class

Next we will build the code used by the genetic engine.

```
   import csv
2  import datetime
   import unittest

4
   import genetic
```

Test

We'll start by loading the states from the file and building the rules. Since the expected optimal situation will be that all adjacent states have different colors, we can set the optimal value to the number of rules. Our *Chromosome* will have 50 genes, one for each state in alphabetical order. This lets us use the index into its genes as an index into a list of sorted state codes.

```
32      return rulesAdded.keys()

34
   class GraphColoringTests(unittest.TestCase):
36      def test(self):
            states = load_data("adjacent_states.csv")
38          rules = build_rules(states)
            optimalValue = len(rules)
40          stateIndexLookup = {key: index
                              for index, key in enumerate(sorted(states))}
```

Genes

Next, since we want to four-color the 50 states, our genotype can be four color codes (the first letter of each color name).

```
42          colors = ["Orange", "Yellow", "Green", "Blue"]
43          colorLookup = {color[0]: color for color in colors}
44          geneset = list(colorLookup.keys())
```

Now add the usual function definitions and call *get_best*.

```
46    startTime = datetime.datetime.now()

48    def fnDisplay(candidate):
          display(candidate, startTime)

50    def fnGetFitness(genes):
          return get_fitness(genes, rules, stateIndexLookup)

52
      best = genetic.get_best(fnGetFitness, len(states), optimalValue,
54                             geneset, fnDisplay)
      self.assertTrue(not optimalValue > best.Fitness)
```

And at the end we can write out the color of each state.

```
57    keys = sorted(states.keys())
58    for index in range(len(states)):
59        print(keys[index] + " is " + colorLookup[best.Genes[index]])
```

Fitness

Next, we need a fitness function that counts how many constraints the gene sequence passed.

```
def get_fitness(genes, rules, stateIndexLookup):
36    rulesThatPass = sum(1 for rule in rules
                          if rule.IsValid(genes, stateIndexLookup))
38    return rulesThatPass

40
class GraphColoringTests(unittest.TestCase):
```

This uses a new function in the *Rule* class:

```
      def __str__(self):
82        return self.Node + " -> " + self.Adjacent

84    def IsValid(self, genes, nodeIndexLookup):
          index = nodeIndexLookup[self.Node]
86        adjacentStateIndex = nodeIndexLookup[self.Adjacent]
          return genes[index] != genes[adjacentStateIndex]
```

Display

As for the display function, it should be sufficient to output the genes because they are also color codes.

```python
def display(candidate, startTime):
    timeDiff = datetime.datetime.now() - startTime
    print("{}\t{}\t{}".format(
        ''.join(map(str, candidate.Genes)),
        candidate.Fitness,
        timeDiff))


class GraphColoringTests(unittest.TestCase):
```

Run

Now when we run our main `test` function we get output like the following. The number to the right of the gene sequence indicates how many rules this gene sequence satisfies.

```
. . .
GOGOYYGOBGYOYYOOOGOBYOGOYYGOBBYOGGYYBBGOBYBYBGOOBOO 103 0:00:00.014000
YOGOYYGOBGYYGYBOOGOBYGGOYYGOBBYOGGYYBBGOBYBYBYOOBOO 105 0:00:00.017001
YOGOYYGOBGYYGYBOOGOBYGGOYYGOBBYOGGYYBBGOBYBYBYOOYBO 106 0:00:00.017001
GOGOYYOGYBYGGYBOOGOBBBBOYYGGBBYOGGYYBBGYOYBYBYOOYOO 107 0:00:00.040002
AK is Green
AL is Orange
AR is Green
AZ is Orange
CA is Yellow
CO is Yellow
CT is Orange
...
TX is Yellow
UT is Blue
VA is Yellow
VT is Orange
WA is Orange
WI is Yellow
WV is Orange
WY is Orange
```

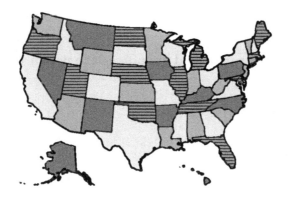

Benchmarking

To benchmark this project we're going to use R100_1gb, one of the graph color-ing problem sets available from https://turing.cs.hbg.psu.edu/txn131/graphcoloring.html The file format is line based, with each line prefixed with its type. The lines we're interested in start with e, for edge, followed by the numeric IDs of the two nodes con-nected by that edge, as follows:

```
e 16 10
```

If we change the format of our adjacent state file to the same format, then we'll be able to reuse a lot of code. We'll start by adding a utility test-function that reads our current file and outputs the contents in the new format.

Convert the state file

```
class GraphColoringTests(unittest.TestCase):
50      @staticmethod
        def test_convert_file():
52          states = load_data("adjacent_states.csv")
            output = []
54          nodeCount = edgeCount = 0
            for state, adjacents in states.items():
56              nodeCount += 1
                for adjacent in adjacents:
58                  if adjacent == '':
                        output.append("n {} 0".format(state))
60                  else:
                        output.append("e {} {}".format(state, adjacent))
62                      edgeCount += 1
            with open('./adjacent_states.col', mode='w+') as outfile:
64              print("p edge {} {}".format(nodeCount, edgeCount), file=outfile)
                for line in sorted(output):
66                  print(line, file=outfile)
```

When we run this test we end up with a file whose content looks like the following:

```
p edge 51 214
e AL FL
e AL GA
. . .
e WY UT
n AK 0
n HI 0
```

Alaska and Hawaii do not have edges, so the only way we know about them is from their node (n) records.

The utility function and `import csv` can be removed after the file is converted.

Read the new file format

Next we need to update *load_data* to read the new file format.

```
    def load_data(localFileName):
8       """ expects: T D1 [D2 ... DN]
            where T is the record type
10          and D1 .. DN are record-type appropriate data elements
        """
12      rules = set()
        nodes = set()
14      with open(localFileName, mode='r') as infile:
            content = infile.read().splitlines()
16      for row in content:
            if row[0] == 'e':  # e aa bb, aa and bb are node ids
18              nodeIds = row.split(' ')[1:3]
                rules.add(Rule(nodeIds[0], nodeIds[1]))
20              nodes.add(nodeIds[0])
                nodes.add(nodeIds[1])
22              continue
            if row[0] == 'n':  # n aa ww, aa is a node id, ww is a weight
24              nodeIds = row.split(' ')
                nodes.add(nodeIds[1])
26      return rules, nodes
```

ⓘ Now we're returning a set of *Rule* objects *and* a set of node names. We'll capture those in variables in the test function. Since we have `__hash__` and `__eq__` functions on the *Rule* class, putting the rules in a set automatically eliminates the bi-directional equivalents.

Extract parameters

We'll also take this opportunity to rename the test function to *color* and make the file name and color list into parameters. Then we'll also add a *test_states* function that uses the *color* function.

```
class GraphColoringTests(unittest.TestCase):
44    def test_states(self):
          self.color("adjacent_states.col",
46                    ["Orange", "Yellow", "Green", "Blue"])

48    def color(self, file, colors):
          rules, nodes = load_data(file)
50        optimalValue = len(rules)
          colorLookup = {color[0]: color for color in colors}
```

Remove the following line from the *color* function since the list of colors is now a parameter.

```
colors = ["Orange", "Yellow", "Green", "Blue"]
```

Node indexes

The next change to the *color* function affects how we get the node indexes.

```
52        geneset = list(colorLookup.keys())
          startTime = datetime.datetime.now()
54        nodeIndexLookup = {key: index
                             for index, key in enumerate(sorted(nodes))}    <==
56
          def fnDisplay(candidate):
58            display(candidate, startTime)

60        def fnGetFitness(genes):
              return get_fitness(genes, rules, nodeIndexLookup)            <==
```

Update the final output

Finally, we have to update the way we write out the results at the end of the test function:

```
          best = genetic.get_best(fnGetFitness, len(nodes), optimalValue,
64                                 geneset, fnDisplay)
          self.assertTrue(not optimalValue > best.Fitness)
66
          keys = sorted(nodes)                                            <==
68        for index in range(len(nodes)):                                 <==
              print(keys[index] + " is " + colorLookup[best.Genes[index]])
```

Be sure to run the state test to verify that it still works.

Add the benchmark test

Next we can add a test for the `R100_1gb` data as follows:

```
                        ["Orange", "Yellow", "Green", "Blue"])
64
       def test_R100_1gb(self):
66           self.color("R100_1gb.col",
                   ["Red", "Orange", "Yellow", "Green", "Blue", "Indigo"])
```

Benchmarks

When we run the test it is able to find a way to color the graph using 6 colors relatively quickly. It can also find a solution using 5 colors but that takes longer than we want to spend on a benchmark, so we'll stay with 6 colors. We'll use this test as our benchmark for graph coloring.

```
69     def test_benchmark(self):
70         genetic.Benchmark.run(lambda: self.test_R100_1gb())
71
72     def color(self, file, colors):
```

Benchmark

average (seconds)	standard deviation
0.74	0.42

Summary

In this project we read from a file and built constraints that can be applied to each candidate to determine its fitness. This was also the first project where we used test data from a standard set. Reading about others' solutions to the same standard problem is a good way to learn advanced techniques and to get inspiration for improving your fitness function and genotype.

Card Problem

In this project we will solve the Card Problem. We start off with the set of cards, Ace and 2-10, which we separate into 2 groups of 5 cards. The cards in each group have different constraints. The card values in one group must have a product of 360. The card values in the other group must sum to 36. We can only use each card once. First try it by hand with a deck of cards. Then at least think about what genes you would use, and how you would evaluate fitness.

Test class and genes

For this project our genotype and phenotype can be the same, integers. Thus we can avoid an encode/decode step.

cardTests.py

```
   import datetime
2  import unittest

4  import genetic

6
   class CardTests(unittest.TestCase):
8      def test(self):
           geneset = [i + 1 for i in range(10)]
```

Fitness

This keeps fitness calculation relatively easy because we can sum one range of genes and multiply the rest. In this project we have 3 values to include in the fitness. One is the sum of the numbers in the first group. Another is the product of the numbers in the second group. The last is a count of the duplicated numbers in the list; we don't want any duplicates.

```python
3  import operator
4  import unittest
```

```python
   def get_fitness(genes):
10     group1Sum = sum(genes[0:5])
       group2Product = functools.reduce(operator.mul, genes[5:10])
12     duplicateCount = (len(genes) - len(set(genes)))
       return Fitness(group1Sum, group2Product, duplicateCount)

14

16 class CardTests(unittest.TestCase):
```

Once again we'll use a *Fitness* class.

```python
   class Fitness:
22     def __init__(self, group1Sum, group2Product, duplicateCount):
           self.Group1Sum = group1Sum
24         self.Group2Product = group2Product
           sumDifference = abs(36 - group1Sum)
26         productDifference = abs(360 - group2Product)
           self.TotalDifference = sumDifference + productDifference
28         self.DuplicateCount = duplicateCount
```

When comparing two fitnesses, we'll prefer gene sequences with fewer duplicates, and when those are the same, we'll prefer the one whose sum and product values are closer to the optimal values.

```python
30     def __gt__(self, other):
           if self.DuplicateCount != other.DuplicateCount:
32             return self.DuplicateCount < other.DuplicateCount
           return self.TotalDifference < other.TotalDifference

34

36 if __name__ == '__main__':
       unittest.main()
```

Display

In the display function we'll separate the two groups visually with a dash.

```python
16  def display(candidate, startTime):
        timeDiff = datetime.datetime.now() - startTime
18      print("{} - {}\t{}\t{}".format(
            ', '.join(map(str, candidate.Genes[0:5])),
20          ', '.join(map(str, candidate.Genes[5:10])),
            candidate.Fitness,
22          timeDiff))

24
    class CardTests(unittest.TestCase):
```

We need to add a `__str__` function to the *Fitness* class:

```python
44      def __str__(self):
            return "sum: {} prod: {} dups: {}".format(
46              self.Group1Sum,
                self.Group2Product,
48              self.DuplicateCount)

50
    if __name__ == '__main__':
```

Test

Here's the rest of the test harness:

```python
26      def test(self):
            geneset = [i + 1 for i in range(10)]
28          startTime = datetime.datetime.now()

30          def fnDisplay(candidate):
                display(candidate, startTime)
32
            def fnGetFitness(genes):
34              return get_fitness(genes)

36          optimalFitness = Fitness(36, 360, 0)
            best = genetic.get_best(fnGetFitness, 10, optimalFitness, geneset,
38                                   fnDisplay)
            self.assertTrue(not optimalFitness > best.Fitness)
```

Run

Now we're ready to try it.

sample output

```
2, 3, 1, 6, 4 - 8, 5, 9, 7, 10   sum: 16 prod: 25200 dups: 0 0:00:00
```

Study the result

We can see that the mutation function quickly eliminates the duplicate values, but the algorithm almost always gets stuck immediately thereafter. The reason is, in order to make progress it has to be able to change 2 numbers. But, it can only change 1 at a time and the priority of eliminating duplicates keeps it from moving forward.

Introducing custom mutation

We need to find a way to let the engine make two changes at once, ideally without introducing duplication in the process. This means changing the way mutation works. The most flexible way to do that is to introduce an optional parameter called *custom_mutate* into *get_best* that allows us to perform the mutation ourselves. Then we replace the current definition of *fnMutate* with a different one depending on whether or not *custom_mutate* is provided.

genetic.py

```
26  def get_best(get_fitness, targetLen, optimalFitness, geneSet, display,
                custom_mutate=None):

28      if custom_mutate is None:
            def fnMutate(parent):
30              return _mutate(parent, geneSet, get_fitness)
        else:
32          def fnMutate(parent):
                return _mutate_custom(parent, custom_mutate, get_fitness)
```

We'll use a variant of *_mutate* instead of the built-in implementation when *custom_mutate* is used.

```
16  def _mutate_custom(parent, custom_mutate, get_fitness):
        childGenes = parent.Genes[:]
18      custom_mutate(childGenes)
        fitness = get_fitness(childGenes)
20      return Chromosome(childGenes, fitness)

22
    def _generate_parent(length, geneSet, get_fitness):
```

Mutate

Now back in our genetic algorithm we can add a mutation function that changes 1 random gene if there are duplicates, but otherwise swaps 2 genes.

cardTests.py

```
 3  import operator
 4  import random
```

```
26  def mutate(genes, geneset):
        if len(genes) == len(set(genes)):
28          indexA, indexB = random.sample(range(len(genes)), 2)
            genes[indexA], genes[indexB] = genes[indexB], genes[indexA]
30      else:
            indexA = random.randrange(0, len(genes))
32          indexB = random.randrange(0, len(geneset))
            genes[indexA] = geneset[indexB]
34

36  class CardTests(unittest.TestCase):
```

Then we pass that function to *get_best* in the test harness.

```
        def fnMutate(genes):                                      <==
48          mutate(genes, geneset)

50      optimalFitness = Fitness(36, 360, 0)
        best = genetic.get_best(fnGetFitness, 10, optimalFitness, geneset,
52                          fnDisplay, custom_mutate=fnMutate)        <==
        self.assertTrue(not optimalFitness > best.Fitness)
```

Run 2

Now when we run the test, it can find the solution about 20 percent of the time. The rest of the time it still gets stuck.

sample output

```
8, 10, 7, 6, 4 - 9, 3, 2, 1, 5  sum: 35 prod: 270 dups: 0   0:00:00
10, 5, 6, 4, 8 - 3, 9, 2, 1, 7  sum: 33 prod: 378 dups: 0   0:00:00.001033
```

Study the result

When we compare the last line in these results with the optimal solution, we can see that the test needs to be able to swap 2 elements on the left side with 2 on the right.

Engineer a solution

We can solve that by looping the swap portion of the mutation function a random number of times.

```
26  def mutate(genes, geneset):
        if len(genes) == len(set(genes)):
28          count = random.randint(1, 4)
            while count > 0:
30              count -= 1
                indexA, indexB = random.sample(range(len(genes)), 2)
32              genes[indexA], genes[indexB] = genes[indexB], genes[indexA]
        else:
34          indexA = random.randrange(0, len(genes))
            indexB = random.randrange(0, len(geneset))
36          genes[indexA] = geneset[indexB]
```

We'll see this pattern again in other projects.

Run 3

Now, when we run the test it finds the optimal solution every time.

sample output

```
7, 4, 6, 10, 9 - 8, 3, 5, 1, 2  sum: 36 prod: 240 dups: 0   0:00:00
7, 4, 9, 8, 6 - 1, 3, 5, 2, 10  sum: 34 prod: 300 dups: 0   0:00:00
9, 8, 3, 7, 6 - 5, 4, 1, 2, 10  sum: 33 prod: 400 dups: 0   0:00:00.002000
9, 10, 3, 7, 6 - 5, 4, 1, 2, 8  sum: 35 prod: 320 dups: 0   0:00:00.002000
9, 7, 10, 5, 3 - 6, 1, 2, 8, 4  sum: 34 prod: 384 dups: 0   0:00:00.003000
5, 8, 10, 3, 9 - 4, 1, 7, 2, 6  sum: 35 prod: 336 dups: 0   0:00:00.003000
3, 6, 10, 7, 8 - 9, 2, 5, 1, 4  sum: 34 prod: 360 dups: 0   0:00:00.015001
7, 9, 2, 8, 10 - 6, 3, 1, 5, 4  sum: 36 prod: 360 dups: 0   0:00:00.023001
```

Retrospective

In all previous projects the only ability we've had to guide the algorithm towards a solution has been the fitness value. We've seen that the fitness alone can usually be used to work around structural constraints in the genes. In this project we started using mutation to work around structural constraints as well, but custom mutation is much more powerful than that. It can also take advantage of problem-specific knowledge to narrow the search scope toward better solutions, away from unworkable ones, or both. When we start using mutation that way we're no longer building a simple genetic algorithm, we're building a memetic algorithm.

Memetic algorithms are capable of solving a wider range of problems than random-population-based genetic algorithms because they accelerate the search. Take some time and try to use custom mutation to improve the speed of previous project solutions.

Your mutate function for the 8 Queens Puzzle can now take advantage of problem-specific knowledge such as: no 2 queens will be in the same row or column. So, like this project's mutate function, if there is a duplicate row index, change a random row index, otherwise swap 2 row indexes. The same can be done for the column indexes.

In the Password and One Max projects you might try changing a random number of genes. Another option is to create an empty dictionary of index-to-known in the test harness and pass it to your mutation function. Then each time you make a random change, check the fitness and compare it with the initial fitness from when the mutation function was called. If the random change makes the fitness worse, then you'll know that the previous value at that index was the correct one. Add it to the dictionary and only change that location if it doesn't match what is in the dictionary. There's a lot you could do with this concept, so experiment.

The speed of the Sorted Numbers project could be improved in several ways. For example, we could increment all the values in the final run of the array by 1 if possible, or decrement all the values in the first run by 1 if possible, or change 1 value on both sides of a discontinuity to bring the lines together faster. You will likely think of more.

Also, in Graph Coloring you could take advantage of the adjacency rules to choose a compatible color for a particular gene index.

> Memetic algorithm DOs and DON'Ts: It is important to balance keeping the algorithm fast with letting it take advantage of problem-specific knowledge. It is OKAY to check the fitness as long as that runs fast. DO NOT make a lot of changes without checking the fitness. If checking fitness, DO return the first improvement you find. DO NOT try to solve the entire problem, let the genetic engine and the random number generator do their jobs.

Benchmarks

```
58    def test_benchmark(self):
          genetic.Benchmark.run(lambda: self.test())
60

62  class Fitness:
```

Because we changed the `genetic` module we'll update all of the benchmarks.

Updated Benchmarks

project	average (seconds)	standard deviation
Guess Password	1.23	0.28
One Max	1.24	0.17
Sorted Numbers	1.15	0.66
Queens	1.45	1.07
Graph Coloring	0.79	0.41
Cards	0.01	0.01

Summary

In this project we added the very useful ability to take over mutation from the engine. We also learned about memetic algorithms and how the custom mutation function can be used to take advantage of problem-specific knowledge. Finally, we used the sum-of-difference technique, which is a commonly used in numerical problems.

Knights Problem

The next project is to figure out the minimal number of chess knights necessary to attack every square on a chess board. This means our chessboard must be at least 3x4 for some number of knights to be able to attack all squares on the board because a knight can only attack certain squares relative to its own location:

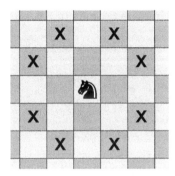

The knight can attack, at most, 8 squares, fewer when positioned along an edge.

Stop here and at least think about what genes you would use, and how you would evaluate fitness.

Genes

For our genotype we could use the same number as squares on our chessboard so that each represents a location. That has the advantage of preventing duplication. Its major disadvantage is that most of the positions will be empty. A better option is for each gene to be a knight location, just like we did in the 8 Queens project. This works as long as we know how many knights are required, which we do for square boards as you'll see later.

Position

This time we're going to use a *Position* class with X and Y coordinates.

knightsTests.py

```
1  class Position:
2      def __init__(self, x, y):
3          self.X = x
4          self.Y = y
```

Attacks

We're going to need a utility function that returns all the squares a knight could attack from a given location, respecting the bounds of the chessboard.

```
   def get_attacks(location, boardWidth, boardHeight):
2      return [i for i in set(
           Position(x + location.X, y + location.Y)
4          for x in [-2, -1, 1, 2] if 0 <= x + location.X < boardWidth
           for y in [-2, -1, 1, 2] if 0 <= y + location.Y < boardHeight
6          and abs(y) != abs(x))]

8
   class Position:
```

Introducing *custom_create*

We have a problem in that the engine doesn't know how to create a Position object. We could pass a list of all possible positions to the engine but there are a lot of them and there's a better way. We could also add an optional function that can be called to create an individual gene, but a more efficient and flexible solution is to provide a function for creating the entire set of genes for a *Chromosome*.

genetic.py

```
32  def get_best(get_fitness, targetLen, optimalFitness, geneSet, display,
33              custom_mutate=None, custom_create=None):
34  ...
```

```
40                    return _mutate_custom(parent, custom_mutate, get_fitness)

42      if custom_create is None:                                        <==
            def fnGenerateParent():
44              return _generate_parent(targetLen, geneSet, get_fitness)
        else:
46          def fnGenerateParent():                                      <==
                genes = custom_create()
48              return Chromosome(genes, get_fitness(genes))

50      for improvement in _get_improvement(fnMutate, fnGenerateParent):
    ...
```

Create

Now we can add a *create* function to the algorithm file. It will assign a specific number of knights to unique board positions.

knightsTests.py

```
  def create(fnGetRandomPosition, expectedKnights):
2     genes = [fnGetRandomPosition() for _ in range(expectedKnights)]
      return genes

4
6 def get_attacks(location, boardWidth, boardHeight):
```

Mutate

We chose not to provide all possible genes to the engine, so we need to use a custom mutation function as well.

```
  import random
2

4 def mutate(genes, fnGetRandomPosition):
      index = random.randrange(0, len(genes))
6     genes[index] = fnGetRandomPosition()

8
  def create(fnGetRandomPosition, expectedKnights):
```

Display

Since we want to show the board in the display function, we'll adapt the *Board* class from our 8 Queens Puzzle implementation.

```python
28  class Board:
        def __init__(self, positions, width, height):
30          board = [['.'] * width for _ in range(height)]

32          for index in range(len(positions)):
                knightPosition = positions[index]
34              board[knightPosition.Y][knightPosition.X] = 'N'
            self._board = board
36          self._width = width
            self._height = height

38
        def print(self):
40          # 0,0 prints in bottom left corner
            for i in reversed(range(self._height)):
42              print(i, "\t", ' '.join(self._board[i]))
            print(" \t", ' '.join(map(str, range(self._width))))
```

```python
    import datetime
2   import random

4
    def display(candidate, startTime, boardWidth, boardHeight):
6       timeDiff = datetime.datetime.now() - startTime
        board = Board(candidate.Genes, boardWidth, boardHeight)
8       board.print()

10      print("{}\n\t{}\t{}".format(
            ' '.join(map(str, candidate.Genes)),
12          candidate.Fitness,
            timeDiff))
```

We also want the display function to show us the positions of the knights as coordinates. Since we use map to convert the *Position* objects to strings, we have to implement __str__.

```python
37          self.Y = y
38
39      def __str__(self):
40          return "{},{}".format(self.X, self.Y)
```

Fitness

For fitness we can just count the unique squares that can be attacked by the knights.

```python
def get_fitness(genes, boardWidth, boardHeight):
    attacked = set(pos
                   for kn in genes
                   for pos in get_attacks(kn, boardWidth, boardHeight))
    return len(attacked)


def display(candidate, startTime, boardWidth, boardHeight):
```

In order to put the *Position* objects into a set, we also have to implement __hash__ and __eq__.

```python
    def __eq__(self, other):
        return self.X == other.X and self.Y == other.Y

    def __hash__(self):
        return self.X * 1000 + self.Y


class Board:
```

Test

Finally, we're going to try this out on a chessboard we can check by hand.

```
2    N N N .
1    . . . .
0    . N N N
     0 1 2 3
```

Note, indexes rise starting from the bottom left corner.

Here's the test harness:

```python
import random
import unittest

import genetic
```

```
44 class KnightsTests(unittest.TestCase):
       def test_3x4(self):
46         width = 4
           height = 3
48         # 1,0   2,0   3,0
           # 0,2   1,2   2,2
50         # 2      N N N .
           # 1       . . . .
52         # 0       . N N N
           #         0 1 2 3
54         self.find_knight_positions(width, height, 6)
```

```
56     def find_knight_positions(self, boardWidth, boardHeight, expectedKnights):
           startTime = datetime.datetime.now()
58
           def fnDisplay(candidate):
60             display(candidate, startTime, boardWidth, boardHeight)
62         def fnGetFitness(genes):
               return get_fitness(genes, boardWidth, boardHeight)
64
           def fnGetRandomPosition():
66             return Position(random.randrange(0, boardWidth),
                               random.randrange(0, boardHeight))
```

```
68         def fnMutate(genes):
               mutate(genes, fnGetRandomPosition)
70
           def fnCreate():
72             return create(fnGetRandomPosition, expectedKnights)
74         optimalFitness = boardWidth * boardHeight
           best = genetic.get_best(fnGetFitness, None, optimalFitness, None,
76                             fnDisplay, fnMutate, fnCreate)
           self.assertTrue(not optimalFitness > best.Fitness)
```

Run

When we run test_3x4 we get output like the following:
sample output

```
2    N . . .
1    N N N .
0    . N . N
     0 1 2 3
0,1 2,1 3,0 0,2 1,0 1,1
    10  0:00:00.001002
```

```
2      . . N N
1      . N . .
0      N N N .
       0 1 2 3
1,0 2,2 3,2 2,0 0,0 1,1
    11  0:00:00.003007
```

```
2      . . N N
1      . . N .
0      N N N .
       0 1 2 3
3,2 2,2 2,0 1,0 2,1 0,0
    12  0:00:00.006015
```

As expected it finds a solution equivalent to our hand coded one.

Test 8x8

We can use OEIS (see: https://oeis.org/A261752) to learn that 14 knights are required
to attack all squares on a standard 8x8 chessboard. Let's see if we can verify it.

```
56    def test_8x8(self):
          width = 8
58        height = 8
          self.find_knight_positions(width, height, 14)
60
      def find_knight_positions(self, boardWidth, boardHeight, expectedKnights):
```

Run

sample output

```
. . .
7      . . . . . . . .
6      . . . . . . . .
5      . N N . . N N .
4      . . N N N N . .
3      . . . . . N . .
2      . . N N N N . .
1      . . N . . . . .
0      . . . . . . . .
       0 1 2 3 4 5 6 7
2,5 3,2 6,5 4,2 3,4 1,5 2,1 5,3 2,2 5,2 4,4 5,5 2,4 5,4
    63  0:00:00.117311
```

```
7     . . . . . . . .
6     . . . . . . . .
5     . N N . . N N .
4     . . N N N N . .
3     . . . . . . . .
2     . . N N N N . .
1     . . N . . N . .
0     . . . . . . . .
      0 1 2 3 4 5 6 7
2,5 3,2 6,5 5,1 3,4 1,5 2,1 4,2 2,2 5,2 4,4 5,5 2,4 5,4
      64  0:00:00.414100
```

It finds an optimal solution every time.

Try 10x10

Let's try it on a 10x10 board. OEIS says the optimal solution requires 22 knights.

```python
    def test_10x10(self):
        width = 10
        height = 10
        self.find_knight_positions(width, height, 22)

    def find_knight_positions(self, boardWidth, boardHeight, expectedKnights):
```

Run

```
9     . . . . . . . . . .
8     . N . . . . . . . .
7     . N N . . N N N N .
6     . . N N . . . . . .
5     . . . N . . . N N .
4     . . . . . . . . . .
3     . . N N . N N . . .
2     . . N . . . N N . .
1     . . N . N . . N . .
0     . . . . . . . . . .
      0 1 2 3 4 5 6 7 8 9
8,7 7,2 2,1 7,5 3,6 3,5 2,2 2,7 3,3
6,3 2,3 8,5 5,7 2,6 5,3 4,1 6,7 1,7
6,2 7,1 1,8 7,7
        100 knights: 22  0:00:16.277931
```

It finds a solution, but it takes a while.

Performance

Let's see if we can improve the performance. First we'll benchmark it:

```
98          self.assertTrue(not optimalFitness > best.Fitness)
99
100     def test_benchmark(self):
101         genetic.Benchmark.run(lambda: self.test_10x10())
```

> ℹ When you run this benchmark you might find that it cannot complete all 100 rounds. This can happen if it ends up with a knight configuration where moving any knight to any location results in a worse fitness. This is called a local minimum, or local maximum, depending on whether you are trying to find a lower or higher fitness, respectively.

The change we are about to make is one way to work around the local maximum.

```
26 def mutate(genes, fnGetRandomPosition):
       count = 2 if random.randint(0, 10) == 0 else 1
28     while count > 0:
           count -= 1
30         index = random.randrange(0, len(genes))
           genes[index] = fnGetRandomPosition()
```

This does not fix the local maximum issue. It simply gives a 1/10 chance of making two changes instead of one, which means the engine now has a random chance of finding the right pair of moves to get past a local maximum. However, as the board size increases, the chance of making the right two moves in a row drops precipitously.

Here's my starting benchmark for the 10x10 board.

average (seconds)	standard deviation
15.49	15.52

Study the result

If you study the optimal 8x8 and 10x10 board layouts you may notice the following pattern: knights are never located on edge rows or columns. This makes sense because a knight can attack, at most, 4 squares from an edge whereas being located just one square away from any edge increases that to 6 squares.

♀When we exploit that pattern our genetic algorithm becomes a memetic algorithm because we're taking advantage of problem-specific knowledge.

Engineer a solution

Our first performance improvement will be to only use non-edge locations for knights.

```
78        allPositions = [Position(x, y)
                          for y in range(boardHeight)
80                        for x in range(boardWidth)]

82        if boardWidth < 6 or boardHeight < 6:
              nonEdgePositions = allPositions
84        else:
              nonEdgePositions = [i for i in allPositions
86                                 if 0 < i.X < boardWidth - 1 and
                                      0 < i.Y < boardHeight - 1]

88
          def fnGetRandomPosition():
90            return random.choice(nonEdgePositions)
```

Run

Updated Benchmark

average (seconds)	standard deviation
3.76	3.84

The pattern we discovered netted us a nice performance improvement. Not only did we improve the knights' chances of hitting, we also reduced the search space on a 10x10 board by removing more than 1/3 of the potential knight positions. That is the virtuous cycle I mentioned back in the first project in action.

Choose wisely

We can get another performance boost by moving knights whose attacks are all covered by other knights to a position where they can attack a square that is not currently under attack. There's a performance hit for checking all the squares and knight attacks but it is more than compensated for if it results in an improvement. Consider that for a 10x10 board the chances of picking the right knight (1 in 22) and moving it to bring a new square under attack (1 in 32 at worst because even the corner square can be attacked from 2 positions in the non-edge 8x8 center) is 1 in 704.

We start off as before but with some additional parameters.

```
26  def mutate(genes, boardWidth, boardHeight, allPositions, nonEdgePositions):
27      count = 2 if random.randint(0, 10) == 0 else 1
28      while count > 0:
29          count -= 1
30  ...
```

The parameters come from *find_knight_positions* as follows:

```
123          def fnMutate(genes):
124              mutate(genes, boardWidth, boardHeight, allPositions,
125                  nonEdgePositions)
126  ...
```

Now continuing to modify the mutation function, the next thing we do is figure out which knights are attacking which squares. The array in the dictionary has each knight's gene index.

```
30          positionToKnightIndexes = dict((p, []) for p in allPositions)
31          for i, knight in enumerate(genes):
32              for position in get_attacks(knight, boardWidth, boardHeight):
33                  positionToKnightIndexes[position].append(i)
34  ...
```

Then we get a list of indexes of knights whose attacks are all covered by some other knight, and while we're at it we build a list of the squares that are not under attack.

```
        knightIndexes = set(i for i in range(len(genes)))
36      unattacked = []
        for kvp in positionToKnightIndexes.items():
38          if len(kvp[1]) > 1:
                continue
40          if len(kvp[1]) == 0:
                unattacked.append(kvp[0])
42              continue
            for p in kvp[1]:   # len == 1
44              if p in knightIndexes:
                    knightIndexes.remove(p)
46  ...
```

Next we build the list of locations from which the *unattacked* squares can be attacked. We keep the duplicates because that makes them more likely to be selected, resulting in attacking multiple new squares at once.

```
48        potentialKnightPositions = \
             [p for positions in
50              map(lambda x: get_attacks(x, boardWidth, boardHeight),
                    unattacked)
52              for p in positions if p in nonEdgePositions] \
                    if len(unattacked) > 0 else nonEdgePositions
   ...
```

Then we choose a gene (knight) to replace.

```
54        geneIndex = random.randrange(0, len(genes)) \
55            if len(knightIndexes) == 0 \
56            else random.choice([i for i in knightIndexes])
57 ...
```

Lastly, we replace that knight with one likely to improve the fitness.

```
58        position = random.choice(potentialKnightPositions)
59        genes[geneIndex] = position
```

Run 2

Updated Benchmark

average (seconds)	standard deviation
0.79	1.02

Retrospective

The ability to control Chromosome creation often goes hand-in-hand with a custom mutation function. With both tools at your disposal you can simplify mutation functions in previous problems, such as in the Card, Sorted Numbers and 8 Queens projects. Use *custom_create* to prevent the creation of invalid sequences so you don't have to correct for them during mutation or in the fitness value. As with custom mutation, don't try to force a solution in this function. Let the genetic engine do its job.

Benchmarks

We made another change to `genetic` so we'll update the benchmarks.

project	average (seconds)	standard deviation
Guess Password	1.21	0.31
One Max	1.23	0.16
Sorted Numbers	1.15	0.60
Queens	1.61	1.18
Graph Coloring	0.77	0.40
Cards	0.01	0.01
Knights	0.79	1.02

Summary

This was our first use of a custom object instead of a letter or number for our genotype. This led to the introduction of the ability to customize gene sequence creation in the `genetic` module. Custom creation and custom mutation are frequently used together. We'll use both of these techniques together again in future projects.

Magic Squares

Magic squares are squares of numbers where each of the rows and columns and both major diagonals sum to the same value, and all of the numbers between 1 and n^2 are used only once.

example

$$\begin{array}{ccc} 6 & 7 & 2 \\ 1 & 5 & 9 \\ 8 & 3 & 4 \end{array}$$

Take a break here and at least think about what genes you would use, and how you would evaluate fitness.

Test class

We'll start with the test stub.

magicSquareTests.py

```python
import datetime
import random
import unittest

import genetic


class MagicSquareTests(unittest.TestCase):
    def test_size_3(self):
        self.generate(3)
```

Test harness

In the test harness we'll determine the range of numbers to use to fill the magic square from its diagonal size then calculate the expected sum. We then pass those to the fitness function.

```
12    def generate(self, diagonalSize):
          nSquared = diagonalSize * diagonalSize
14        geneset = [i for i in range(1, nSquared + 1)]
          expectedSum = diagonalSize * (nSquared + 1) / 2
16
          def fnGetFitness(genes):
18            return get_fitness(genes, diagonalSize, expectedSum)
    ...
```

Fitness

For fitness we can count the number of rows, columns, and diagonals where the sum is equal to the expected sum.

```
8  def get_fitness(genes, diagonalSize, expectedSum):
       rowSums = [0 for _ in range(diagonalSize)]
10     columnSums = [0 for _ in range(diagonalSize)]
       southeastDiagonalSum = 0
12     northeastDiagonalSum = 0

14     for row in range(diagonalSize):
           for column in range(diagonalSize):
16             value = genes[row * diagonalSize + column]
               rowSums[row] += value
18             columnSums[column] += value
           southeastDiagonalSum += genes[row * diagonalSize + row]
20         northeastDiagonalSum += genes[row * diagonalSize +
                                         (diagonalSize - 1 - row)]
22
       fitness = sum(1 for s in rowSums + columnSums +
24                 [southeastDiagonalSum, northeastDiagonalSum]
                   if s == expectedSum)
26
       return fitness
28

30 class MagicSquareTests(unittest.TestCase):
```

Unfortunately, that means if we want to display the sums we have to recalculate them. So, let's extract a reusable function.

```python
def get_sums(genes, diagonalSize):
    rows = [0 for _ in range(diagonalSize)]
    columns = [0 for _ in range(diagonalSize)]
    southeastDiagonalSum = 0
    northeastDiagonalSum = 0
    for row in range(diagonalSize):
        for column in range(diagonalSize):
            value = genes[row * diagonalSize + column]
            rows[row] += value
            columns[column] += value
        southeastDiagonalSum += genes[row * diagonalSize + row]
        northeastDiagonalSum += genes[row * diagonalSize +
                                      (diagonalSize - 1 - row)]
    return rows, columns, northeastDiagonalSum, southeastDiagonalSum


class MagicSquareTests(unittest.TestCase):
```

Then call it from the fitness function:

```python
def get_fitness(genes, diagonalSize, expectedSum):
    rows, columns, northeastDiagonalSum, southeastDiagonalSum = \
        get_sums(genes, diagonalSize)

    fitness = sum(1 for s in rows + columns +
                  [southeastDiagonalSum, northeastDiagonalSum]
                  if s == expectedSum)

    return fitness
```

Display

We can call that function from the display function too.

```
def display(candidate, diagonalSize, startTime):
    timeDiff = datetime.datetime.now() - startTime

    rows, columns, northeastDiagonalSum, southeastDiagonalSum = \
        get_sums(candidate.Genes, diagonalSize)

    for rowNumber in range(diagonalSize):
        row = candidate.Genes[
            rowNumber * diagonalSize:(rowNumber + 1) * diagonalSize]
        print("\t ", row, "=", rows[rowNumber])
    print(northeastDiagonalSum, "\t", columns, "\t", southeastDiagonalSum)
    print(" - - - - - - - - - -", candidate.Fitness, timeDiff)


def get_sums(genes, diagonalSize):
```

This will produce output like the following:

sample output

```
    [5, 1, 8] = 14
    [6, 4, 9] = 19
    [3, 7, 2] = 12
15  [14, 12, 19]   11
- - - - - - - - - - - 1 0:00:00.001000
```

ⓘWe could use format strings to justify the numbers but that involves converting each number to a string, finding the longest one, and then dynamically building a format string. However, all we really want is an idea of what is happening; a comma in the output works fine for that.

Now, since one of the constraints is that we have to use all the numbers between 1 and n^2, we'll pass a *custom creation* function that produces a random permutation of all values in that range

```
58        def fnGetFitness(genes):
              return get_fitness(genes, diagonalSize, expectedSum)
60
          def fnCustomCreate():
62            return random.sample(geneset, len(geneset))

64        optimalValue = 2 + 2 * diagonalSize
          startTime = datetime.datetime.now()
66        best = genetic.get_best(fnGetFitness, nSquared, optimalValue,
                                   geneset, fnDisplay, fnMutate, fnCustomCreate)
68
          self.assertTrue(not optimalValue > best.Fitness)
70

72 if __name__ == '__main__':
       unittest.main()
```

Mutate

We'll also pass a companion *custom mutation* function so we don't have to worry about duplication being introduced by the engine's built-in mutation function. We could simply swap two genes but for performance we're going to pass in the index options. This can often provide a good performance boost versus generating a list of indexes each time we enter the function.

```
def mutate(genes, indexes):
50     indexA, indexB = random.sample(indexes, 2)
       genes[indexA], genes[indexB] = genes[indexB], genes[indexA]
52
54 class MagicSquareTests(unittest.TestCase):
```

Here's the rest of the test harness.

```
          def fnGetFitness(genes):
64            return get_fitness(genes, diagonalSize, expectedSum)

66        def fnDisplay(candidate):
              display(candidate, diagonalSize, startTime)
68
          geneIndexes = [i for i in range(0, len(geneset))]
70
          def fnMutate(genes):
72            mutate(genes, geneIndexes)

74        def fnCustomCreate():
```

Run

And, when we run it we get a result like the following:

sample result

```
. . .
     [8, 3, 4] = 15
     [1, 9, 5] = 15
     [2, 7, 6] = 15
15   [11, 19, 15]    23
- - - - - - - - - - - 5 0:00:00.001001
```

We can run the test many times but it will rarely find a valid solution.

Use sum of differences

The problem is the fitness function is written exclusively rather than inclusively. It only gives credit when the sum exactly matches the expected sum, so there's no partial credit for the genetic engine to take advantage of. This is a problem we've encountered before. The solution is to take the sum of the differences between the actual sum and the expected sum for each row, column, and diagonal. That makes zero optimal, so we'll need a *Fitness* object to help reverse the greater-than logic used to compare fitnesses in the engine.

```
86  class Fitness:
        def __init__(self, sumOfDifferences):
88          self.SumOfDifferences = sumOfDifferences

90      def __gt__(self, other):
            return self.SumOfDifferences < other.SumOfDifferences
92
        def __str__(self):
94          return "{}".format(self.SumOfDifferences)

96
    if __name__ == '__main__':
```

Next we update *get_fitness*:

```
 8  def get_fitness(genes, diagonalSize, expectedSum):
        rows, columns, northeastDiagonalSum, southeastDiagonalSum = \
10          get_sums(genes, diagonalSize)

12      sumOfDifferences = sum(int(abs(s - expectedSum))
                               for s in rows + columns +
14                             [southeastDiagonalSum, northeastDiagonalSum]
                               if s != expectedSum)

16
        return Fitness(sumOfDifferences)
```

And the optimal fitness value in our test.

```
78          optimalValue = Fitness(0)
79          startTime = datetime.datetime.now()
```

Run 2

Now when we run the test we get a valid solution about 60% of the time but only because it just happens to find a sequence of swaps that drive improvement. When it doesn't find a sequence

sample result

```
        [4, 8, 3] = 15
        [2, 6, 7] = 15
        [9, 1, 5] = 15
18      [15, 15, 15]    15
- - - - - - - - - - - 3 0:00:00.002005
```

it gets stuck at a position where it requires at least 2 swaps to make progress. We're hitting a local minimum.

Fixing the local minimum / maximum issue

To fix the local minimum/local maximum issue we're going to allow the current genetic line to die out. The first step in that is tracking how many generations have passed since the last improvement. We'll call this its *Age*.

genetic.py

```
    class Chromosome:
70      def __init__(self, genes, fitness):
            self.Genes = genes
72          self.Fitness = fitness
            self.Age = 0
```

Next, we'll add an optional parameter that allows us to set an upper limit on the age of a genetic line. That parameter will be passed through to _get_improvement.

```
32 def get_best(get_fitness, targetLen, optimalFitness, geneSet, display,
33           custom_mutate=None, custom_create=None, maxAge=None):
34 ...
```

```
49     for improvement in _get_improvement(fnMutate, fnGenerateParent, maxAge):
```

For the next part we need to import a couple of functions from other modules.

```
4 import time
5 from bisect import bisect_left
6 from math import exp
```

Then we need to separate the best parent from the current parent so that we still have something to compare to when a genetic line dies out. We're also going to keep a list containing the fitnesses of the historical best parents.

```
57 def _get_improvement(new_child, generate_parent, maxAge):
58     parent = bestParent = generate_parent()
59     yield bestParent
60     historicalFitnesses = [bestParent.Fitness]
```

Next, we want to make sure we retain the current functionality if the maximum age is not provided.

```
   while True:
62         child = new_child(parent)
       if parent.Fitness > child.Fitness:
64             if maxAge is None:
                   continue
```

However, when the child's fitness is worse than that of its parent, the most traveled path through the code, and a maximum age is provided, then we need to check whether or not the genetic line's age has reached the maximum.

```
66             parent.Age += 1
67             if maxAge > parent.Age:
68                 continue
```

If so, we may allow the genetic line to die and replace it with something else. We're going to do that using simulated annealing.

Annealing is a method used to reduce internal stresses in materials like metal. At a high level, it works by heating the metal to a high temperature then allowing it to cool slowly. As you know, heat causes metal to expand. So the metal expands, loosening the bonds between materials in the metal, allowing them to move around. Then the metal is allowed to cool slowly. As the metal cools the bonds tighten again and the impurities get pushed along by the increasing pressure until they find something to bond with or until there is no more wiggle-room, thus reducing overall stress in the system.

The standard global search algorithm only allows a parent to be replaced by a child with equal or better fitness. This makes it very difficult to break out of a local minimum or maximum because the only way out is through chance discovery of an equal or better gene sequence that is different enough from the current gene sequence to escape the local minimum/maximum, an unlikely event.

Simulated annealing resolves this by slowly increasing the *probability* of replacing the parent with a different gene sequence, even if that gene sequence has a worse fitness, based in part on *how long* we've been using that parent to try to make the next generation. Thus, the implementation in this book uses the term *age* to control the simulated annealing process.

In order to keep the labels semantically close to those associated with annealing metal, however, the community tends to use the terms *heat*, *temperature*, and *energy* where I use *age* and *probability*. I find the terms *heat* and *energy* to be leaky equivalents when explaining the algorithm because it isn't obvious how to apply them to a gene sequence. Unfortunately *age* is also a leaky equivalent because the growth in probability is nonlinear. However, the resultant implementation is the same if you ignore the variable names: the probability of replacing the parent depends on how long we've been using the same parent and how different the new gene sequence is from the parent.

We need to determine how far away the child's fitness is from the best fitness. If we had a numeric fitness it would be a simple calculation. But our fitnesses aren't always numeric. No problem, we'll figure out where it would be in the realm of historical fitnesses.

```
69    index = bisect_left(historicalFitnesses, child.Fitness, 0,
70                        len(historicalFitnesses))
```

Whether calculating the difference directly from the fitness, or by using its index into the historical fitnesses as we do here, we get a proportion by dividing the child's index by the index of the best value, in this case the highest index.

```
71    proportionSimilar = index / len(historicalFitnesses)
```

Then we raise Euler's number (e), roughly 2.718, to the power of the proportion negated. The result is a floating point number that approaches 1 if the child's fitness is far away from the best fitness, but approaches ~0.36 when its fitness is very close to the best fitness. In the following sample chart assume the maximum current index is 50:

index	difference	proportion similar	$e^{-proportion}$
0	50	0.0	1.00
5	45	0.1	0.90
10	40	0.2	0.82
40	10	0.8	0.45
45	5	0.9	0.41
50	0	1.0	0.37

A child whose fitness is close to the current best will have a high index (because the higher/better fitnesses are at the end of the array) and a low difference from the best fitness. As a result, it will have a lower chance of becoming the new parent. A child that has a fitness far from the current best will have a low index and high difference, and thus a high chance of becoming the new parent.

Next we pick a random number and if that random number is smaller than $e^{-proportion}$ then the child becomes the new parent.

```
72        if random.random() < exp(-proportionSimilar):
73            parent = child
74            continue
```

Otherwise we replace the parent with the best parent and reset its age to zero so it has time to anneal.

```
75            bestParent.Age = 0
76            parent = bestParent
77            continue
```

Next we consider what to do if the child's fitness is not lower than that of its parent.

```
78      if not child.Fitness > parent.Fitness:
            # same fitness
80          child.Age = parent.Age + 1
            parent = child
82          continue
```

When the child has a better fitness than its parent, we reset its age to zero and make it the new parent.

```
83          child.Age = 0
84          parent = child
```

Finally, when we find a child whose fitness is better than that of the best parent, we replace the best parent and append its fitness to the list of historical fitnesses.

```
85      if child.Fitness > bestParent.Fitness:
86          bestParent = child
87          yield bestParent
88          historicalFitnesses.append(bestParent.Fitness)
```

Set the maximum age

Now, to use it in our test harness we just need to set the maxiumum age. But what value should we use? How do we pick a good maximum age? Let's sample the average run times for the projects where we've encountered local minimums or maximums.

	50	500	5000	no max
Knights	0.63 +/- 0.47	0.68 +/- 0.52	0.66 +/- 0.53	0.61 +/- 0.46
Magic Square	0.01 +/- 0.01	0.04 +/- 0.06	0.39 +/- 0.47	*

* could not complete.

That's interesting. The Knights project doesn't appear to benefit from allowing genetic lines to age out. Magic squares, however, clearly benefits not only from having a maximum age but also from having a low one.

magicSquareTests.py

```
class MagicSquareTests(unittest.TestCase):
56      def test_size_3(self):
            self.generate(3, 50)
58
        def generate(self, diagonalSize, maxAge):
```

```
80        best = genetic.get_best(fnGetFitness, nSquared, optimalValue,
81                        geneset, fnDisplay, fnMutate, fnCustomCreate,
82                        maxAge)
```

Run 3

Now the test can quickly find a solution for a size-3 magic square every time.

```
    [6, 7, 2] = 15
    [1, 5, 9] = 15
    [8, 3, 4] = 15
15  [15, 15, 15]    15
- - - - - - - - - - 0 0:00:00.008000
```

Size-5 Magic Squares

Size-5 magic squares need a higher maximum age.

```
59    def test_size_5(self):
60        self.generate(5, 500)
61
62    def generate(self, diagonalSize, maxAge):
```

Run

It can find a magic square every time but we're really giving the simulated annealing code a workout to get it.

sample result

```
    [25, 3, 10, 4, 23] = 65
    [9, 21, 8, 14, 13] = 65
    [22, 6, 5, 15, 17] = 65
    [2, 16, 24, 12, 11] = 65
    [7, 19, 18, 20, 1] = 65
65  [65, 65, 65, 65, 65]    64
- - - - - - - - - - - 1 0:00:00.285760
    [13, 16, 7, 4, 25] = 65
    [22, 19, 5, 9, 10] = 65
    [20, 3, 17, 14, 11] = 65
    [2, 6, 24, 15, 18] = 65
    [8, 21, 12, 23, 1] = 65
65  [65, 65, 65, 65, 65]    65
- - - - - - - - - - - 0 0:00:00.921482
```

Size-10 Magic Squares

```
65    def test_size_10(self):
66        self.generate(10, 5000)
67
68    def generate(self, diagonalSize, maxAge):
```

Given time, it can build larger squares too:
note: alignment manually adjusted for clarity

```
        [31,   9,  50,  21,  81,  92,  27,  34,  97, 63] = 505
        [ 8,  80,  86,  29,  40,  24, 100,  55,  72, 11] = 505
        [87,  53,  69,  95,  15,  67,  94,   6,  17,  2] = 505
        [79,  30,  37,  28,  38,  71,  42,  96,  62, 22] = 505
        [54,  46,  56,  93,   3,  74,  59,  52,  23, 45] = 505
        [35,  89,  98,  83,  32,   4,  10,   5,  58, 91] = 505
        [19,  75,   1,  41,  61,  70,  33,  76,  47, 82] = 505
        [20,  44,  78,  12,  85,  36,  65,  99,  18, 48] = 505
        [88,  13,  14,  64,  73,  60,  49,  25,  68, 51] = 505
        [84,  66,  16,  39,  77,   7,  26,  57,  43, 90] = 505
505     [505, 505, 505, 505, 505, 505, 505, 505, 505, 505]    505
- - - - - - - - - - - 0 0:04:24.477191
```

Retrospective

We saw that using various maximum ages on the Knight's project had no particular effect. What do you think will happen if you use a maximum age for the other projects? Try it.

Benchmarks

We'll benchmark this project with size-4 magic squares because size-5 runs a bit slower than I like in a benchmark.

```
59    def test_size_4(self):
60        self.generate(4, 50)
61
62    def test_size_5(self):
```

```
68    def test_benchmark(self):
69        genetic.Benchmark.run(self.test_size_4)
70
71    def generate(self, diagonalSize, maxAge):
```

We rewrote a core function of the genetic module so we'll update the benchmarks to make sure there was no unintended slowdown in the ability to solve the previous projects.

Updated Benchmarks

project	average (seconds)	standard deviation
Guess Password	1.31	0.41
One Max	1.22	0.17
Sorted Numbers	1.23	0.83
Queens	1.39	1.03
Graph Coloring	0.78	0.34
Cards	0.01	0.01
Knights	0.61	0.46
Magic Square	0.33	0.56

Summary

In this project we encountered the first project where our forward progress was significantly impacted by a local minimum. We resolved this by adding an option to the engine that allows it to escape local minimums/maximums through the use of simulated annealing. This is also the first time we passed the gene indexes to the mutate function. We'll be using this again.

Knapsack Problem

The goal of this project is to put as much stuff into a container as it will hold while optimizing for constraints such as item weight, size, shape, and value, and in variations of the problem, for the shape of the container. The bounded knapsack problem has a limitation on the number of each particular item available. In the 1/0 knapsack problem you can take no more than 1 of any given item. In the unbounded variant of the knapsack problem you are only limited by the container. We'll try a simple version of the unbounded knapsack problem so we can understand how it works.

Resources

We'll start by defining some resources:

Name	Value	Weight(kg)	Volume(L^3)
Flour	1680	0.265	0.41
Butter	1440	0.5	0.13
Sugar	1840	0.441	0.29

This implies a *Resource* class.

knapsackTests.py

```
class Resource:
    def __init__(self, name, value, weight, volume):
        self.Name = name
        self.Value = value
        self.Weight = weight
        self.Volume = volume
```

111

Test

We will hard code the resources into our test.

```
   import datetime
 2 import unittest

 4 import genetic

 6
   class KnapsackTests(unittest.TestCase):
 8     def test_cookies(self):
           items = [
10                 Resource("Flour", 1680, 0.265, .41),
                   Resource("Butter", 1440, 0.5, .13),
12                 Resource("Sugar", 1840, 0.441, .29)
               ]

14

16 class Resource:
```

For the container limits, let's say the knapsack contents cannot weigh more than 10 kilograms and its maximum volume is 4 cubic liters.

```
13         ]
14         maxWeight = 10
15         maxVolume = 4
```

Our goal is to maximize the value of the contents of the knapsack within those constraints. Think about how you would implement this before proceeding.

Let's think about how we would accomplish that by hand. We want a high ratio of value to weight and value to volume so we can get the highest possible total value. When we can't stuff any more of the resource with the best ratio into the knapsack, we fill in the remaining space with the next most valuable resource, and so on. Once the knapsack is full we have to consider whether we would be better off replacing one item type with a combination of others in order to increase the total value of the items in the knapsack.

ItemQuantity

This time we'll make the genes instances of an *ItemQuantity* class containing the resource and the quantity of that resource to take.

```python
24          self.Volume = volume

26 class ItemQuantity:
       def __init__(self, item, quantity):
28         self.Item = item
           self.Quantity = quantity
30
       def __eq__(self, other):
32         return self.Item == other.Item and self.Quantity == other.Quantity
```

Fitness

To calculate fitness we need to sum the weight, volume, and value of items in the knapsack.

> ℹ We're going to be careful about how we select genes so that they will never exceed the weight or volume constraints. Therefore, we don't have to check those here.

```python
  def get_fitness(genes):
8     totalWeight = 0
      totalVolume = 0
10    totalValue = 0
      for iq in genes:
12        count = iq.Quantity
          totalWeight += iq.Item.Weight * count
14        totalVolume += iq.Item.Volume * count
          totalValue += iq.Item.Value * count
16
      return Fitness(totalWeight, totalVolume, totalValue)
18
20 class KnapsackTests(unittest.TestCase):
```

We use these values to populate a *Fitness* object.

When comparing *Fitness* instances we will prefer the one with the highest value.

```
              return self.Item == other.Item and self.Quantity == other.Quantity
46

48 class Fitness:
       def __init__(self, totalWeight, totalVolume, totalValue):
50         self.TotalWeight = totalWeight
           self.TotalVolume = totalVolume
52         self.TotalValue = totalValue

54     def __gt__(self, other):
           if self.TotalValue != other.TotalValue:
56             return self.TotalValue > other.TotalValue
           if self.TotalWeight != other.TotalWeight:
58             return self.TotalWeight < other.TotalWeight
           return self.TotalVolume < other.TotalVolume
60
       def __str__(self):
62         return "wt: {:0.2f} vol: {:0.2f} value: {}".format(
                   self.TotalWeight,
64                 self.TotalVolume,
                   self.TotalValue)
66

68 if __name__ == '__main__':
       unittest.main()
```

ℹ️Because we're only comparing one value and using greater-than to do so, we could simply return the total value from *get_fitness*. But having all three in the *Fitness* object is convenient for displaying them.

Max Quantity

We'll limit the quantity to valid ranges for each item.

```
2 import sys
3 import unittest
```

```
   def max_quantity(item, maxWeight, maxVolume):
22     return min(int(maxWeight / item.Weight)
                  if item.Weight > 0 else sys.maxsize,
24                 int(maxVolume / item.Volume)
                  if item.Volume > 0 else sys.maxsize)
26

28 class KnapsackTests(unittest.TestCase):
```

Create

Each time our *custom_create* implementation adds an *ItemQuantity* to the genes, it reduces the remaining weight and volume so it doesn't exceed those limits. When creating a new *Chromosome* we're going to take as much as we can of each item we choose so we fill our container quickly and thus have fewer items to exchange if they aren't the best choices.

```python
import random
import sys
```

```python
def create(items, maxWeight, maxVolume):
    genes = []
    remainingWeight, remainingVolume = maxWeight, maxVolume
    for i in range(random.randrange(1, len(items))):
        newGene = add(genes, items, remainingWeight, remainingVolume)
        if newGene is not None:
            genes.append(newGene)
            remainingWeight -= newGene.Quantity * newGene.Item.Weight
            remainingVolume -= newGene.Quantity * newGene.Item.Volume
    return genes


class KnapsackTests(unittest.TestCase):
```

When adding an item we're going to exclude item types that are already in the knapsack from our options because we don't want to have to sum multiple groups of a particular item type. Then we pick a random item and add as much of that item to the knapsack as we can.

```python
def add(genes, items, maxWeight, maxVolume):
    usedItems = {iq.Item for iq in genes}
    item = random.choice(items)
    while item in usedItems:
        item = random.choice(items)

    maxQuantity = max_quantity(item, maxWeight, maxVolume)
    return ItemQuantity(item, maxQuantity) if maxQuantity > 0 else None


class KnapsackTests(unittest.TestCase):
```

Mutate

We'll start off the mutation function by getting the fitness. We need it so we can calculate the remaining weight and volume.

```
48      return ItemQuantity(item, maxQuantity) if maxQuantity > 0 else None

50
    def mutate(genes, items, maxWeight, maxVolume):
52      fitness = get_fitness(genes)
        remainingWeight = maxWeight - fitness.TotalWeight
54      remainingVolume = maxVolume - fitness.TotalVolume
```

Next, because we don't know how many different items we'll take we don't know how long the gene sequence needs to be. This means our gene sequence will have a variable length, up to the number of different items. So we have to handle adding and removing items in addition to the usual item replacement. We'll implement *removing* first.

We need to give it a small chance of removing an item from the knapsack. We'll only do that if we have more than one item so that the knapsack is never empty. We don't immediately return when removing an item because we know removing an item reduces the fitness.

```
        removing = len(genes) > 1 and random.randint(0, 10) == 0
56      if removing:
            index = random.randrange(0, len(genes))
58          iq = genes[index]
            item = iq.Item
60          remainingWeight += item.Weight * iq.Quantity
            remainingVolume += item.Volume * iq.Quantity
62          del genes[index]
```

We'll always add if the length is zero and when there is weight or volume available. Otherwise, if we haven't used all the item types, we'll give the algorithm a small chance of adding another item type. If it does then we return the result.

```
64      adding = (remainingWeight > 0 or remainingVolume > 0) and \
                (len(genes) == 0 or
66                (len(genes) < len(items) and random.randint(0, 100) == 0))

68      if adding:
            newGene = add(genes, items, remainingWeight, remainingVolume)
70          if newGene is not None:
                genes.append(newGene)
72              return
```

Next we need to implement item replacement by picking a random item that is already in the knapsack then adding its quantity weight and volume to our total available.

```
74      index = random.randrange(0, len(genes))
        iq = genes[index]
76      item = iq.Item
        remainingWeight += item.Weight * iq.Quantity
78      remainingVolume += item.Volume * iq.Quantity
```

Then we give the algorithm a chance to pick a different item type. If we do replace it, we prevent the item type we're replacing from being selected.

```
80      changeItem = len(genes) < len(items) and random.randint(0, 4) == 0
81      if changeItem:
82          itema, itemb = random.sample(items, 2)
83          item = itema if itema != item else itemb
```

Either way we replace the current gene unless the maximum quantity is zero, in which case we remove the gene.

```
84      maxQuantity = max_quantity(item, remainingWeight, remainingVolume)
        if maxQuantity > 0:
86          quantity = random.randint(1, maxQuantity)
            genes[index] = ItemQuantity(item, quantity)
88      else:
            del genes[index]
```

💡We receive a shallow copy of the list of genes from the engine, so we must be careful to create a new *ItemQuantity* object instead of simply changing the quantity on the existing object, which would unintentionally change the parent's gene too.

Display

In the display function we'll show the resource names and quantities so we know what to buy, and their total value, weight, and volume.

```python
22  def display(candidate, startTime):
        timeDiff = datetime.datetime.now() - startTime
24      genes = candidate.Genes[:]
        genes.sort(key=lambda iq: iq.Quantity, reverse=True)
26
        descriptions = [str(iq.Quantity) + "x" + iq.Item.Name for iq in genes]
28      if len(descriptions) == 0:
            descriptions.append("Empty")
30      print("{}\t{}\t{}".format(
            ', '.join(descriptions),
32          candidate.Fitness,
            timeDiff))
34
36  def max_quantity(item, maxWeight, maxVolume):
```

The output should look like this:

```
13xSugar, 1xButter  wt: 6.23 vol: 3.90 value: 25360 0:00:00.001002
```

Test

Here's the full test function

```python
        def test_cookies(self):
108         items = [
                Resource("Flour", 1680, 0.265, .41),
110             Resource("Butter", 1440, 0.5, .13),
                Resource("Sugar", 1840, 0.441, .29)
112         ]
            maxWeight = 10
114         maxVolume = 4
            optimal = get_fitness(
116             [ItemQuantity(items[0], 1),
                 ItemQuantity(items[1], 14),
118              ItemQuantity(items[2], 6)])
            self.fill_knapsack(items, maxWeight, maxVolume, optimal)
```

and the test harness:

```
120          self.fill_knapsack(items, maxWeight, maxVolume, optimal)

       def fill_knapsack(self, items, maxWeight, maxVolume, optimalFitness):
122          startTime = datetime.datetime.now()

124          def fnDisplay(candidate):
                 display(candidate, startTime)
126
             def fnGetFitness(genes):
128              return get_fitness(genes)

130          def fnCreate():
                 return create(items, maxWeight, maxVolume)
132
             def fnMutate(genes):
134              mutate(genes, items, maxWeight, maxVolume)

136          best = genetic.get_best(fnGetFitness, None, optimalFitness, None,
                                     fnDisplay, fnMutate, fnCreate)
138          self.assertTrue(not optimalFitness > best.Fitness)
```

Run

When we run *test_cookies*

sample output

```
19xButter, 1xSugar  wt: 9.94 vol: 2.76 value: 29200 0:00:00.003007
```

it gets stuck. From previous experience we know this means it is hitting a local maximum. We also know the fix is to use simulated annealing to escape from the local maximum.

Use simulated annealing

```
136          best = genetic.get_best(fnGetFitness, None, optimalFitness, None,
137                                   fnDisplay, fnMutate, fnCreate, maxAge=50)
```

Run 2

Now when we run the test it can find the optimal solution every time.

sample output

```
5xFlour, 1xSugar    wt: 1.77 vol: 2.34 value: 10240 0:00:00
9xFlour, 1xSugar    wt: 2.83 vol: 3.98 value: 16960 0:00:00
13xSugar    wt: 5.73 vol: 3.77 value: 23920 0:00:00
12xSugar, 2xButter  wt: 6.29 vol: 3.74 value: 24960 0:00:00.002977
12xSugar, 4xButter  wt: 7.29 vol: 4.00 value: 27840 0:00:00.002977
20xButter   wt: 10.00 vol: 2.60 value: 28800    0:00:00.004022
19xButter, 1xSugar  wt: 9.94 vol: 2.76 value: 29200 0:00:01.682475
12xButter, 8xSugar  wt: 9.53 vol: 3.88 value: 32000 0:00:01.868943
15xButter, 5xSugar, 1xFlour wt: 9.97 vol: 3.81 value: 32480 0:00:01.921079
14xButter, 6xSugar, 1xFlour wt: 9.91 vol: 3.97 value: 32880 0:00:02.828494
```

Excellent! But does it work on larger problem sets?

Solving a harder problem

Like other projects we've seen, knapsack problems are very popular and as a result there are standard problem sets available. One such set, named exnsd16, is available from PYAsUKP:

https://github.com/henriquebecker91/masters/tree/master/data/ukp

File format

The problem files have the following format:

```
. . .
c: 8273            <-- constraint
...
begin data         <-- resource data starts
12 34              <-- weight and value
6 79

...
43 25
end data           <-- resource data ends
...
sol:               <-- begin optimal solution
    13   54   87   23 <-- resource index, count, quantity weight, quantity value
    55   32   78   69

                   <-- empty line
...
```

Parse the file

Writing a parser for this data format is easy. We start with a container:

```
178 class KnapsackProblemData:
        def __init__(self):
180         self.Resources = []
            self.MaxWeight = 0
182         self.Solution = []

184
    if __name__ == '__main__':
```

Next we need a function that reads all the lines from the file and manages the parsing:

```
138         self.assertTrue(not optimalFitness > best.Fitness)

140
    def load_data(localFileName):
142     with open(localFileName, mode='r') as infile:
            lines = infile.read().splitlines()
144     data = KnapsackProblemData()
        f = find_constraint
146
        for line in lines:
148         f = f(line.strip(), data)
            if f is None:
150             break
        return data
```

The initial parse function *find_constraint* looks for the constraint marker:

```
154 def find_constraint(line, data):
        parts = line.split(' ')
156     if parts[0] != "c:":
            return find_constraint
158     data.MaxWeight = int(parts[1])
        return find_data_start
```

Once the constraint is found it hands off to *find_data_start* to start watching for the start of the data section.

```
162 def find_data_start(line, data):
163     if line != "begin data":
164         return find_data_start
165     return read_resource_or_find_data_end
```

The next function in the chain reads the *Resources* until the end of the data section is detected. We name the resources by their 1-based resource index.

```
168  def read_resource_or_find_data_end(line, data):
         if line == "end data":
170          return find_solution_start
         parts = line.split('\t')
172      resource = Resource("R" + str(1 + len(data.Resources)), int(parts[1]),
                             int(parts[0]), 0)
174      data.Resources.append(resource)
         return read_resource_or_find_data_end
```

Then we transition to looking for the start of the solution section.

```
178  def find_solution_start(line, data):
179      if line == "sol:":
180          return read_solution_resource_or_find_solution_end
181      return find_solution_start
```

Once we find the solution, we read the resource index and quantity and create the genes for the optimal solution. When we encounter an empty line we're done.

```
184  def read_solution_resource_or_find_solution_end(line, data):
         if line == "":
186          return None
         parts = [p for p in line.split('\t') if p != ""]
188      resourceIndex = int(parts[0]) - 1  # make it 0 based
         resourceQuantity = int(parts[1])
190      data.Solution.append(
             ItemQuantity(data.Resources[resourceIndex], resourceQuantity))
192      return read_solution_resource_or_find_solution_end
```

The parser is complete.

Test exnsd16

Next we need a test that uses the parser and a problem file.

```
     def test_exnsd16(self):
122      problemInfo = load_data("exnsd16.ukp")
         items = problemInfo.Resources
124      maxWeight = problemInfo.MaxWeight
         maxVolume = 0
126      optimal = get_fitness(problemInfo.Solution)
         self.fill_knapsack(items, maxWeight, maxVolume, optimal)
128
     def fill_knapsack(self, items, maxWeight, maxVolume, optimalFitness):
```

Run

When we run the test it can find the solution every time but it can take a couple of minutes.

sample output

```
. . .
156xR288, 1xR55 wt: 889237.00 vol: 0.00 value: 1029553  0:02:42.741197
156xR288, 1xR410   wt: 889244.00 vol: 0.00 value: 1029582  0:02:42.922804
156xR288, 1xR65 wt: 889276.00 vol: 0.00 value: 1029640  0:02:42.978019
156xR288, 1xR987   wt: 889303.00 vol: 0.00 value: 1029680  0:02:43.035709
```

Performance

Performance on the knapsack problem is frequently improved by using the branch and bound algorithm.

> At a high level, the branch and bound algorithm involves a gene-specific decision and the associated consequences, or costs, of making that decision. Making a decision may allow/force you to eliminate many other potential decisions. For example, choosing a particular shirt/blouse to wear today may imply cultural constraints on your pant/skirt options. And your choice of pant/skirt combined with your blouse/shirt may limit your shoe and sock options. It is a chain reaction. This is why you often see the branch and bound algorithm depicted as a decision tree. Belt/no belt. Tie/no tie. Do I need an undershirt/slip with this? You can start anywhere on the decision tree but as soon as you make a decision your options for the next decision are reduced. The branch is the decision point. The bound is the limitations introduced by that decision. If your options can be ordered numerically then your next decision can generally be found very quickly via binary search.

To facilitate our ability to find the next improvement from a current partial solution we're going to sort the items by value. We're also going to use a sliding window to limit how far above and below the current item it can go to select a replacement in the mutation function. We pass the sorted items and the window to the mutation function.

```
     def fill_knapsack(self, items, maxWeight, maxVolume, optimalFitness):
130      startTime = datetime.datetime.now()
         window = Window(1,
132                     max(1, int(len(items) / 3)),
                        int(len(items) / 2))
134
         sortedItems = sorted(items, key=lambda item: item.Value)
136
         def fnDisplay(candidate):
138 ...
```

```
146      def fnMutate(genes):
147          mutate(genes, sortedItems, maxWeight, maxVolume, window)
```

Here's the implementation of *Window*:

```
252 class Window:
        def __init__(self, minimum, maximum, size):
254         self.Min = minimum
            self.Max = maximum
256         self.Size = size

258     def slide(self):
            self.Size = self.Size - 1 if self.Size > self.Min else self.Max
260

262 if __name__ == '__main__':
        unittest.main()
```

In the mutation function the first thing we do is slide the window.

```
65 def mutate(genes, items, maxWeight, maxVolume, window):
66     window.slide()
67     fitness = get_fitness(genes)
68 ...
```

Then in the section where we have the option to replace a gene item we pick the new item from those within *window* range of the current item. And then take the maximum possible quantity of that item.

```
96   if changeItem:
         itemIndex = items.index(iq.Item)
98       start = max(1, itemIndex - window.Size)
         stop = min(len(items) - 1, itemIndex + window.Size)
100      item = items[random.randint(start, stop)]
     maxQuantity = max_quantity(item, remainingWeight, remainingVolume)
102  if maxQuantity > 0:
         genes[index] = ItemQuantity(item, maxQuantity
104      if window.Size > 1 else random.randint(1, maxQuantity))
     else:
106      del genes[index]
```

That's it.

Run

Now it finds the solution in about a second on average.

```
155xR288, 5xR409, 1xR112    wt: 889269.00 vol: 0.00 value: 1029497  0:00:00.344953
155xR288, 5xR409, 1xR1060   wt: 889286.00 vol: 0.00 value: 1029520  0:00:00.344953
155xR288, 5xR409, 1xR1028   wt: 889298.00 vol: 0.00 value: 1029525  0:00:00.378039
156xR288, 1xR987    wt: 889303.00 vol: 0.00 value: 1029680  0:00:00.435156
```

Outstanding!

Retrospective

Try using the sum of difference technique when calculating the fitness.

Benchmarks

Benchmark it with:

```
133  def test_benchmark(self):
134      genetic.Benchmark.run(lambda: self.test_exnsd16())
135
136  def fill_knapsack(self, items, maxWeight, maxVolume, optimalFitness):
```

We did not change `genetic` so here's the final benchmark.

Benchmark

average (seconds)	standard deviation
1.06	1.14

Summary

In this project we solved the unbounded version of the knapsack problem and learned about the branch and bound algorithm.

Solving Linear Equations

Solving systems of equations is a common problem in engineering and you can find hundreds of papers online presenting ways to solve them. The methods fall into two broad classes: mathematical and iterative. The first includes methods like LU factorization, Gaussian elimination, and QR decomposition. The issue with these is that rounding errors are compounded at each step so methods must be used to correct for the errors. The iterative class uses successive approximation to find better solutions without the rounding errors. Genetic algorithms fall into this class.

In this project we're going to see how genetic algorithms can be used to find the unknowns in a system of linear equations. For example:

$$\left\| \begin{array}{l} x + 2y = 4 \\ 4x + 4y = 12 \end{array} \right\|$$

We want to figure out which x and y values we can use to solve both equations simultaneously. Stop here and think about how you would solve this problem with a genetic algorithm.

We can do this with our genetic engine using one gene for each unknown and a gene set containing all numbers in the range of expected values. Let's try it.

Test class, test, and genes

We'll start off with the usual stub code.

linearEquationTests.py

```
import datetime
import unittest

import genetic


class LinearEquationTests(unittest.TestCase):
    def test(self):
        geneset = [i for i in range(10)]
        startTime = datetime.datetime.now()

        def fnDisplay(candidate):
            display(candidate, startTime)

        def fnGetFitness(genes):
            return get_fitness(genes)
```

Fitness

In *get_fitness* we can substitute the gene values directly into *x* and *y*, but what should we return as the fitness so the engine can make progress? A good solution is to rewrite the equations so we're looking for zero.

```
x + 2y - 4 = 0

4x + 4y - 12 = 0
```

This allows us to use the sum of differences technique that we used in the Cards project.

```
def get_fitness(genes):
    x, y = genes[0:2]

    e1 = x + 2 * y - 4
    e2 = 4 * x + 4 * y - 12
    fitness = Fitness(abs(e1) + abs(e2))

    return fitness


class LinearEquationTests(unittest.TestCase):
```

Fitness class

With the *Fitness* class defined as:

```
class Fitness:
    def __init__(self, totalDifference):
        self.TotalDifference = totalDifference

    def __gt__(self, other):
        return self.TotalDifference < other.TotalDifference

    def __str__(self):
        return "diff: {:0.2f}".format(float(self.TotalDifference))


if __name__ == '__main__':
    unittest.main()
```

Optimal fitness

That means the optimal fitness value in our test is going to be zero.

```
        return get_fitness(genes)

    optimalFitness = Fitness(0)
    best = genetic.get_best(fnGetFitness, 2, optimalFitness, geneset,
                            fnDisplay)
    self.assertTrue(not optimalFitness > best.Fitness)
```

Display

Finally, in the display function, we can write out the *x* and *y* values.

linearEquationTests.py

```
def display(candidate, startTime):
    timeDiff = datetime.datetime.now() - startTime
    x, y = candidate.Genes[0:2]
    print("x = {}, y = {}\t{}\t{}".format(
        x,
        y,
        candidate.Fitness,
        timeDiff))


class LinearEquationTests(unittest.TestCase):
```

Run

Now when we run the test...

```
x = 5, y = 2    diff: 21.00 0:00:00
x = 0, y = 2    diff: 4.00  0:00:00
x = 0, y = 3    diff: 2.00  0:00:00.001000
```

it almost always stalls. Why? Consider the values of x and y in the above output. What has to happen for it to make progress? Both x and y have to change to new values at the same time. We've encountered another local minimum.

Use simulated annealing

We've hit a local minimum so we'll see if adding a maximum age fixes it.

```
39        best = genetic.get_best(fnGetFitness, 2, optimalFitness, geneset,
40                                   fnDisplay, maxAge=50)
```

Run 2

Now when we run the test, it finds the correct solution every time.

sample output

```
x = 7, y = 0    diff: 19.00 0:00:00
x = 5, y = 0    diff: 9.00  0:00:00
x = 4, y = 0    diff: 4.00  0:00:00
x = 3, y = 0    diff: 1.00  0:00:00
x = 2, y = 1    diff: 0.00  0:00:00.003007
```

We can verify the solution by manually substituting the values it found back into the original equations.

```
(2) + 2*(1) = 4

4*(2) + 4*(1) = 12
```

Great!

Fractions and 3 Unknowns

Now, what if *x* and *y* are fractions or mixed numbers and we have more unknowns? Well, let's try a system with 3 unknowns and some fractions and see what happens.

```
6x - 2y + 8z = 20

y + 8x * z = -1

2z * 6/x + 3y/2 = 6

expected:
x = 2/3
y = -5
z = 3/4
```

Since some of the unknowns are fractions, our genotype will be 2 genes, one for the numerator and one for the denominator, for each unknown. This means we need 6 genes to solve the equations above. Based on the expected values, we're going to let the gene set contain values in the range -5 to 5, excluding 0. The display and fitness functions will also have to change.

Refactoring

We would like to have common fitness, display, and mutate functions used by tests that are solving for a different number of unknowns, and with different genotypes. Let's start by moving the gene set and equation details to the test function.

```
class LinearEquationTests(unittest.TestCase):
    def test_2_unknowns(self):
        geneset = [i for i in range(-5, 5) if i != 0]

        def fnGenesToInputs(genes):
            return genes[0], genes[1]

        def e1(genes):
            x, y = fnGenesToInputs(genes)
            return x + 2 * y - 4

        def e2(genes):
            x, y = fnGenesToInputs(genes)
            return 4 * x + 4 * y - 12

        equations = [e1, e2]
        self.solve_unknowns(2, geneset, equations, fnGenesToInputs)
```

Then rename the previous test harness function to *solve_unknowns* and send it the gene set, equations, and a function that converts the genotype to whatever phenotype the equations need.

```python
            self.solve_unknowns(2, geneset, equations, fnGenesToInputs)

    def solve_unknowns(self, numUnknowns, geneset, equations,
                       fnGenesToInputs):
        startTime = datetime.datetime.now()

        def fnDisplay(candidate):
            display(candidate, startTime, fnGenesToInputs)

        def fnGetFitness(genes):
            return get_fitness(genes, equations)

        optimalFitness = Fitness(0)
        best = genetic.get_best(fnGetFitness, numUnknowns, optimalFitness,
                                geneset, fnDisplay, maxAge=50)
        self.assertTrue(not optimalFitness > best.Fitness)
```

Now we can simplify the fitness function by making it only responsible for summing the absolute values of the equation results.

```python
def get_fitness(genes, equations):
    fitness = Fitness(sum(abs(e(genes)) for e in equations))
    return fitness
```

The display function will still show the unknowns, fitness and elapsed time. It will also do so without having to know how many unknowns there are.

```python
def display(candidate, startTime, fnGenesToInputs):
    timeDiff = datetime.datetime.now() - startTime
    symbols = "xyz"
    result = ', '.join("{} = {}".format(s, v)
                       for s, v in
                       zip(symbols, fnGenesToInputs(candidate.Genes)))
    print("{}\t{}\t{}".format(
        result,
        candidate.Fitness,
        timeDiff))
```

Test

Next we can add the new test for solving 3 unknowns. In the test for 2 unknowns the genotype *was* the phenotype. But in this test we need to convert every pair of genes to a fraction. Also, we're not going to use simple division because floating point values can be difficult to mentally map to fractions. Instead we'll use the Fraction class so we see 1/4 instead of .25, for example. We have to do the same thing to any fractions in the equations.

```python
2  import fractions
3  import unittest
```

```python
     def test_3_unknowns(self):
44       geneset = [i for i in range(-5, 5) if i != 0]

46       def fnGenesToInputs(genes):
             return [fractions.Fraction(genes[i], genes[i + 1])
48                   for i in range(0, len(genes), 2)]

50       def e1(genes):
             x, y, z = fnGenesToInputs(genes)
52           return 6 * x - 2 * y + 8 * z - 20

54       def e2(genes):
             x, y, z = fnGenesToInputs(genes)
56           return y + 8 * x * z + 1

58       def e3(genes):
             x, y, z = fnGenesToInputs(genes)
60           return 2 * z * fractions.Fraction(6, x) \
                    + 3 * fractions.Fraction(y, 2) - 6
62
         equations = [e1, e2, e3]
64
         self.solve_unknowns(6, geneset, equations, fnGenesToInputs)
66
     def solve_unknowns(self, numUnknowns, geneset, equations,
```

And we're ready to run the test.

Run

```
. . .
x = 3/5, y = -5, z = 2/3    diff: 2.03  0:00:00.932517
x = 2/3, y = -5, z = 4/5    diff: 1.57  0:00:09.709865
. . .
```

It occasionally has a delay while working around a local minimum. When we compare the above values of x, y and z with the expected values, we discover that we're hitting a local minimum again. Except now, instead of needing to make 2 changes in order to move forward, we need to make 4. The root of the problem is we're changing the numerator and denominator separately when we really need to be able to replace the fraction they represent with a new fraction.

Use Fractions as the Genotype

In order to use fractions as genes, we have to change the gene set to a set of all possible fractions in the range of numbers we want to support. A benefit of this is that our genotype and phenotype are the same again so we can eliminate the conversion step when evaluating the equations.

```
     def test_3_unknowns(self):
44       geneRange = [i for i in range(-5, 5) if i != 0]          <==
         geneset = [i for i in set(                               <==
46           fractions.Fraction(d, e)                             <==
             for d in geneRange                                   <==
48           for e in geneRange if e != 0)]                       <==

50       def fnGenesToInputs(genes):
             return genes                                         <==
52
         def e1(genes):
54           x, y, z = genes                                      <==
             return 6 * x - 2 * y + 8 * z - 20
56
         def e2(genes):
58           x, y, z = genes                                      <==
             return y + 8 * x * z + 1
60
         def e3(genes):
62           x, y, z = genes                                      <==
             return 2 * z * fractions.Fraction(6, x) \
64                   + 3 * fractions.Fraction(y, 2) - 6

66       equations = [e1, e2, e3]
         self.solve_unknowns(3, geneset, equations, fnGenesToInputs)   <==
```

Run 2

Now when it encounters a local minimum like the one we saw above

```
. . .
x = 3/5, y = -5, z = 2/3    diff: 2.03   0:00:00.042112
x = 2/3, y = -5, z = 4/5    diff: 1.57   0:00:00.082218
. . .
```

the engine hardly slows down. Great!

Finding 4 unknowns

Now let's see if it can solve 4 unknowns:

```
1/15x  - 2y  - 15z  -4/5a =  3
-5/2x  - 9/4y + 12z  - a =  17
-13x  + 3/10y - 6z  - 2/5a =  17
1/2x  + 2y  + 7/4z + 4/3a =  -9

x =  -3/2
y =  -7/2
z =  1/3
a =  -11/8
```

Test

We just have to add the new test

```python
    def test_4_unknowns(self):
        geneRange = [i for i in range(-13, 13) if i != 0]
        geneset = [i for i in set(
            fractions.Fraction(d, e)
            for d in geneRange
            for e in geneRange if e != 0)]

        def fnGenesToInputs(genes):
            return genes

        def e1(genes):
            x, y, z, a = genes
            return fractions.Fraction(1, 15) * x \
                   - 2 * y \
                   - 15 * z \
                   - fractions.Fraction(4, 5) * a \
                   - 3

        def e2(genes):
            x, y, z, a = genes
            return -fractions.Fraction(5, 2) * x \
                   - fractions.Fraction(9, 4) * y \
                   + 12 * z \
                   - a \
                   - 17
```

```
96    def e3(genes):
          x, y, z, a = genes
          return -13 * x \
98            + fractions.Fraction(3, 10) * y \
              - 6 * z \
100           - fractions.Fraction(2, 5) * a \
              - 17
102
      def e4(genes):
104       x, y, z, a = genes
          return fractions.Fraction(1, 2) * x \
106           + 2 * y \
              + fractions.Fraction(7, 4) * z \
108           + fractions.Fraction(4, 3) * a \
              + 9
110
      equations = [e1, e2, e3, e4]
112   self.solve_unknowns(4, geneset, equations, fnGenesToInputs)
```

and update the symbols in the display function

```
15    symbols = "xyza"
```

Run

```
. . .
x = -3/2, y = -10/3, z = 1/3, a = -12/7 diff: 0.40  0:00:05.217881
x = -3/2, y = -10/3, z = 1/3, a = -7/4  diff: 0.40  0:00:05.271022
x = -3/2, y = -7/2, z = 1/3, a = -13/10 diff: 0.27  0:00:12.802097
x = -3/2, y = -7/2, z = 1/3, a = -11/8  diff: 0.00  0:00:12.910380
```

It can find the solution every time but it can take a while. Here's the benchmark for finding 4 unknowns.

average (seconds)	standard deviation
5.82	4.87

Performance

What can we do to improve performance? Are there any patterns in the output? Yes, there are. The first is that the sign of an unknown tends to stay the same. Another is that the change between improvements for a given unknown tends to get smaller as we get closer to the solution. We can take advantage of both by limiting our search to a sliding range around the current gene index. Let's use the branch and bound algorithm.

We'll start by moving the maximum age to a variable and use it to determine the minimum window size for adjusting the number of genes.

```
116        startTime = datetime.datetime.now()
           maxAge = 50
118        window = Window(max(1, int(len(geneset) / (2 * maxAge))),
                           max(1, int(len(geneset) / 3)),
120                        int(len(geneset) / 2))
```

We'll borrow the *Window* class from the previous project:

```
class Window:
146    def __init__(self, minimum, maximum, size):
           self.Min = minimum
148        self.Max = maximum
           self.Size = size
150
       def slide(self):
152        self.Size = self.Size - 1 if self.Size > self.Min else self.Max
154
if __name__ == '__main__':
```

Next, in order to make the most efficient use of multiple rounds through the loop, we're going to want to use random.choose so that we only use each gene index once. That means moving the indexes into an array like we did when finding Magic Squares.

```
120                        int(len(geneset) / 2))
121        geneIndexes = [i for i in range(numUnknowns)]
```

We also need the gene options to be sorted so that genes that are numerically close to the current gene are also physically close to it in the array. This allows us to pick from genes within a certain numeric distance of the current one.

```
122        sortedGeneset = sorted(geneset)
123
124        def fnDisplay(candidate):
```

Lastly, pass these new parameters to a mutation function

```
130        def fnMutate(genes):
131            mutate(genes, sortedGeneset, window, geneIndexes)
132
133        optimalFitness = Fitness(0)
```

and use that function in the engine.

```
134            best = genetic.get_best(fnGetFitness, numUnknowns, optimalFitness,
135                              geneset, fnDisplay, fnMutate, maxAge=maxAge)
```

Now in the mutation function, we start by choosing at least one gene to mutate. Then change the window size and start the loop.

```
3  import random
4  import unittest
```

```
       timeDiff))
24

26 def mutate(genes, sortedGeneset, window, geneIndexes):
       indexes = random.sample(geneIndexes, random.randint(1, len(genes))) \
28         if random.randint(0, 10) == 0 else [random.choice(geneIndexes)]
       window.slide()
30     while len(indexes) > 0:
```

Then, each time through the loop we take the next gene from the indexes we picked

```
31         index = indexes.pop()
```

and calculate the search bounds using the window size. This way we limit the number of genes we could pick from and stop if we reach one of the ends of the array.

```
32         genesetIndex = sortedGeneset.index(genes[index])
33         start = max(0, genesetIndex - window.Size)
34         stop = min(len(sortedGeneset) - 1, genesetIndex + window.Size)
```

Finally, we replace the current gene with one picked randomly from the new bounding range.

```
35         genesetIndex = random.randint(start, stop)
36         genes[index] = sortedGeneset[genesetIndex]
```

This accomplishes our goal of taking advantage of patterns in the data. We now try to find replacement genes that are numerically close to the current gene. Depending on how close the gene is to zero and how wide the selection boundaries are, this keeps our choices mostly negative if the current gene is negative, or mostly positive if the current gene is positive. Using branch and bound we can slowly change the search range around the current best gene. This allows the algorithm to find the next improvement should it require the signs of one or more genes to change, as in this example:

```
x = -1/5, y = -3, z = -1/4, a = -1/10   diff: 35.56 0:00:00.003038
x = 1/7, y = -3, z = 5/13, a = -1/10    diff: 34.21 0:00:00.005043
```

Run

Now when we run the test it can find the 4 unknowns much faster.

```
. . .
x = -3/2, y = -11/3, z = 1/3, a = -13/12   diff: 0.41  0:00:01.176128
x = -3/2, y = -11/3, z = 1/3, a = -1     diff: 0.40  0:00:01.248321
x = -3/2, y = -7/2, z = 1/3, a = -13/10 diff: 0.27  0:00:01.605241
x = -3/2, y = -7/2, z = 1/3, a = -11/8  diff: 0.00  0:00:01.609281
```

Benchmarks

We will benchmark this project with the test that finds 4 unknowns.

```
128     def test_benchmark(self):
129         genetic.Benchmark.run(lambda: self.test_4_unknowns())
130
131     def solve_unknowns(self, numUnknowns, geneset, equations,
```

Benchmark

average (seconds)	standard deviation
1.50	1.17

Summary

In this project we learned how to solve an important engineering problem. We were also able to reinforce to ourselves the power of using branch and bound.

Generating Sudoku

Sudoku puzzles are 9x9 logic problems where each row, column, and non-overlapping 3x3 section must have all the digits in the range 1 to 9. The player is given a partially filled grid and the challenge is to use the known digits, the puzzle constraints, and logic to deduce the remaining digits. Here's a sample completed puzzle:

```
8 4 1 | 5 6 7 | 9 2 3
2 7 6 | 9 4 3 | 1 5 8
9 5 3 | 2 8 1 | 7 6 4
----- + ----- + -----
5 1 9 | 7 2 4 | 8 3 6
6 8 4 | 3 1 9 | 5 7 2
7 3 2 | 6 5 8 | 4 9 1
----- + ----- + -----
1 2 5 | 4 9 6 | 3 8 7
4 6 7 | 8 3 5 | 2 1 9
3 9 8 | 1 7 2 | 6 4 5
```

We're going to use a genetic algorithm to generate a Sudoku puzzle. This is a guided exercise so you should be thinking about how to improve the implementation as we go along. Also, if you've never tried to solve one of these puzzles, you should do so as that process may provide valuable insight.

Let's go.

Test class and genes

First off, our genotype will be the digits 1 thru 9.

sudokuTests.py

```python
import datetime
import unittest

import genetic


class SudokuTests(unittest.TestCase):
    def test(self):
        geneset = [i for i in range(1, 9 + 1)]
        startTime = datetime.datetime.now()
```

Fitness

The fitness value will be a count of the rows, columns and sections that have all 9 digits. This means the optimal value will be 9+9+9 or 27.

```
11        optimalValue = 27
```

The fitness function will be called many times so it needs to run fast. We start by creating an empty `set` for each row, column and section.

```
4  import genetic

6
   def get_fitness(candidate):
8      rows = [set() for _ in range(9)]
       columns = [set() for _ in range(9)]
10     sections = [set() for _ in range(9)]
```

Next, we populate the sets while touching each square only once. The section numbers can be calculated in Excel using:

QUOTIENT(B$1,3)+QUOTIENT($A2,3)*3

	0	1	2	3	4	5	6	7	8	column
0	0	0	0	1	1	1	2	2	2	
1	0	0	0	1	1	1	2	2	2	
2	0	0	0	1	1	1	2	2	2	
3	3	3	3	4	4	4	5	5	5	
4	3	3	3	4	4	4	5	5	5	
5	3	3	3	4	4	4	5	5	5	
6	6	6	6	7	7	7	8	8	8	
7	6	6	6	7	7	7	8	8	8	
8	6	6	6	7	7	7	8	8	8	

row

```
12    for row in range(9):
          for column in range(9):
14            value = candidate[row * 9 + column]
              rows[row].add(value)
16            columns[column].add(value)
              sections[int(row / 3) + int(column / 3) + 3].add(value)
```

Lastly, we return the total number or rows, columns and sections that have the correct count.

```
20      fitness = sum(len(row) == 9 for row in rows) + \
                  sum(len(column) == 9 for column in columns) + \
                  sum(len(section) == 9 for section in sections)
22
        return fitness
```

Display

We can easily produce a visual representation of the complete Sudoku puzzle.

```
26 def display(candidate, startTime):
       timeDiff = datetime.datetime.now() - startTime
28
       for row in range(9):
30         line = ' | '.join(
               ' '.join(str(i)
32                     for i in candidate.Genes[row * 9 + i:row * 9 + i + 3])
               for i in [0, 3, 6])
34         print("", line)
           if row < 8 and row % 3 == 2:
36             print(" ----- + ----- + -----")
       print(" - = -   - = -   - = - {}\t{}\n"
38           .format(candidate.Fitness, timeDiff))
40
   class SudokuTests(unittest.TestCase):
```

Here's the expected output:

```
8 4 1 | 5 6 7 | 4 2 4
2 7 2 | 2 4 4 | 9 7 6
2 4 9 | 4 4 1 | 1 3 1
----- + ----- + -----
9 3 2 | 5 5 5 | 8 7 6
1 9 8 | 8 1 3 | 6 5 9
5 1 5 | 8 7 6 | 6 2 3
----- + ----- + -----
6 8 6 | 7 5 7 | 2 4 3
7 8 2 | 9 8 1 | 8 7 3
9 9 3 | 3 5 9 | 3 6 1
- = -   - = -   - = - 17     0:00:00
```

Test

The full test harness for this project is fairly simple.

```
42  def test(self):
        geneset = [i for i in range(1, 9 + 1)]
44      startTime = datetime.datetime.now()
        optimalValue = 27
46
        def fnDisplay(candidate):
48          display(candidate, startTime)

50      def fnGetFitness(genes):
            return get_fitness(genes)
52
        best = genetic.get_best(fnGetFitness, 81, optimalValue, geneset,
54                              fnDisplay)
        self.assertEqual(best.Fitness, optimalValue)
56

58  if __name__ == '__main__':
        unittest.main()
```

Run

Now run it. It makes progress at first but eventually stalls. I ran the code 10 times and it always stalled with a fitness value between 11 and 15.

```
9 5 8 | 3 6 1 | 2 7 4
2 1 4 | 5 6 8 | 3 7 9
5 8 3 | 4 6 9 | 7 1 2
----- + ----- + -----
4 3 9 | 8 2 5 | 6 7 1
8 9 2 | 6 3 4 | 5 7 1
3 4 7 | 1 6 5 | 9 2 8
----- + ----- + -----
5 7 1 | 9 8 3 | 4 6 2
8 6 9 | 2 7 4 | 1 5 3
5 2 4 | 7 6 9 | 8 1 3
- = -   - = -   - = - 15    0:00:02.793290
```

What should we do now?

- Use simulated annealing to fix the local minimum. (turn to the next page)
- Use custom mutation to swap two genes. (go to page 152)
- Use custom creation to start with the correct number of each digit. (go to page 158)

Many options

The remaining sections of this project are not meant to be read straight through. Choose one of the options above and go to that page.

Use simulated annealing

It certainly behaves like it is hitting a local maximum. So let's see if simulated annealing can fix the stall.

```
53        best = genetic.get_best(fnGetFitness, 81, optimalValue, geneset,
54                              fnDisplay, maxAge=5000)
```

With this change the engine can achieve a fitness value of 23 every time, but it requires a relatively high maximum age and a long run time, and it still stalls at that point every time. That is a good indication that we are encountering local maximums and that they are relatively complex to resolve.

```
2 3 6 | 8 7 9 | 5 4 1
8 5 4 | 1 6 3 | 7 9 2
7 1 9 | 4 8 2 | 6 3 5
----- + ----- + -----
6 9 5 | 3 2 8 | 4 1 7
4 7 1 | 6 3 5 | 2 8 9
5 2 7 | 9 1 4 | 8 6 3
----- + ----- + -----
1 8 2 | 7 9 6 | 3 5 4
9 6 3 | 5 4 7 | 1 2 8
3 4 8 | 2 5 1 | 9 7 6
- = -    - = -    - = - 23     0:03:43.065731
```

Let's see if we can help it by removing some of the inefficiency from the process.

What should we do now?

- Add custom creation to start with the correct number of each digit. (go on to the next page)

- Add custom mutation to swap two genes. (go to page 149)

- Restart from the beginning. (go to page 145)

Add custom creation

We can reduce the amount of work the engine has to do if we start with the right number of each digit. We'll do that with a permutation of 9 copies of the digits.

```
 2  import random
 3  import unittest
```

```
54        def fnCreate():
              return random.sample(geneset * 9, 81)
56
          best = genetic.get_best(fnGetFitness, None, optimalValue, geneset,
58                                 fnDisplay, custom_create=fnCreate,
                                   maxAge=5000)
```

Run 3

This change doesn't affect the fitness value, it is still 23 every time, and it still stalls every time.

```
. . .
1 8 7 | 9 5 9 | 1  3 5
9 6 3 | 7 1 4 | 5  8 2
5 2 4 | 8 6 3 | 7  9 1
----- + ----- + -----
8 7 2 | 4 2 6 | 4  7 3
3 9 1 | 5 3 2 | 6  6 8
4 1 5 | 6 8 7 | 2  3 9
----- + ----- + -----
2 4 6 | 1 9 8 | 3  5 7
6 5 9 | 3 7 1 | 8  2 4
7 3 8 | 2 4 5 | 9  1 6
- = -   - = -   - = -  19      0:00:12.411932
```

Add custom mutation

Since our custom creation function ensures we start with the right number of each digit, we can also replace the built-in mutation function with one that just swaps two genes.

```
42  def mutate(genes, geneIndexes):
        indexA, indexB = random.sample(geneIndexes, 2)
44      genes[indexA], genes[indexB] = genes[indexB], genes[indexA]

46
    class SudokuTests(unittest.TestCase):
```

```
62        geneIndexes = [i for i in range(0, 81)]

64        def fnMutate(genes):
              mutate(genes, geneIndexes)
66
          best = genetic.get_best(fnGetFitness, None, optimalValue, None,
68                              fnDisplay, fnMutate, fnCreate, maxAge=5000)
```

Run 4

```
6 3 1 | 5 7 2 | 4 8 9
5 8 7 | 4 6 9 | 3 2 1
4 9 2 | 7 5 3 | 8 1 6
----- + ----- + -----
8 7 5 | 9 1 6 | 2 3 4
1 6 3 | 2 8 4 | 9 5 7
2 4 9 | 1 3 8 | 7 6 5
----- + ----- + -----
9 1 8 | 6 2 7 | 5 4 3
7 2 6 | 3 4 5 | 1 9 8
3 5 4 | 8 9 1 | 6 7 2
- = -   - = -   - = - 23    0:00:39.616364
```

This change removes the remaining inefficiency from the process but it still stalls. To improve further we need to think about fitness another way.

- Use a more granular fitness. (go to page 163)

- Restart from the beginning. (go to page 145)

Add custom mutation

The genetic algorithm is quite capable of producing a gene sequence that has exactly 9 of each of the 9 digits. Once it does, however, it always stalls because the built-in mutation operation can only make one change at a time. To make further progress it needs to at least be able to swap two genes. We know how to do that.

We'll add a variation of the custom mutation function from the Cards project. If the chromosome has too many or too few of a digit we'll randomly replace a gene. It doesn't matter which one as the engine will make it work. Otherwise, when we have the right number of all the digits, we'll just swap two random genes.

```
2  import random
3  import unittest
```

```
42 def mutate(genes, geneset):
       counts = [0 for _ in range(len(geneset) + 1)]
44     for digit in genes:
           counts[digit] += 1
46     correctDigitCount = sum(1 for i in counts if i == 9)
       if correctDigitCount != 9:
48         index = random.randrange(0, len(genes) - 1)
           genes[index] = random.choice(geneset)
50     else:
           indexA, indexB = random.sample(range(len(genes)), 2)
52         genes[indexA], genes[indexB] = genes[indexB], genes[indexA]

54
   class SudokuTests(unittest.TestCase):
```

We also need to wire the test harness to use our custom mutation function.

```
       def fnMutate(genes):
68         mutate(genes, geneset)

70     best = genetic.get_best(fnGetFitness, 81, optimalValue, geneset,
                               fnDisplay, fnMutate, maxAge=5000)
```

Run 3

This change definitely improves the range of fitness values. Now, over ten runs it always ends up with fitness values of 22 or 23.

```
. . .
6 4 9 | 8 3 7 | 1 5 2
5 3 1 | 2 6 9 | 7 8 4
2 7 8 | 5 4 1 | 6 9 3
----- + ----- + -----
9 8 5 | 3 7 4 | 2 6 1
4 6 3 | 9 1 2 | 5 7 8
1 5 7 | 6 2 8 | 4 3 9
----- + ----- + -----
7 2 6 | 1 8 3 | 9 4 5
8 9 2 | 4 5 6 | 3 1 7
3 1 4 | 7 9 5 | 8 2 6
- = -   - = -   - = - 23      0:00:11.885119
```

Add custom creation

Let's add a custom creation function so we don't waste time creating an invalid gene sequence in the first place. Maybe that will resolve the stall.

```
67          def fnCreate():
68              return random.sample(geneset * 9, 81)
69
70          def fnMutate(genes):
71  ...
```

```
73          best = genetic.get_best(fnGetFitness, None, optimalValue, None,
74                             fnDisplay, fnMutate, fnCreate, maxAge=5000)
```

With that change we can simplify the implementation of the mutation function to just perform swaps.

```
42  def mutate(genes, geneIndexes):
43      indexA, indexB = random.sample(geneIndexes, 2)
44      genes[indexA], genes[indexB] = genes[indexB], genes[indexA]
```

Then update the test harness to match the parameter change.

```
62          geneIndexes = [i for i in range(0, 81)]
63
64          def fnMutate(genes):
65              mutate(genes, geneIndexes)
```

Run 4

```
4 7 2 | 8 5 9 | 6 3 1
8 1 5 | 9 4 2 | 3 6 7
6 3 9 | 1 2 5 | 7 8 4
----- + ----- + -----
9 4 7 | 3 6 8 | 1 5 2
1 2 8 | 7 3 6 | 5 4 9
5 6 3 | 4 1 7 | 9 2 8
----- + ----- + -----
2 5 1 | 6 7 4 | 8 9 3
7 9 4 | 5 8 3 | 2 1 6
3 8 6 | 2 9 1 | 4 7 5
- = -   - = -   - = - 23    0:00:30.633457
```

This change removes the remaining inefficiency from the process and makes it so that we achieve a 23 fitness value 10 times out of 10. But it still stalls. To improve further we need to think about fitness another way.

- Use a more granular fitness. (go to page 163)

- Restart from the beginning. (go to page 145)

Use custom mutation

The genetic algorithm is quite capable of producing a gene sequence that has exactly
9 of each of the 9 digits. Once it does, however, it always stalls because the built-in
mutation operation can only make one change at a time. To make further progress it
needs to at least be able to swap two genes. We know how to do that.

We'll add a variation of the custom mutation function from the Cards project. If the
chromosome has too many or too few of a digit we randomly replace a gene. It doesn't
matter which one; the engine will make it work. Otherwise, when we have the right
number of all the digits then we'll just swap two random genes.

```python
2  import random
```

```python
42  def mutate(genes, geneset):
        counts = [0 for _ in range(len(geneset) + 1)]
44      for digit in genes:
            counts[digit] += 1
46      correctDigitCount = sum(1 for i in counts if i == 9)
        if correctDigitCount != 9:
48          index = random.randrange(0, len(genes) - 1)
            genes[index] = random.choice(geneset)
50      else:
            indexA, indexB = random.sample(range(len(genes)), 2)
52          genes[indexA], genes[indexB] = genes[indexB], genes[indexA]
```

We also need to wire the test harness to use our custom mutation function.

```python
56      def test(self):
57  ...
```

```python
        def fnMutate(genes):
68          mutate(genes, geneset)

70      best = genetic.get_best(fnGetFitness, 81, optimalValue, geneset,
                                fnDisplay, fnMutate)
```

Run 2

This change definitely improves the range of fitness values. Now, over ten runs it always ends up with fitness values of 22 or 23.

```
  . . .
6 9 3 | 2 4 5 | 8 1 7
5 8 1 | 7 3 4 | 6 2 9
4 2 7 | 5 6 3 | 9 8 1
----- + ----- + -----
7 3 2 | 1 9 8 | 4 5 6
9 6 5 | 4 8 1 | 3 7 2
8 1 6 | 9 2 7 | 5 4 3
----- + ----- + -----
3 4 8 | 6 7 2 | 1 9 5
1 7 4 | 3 5 9 | 2 6 8
2 5 9 | 8 1 6 | 7 3 4
- = -   - = -   - = - 23    0:00:12.103029
```

What should we do now?

- Add simulated annealing to fix the local maximum. (go to page 156)

- Add custom creation to start with the correct number of each digit. (turn the page)

- Restart from the beginning. (go to page 145)

(Choose one of the options above)

Add custom creation

If we add a custom creation function we can ensure that we start with the right number of each digit.

```
67        def fnCreate():
68            return random.sample(geneset * 9, 81)
69
70        def fnMutate(genes):
71 ...
```

```
73        best = genetic.get_best(fnGetFitness, None, optimalValue, None,
74                                fnDisplay, fnMutate, fnCreate)
```

This also means we can simplify our mutation function to just swap two genes.

```
42 def mutate(genes, geneIndexes):
43     indexA, indexB = random.sample(geneIndexes, 2)
44     genes[indexA], genes[indexB] = genes[indexB], genes[indexA]
```

Now update the test harness to match the parameter change.

```
62        geneIndexes = [i for i in range(0, 81)]
63
64        def fnMutate(genes):
65            mutate(genes, geneIndexes)
```

Run 3

```
6 4 3 | 2 5 7 | 8 9 1
2 1 7 | 3 9 4 | 6 8 5
5 9 8 | 6 2 1 | 7 3 4
----- + ----- + -----
4 3 5 | 8 7 9 | 2 1 6
8 2 1 | 9 3 6 | 4 5 7
7 6 4 | 5 1 8 | 9 2 3
----- + ----- + -----
9 5 6 | 1 4 2 | 3 7 8
1 7 9 | 4 8 3 | 5 6 2
3 8 2 | 7 6 5 | 1 4 9
- = -   - = -   - = - 23    0:00:20.101972
```

This change enables the engine to achieve a fitness value of 22 or 23 every time, and to do so quickly most of the time. But, it still stalls.

Add simulated annealing

In the past when the engine became stuck it was because it hit a local maximum, right? No problem. Let's see if simulated annealing can help.

```
67    best = genetic.get_best(fnGetFitness, None, optimalValue, None,
68                            fnDisplay, fnMutate, fnCreate, maxAge=5000)
```

Run 4

This change makes it so that we achieve a 23 fitness value every time, but it still stalls. That is a good indication that we are encountering local maximums and that they are relatively complex to resolve.

```
. . .
8 9 5 | 6 4 2 | 1  3 7
4 2 3 | 1 9 7 | 6  5 8
1 7 6 | 5 2 8 | 3  4 9
----- + ----- + -----
6 8 2 | 7 5 3 | 9  1 4
3 4 7 | 9 8 1 | 5  2 6
5 1 9 | 3 6 4 | 7  8 2
----- + ----- + -----
2 3 1 | 4 7 9 | 8  6 5
9 5 8 | 2 1 6 | 4  7 3
7 6 4 | 8 3 5 | 2  9 1
- = -   - = -   - = - 23    0:01:19.822566
```

To improve further we need to think about fitness another way.

- Use a more granular fitness. (go to page 163)
- Restart from the beginning. (go to page 145)

Add simulated annealing

In the past when the engine became stuck it was because it hit a local maximum, right? No problem. Let's see if simulated annealing helps.

```
70    best = genetic.get_best(fnGetFitness, 81, optimalValue, geneset,
71                             fnDisplay, fnMutate, maxAge=5000)
```

Run 3

This change makes it so that we achieve a 23 fitness value every time, but it still stalls. That is a good indication that we are encountering local maximums and that they are complex to resolve.

```
. . .
8 9 5 | 6 4 2 | 1 3 7
4 2 3 | 1 9 7 | 6 5 8
1 7 6 | 5 2 8 | 3 4 9
----- + ----- + -----
6 8 2 | 7 5 3 | 9 1 4
3 4 7 | 9 8 1 | 5 2 6
5 1 9 | 3 6 4 | 7 8 2
----- + ----- + -----
2 3 1 | 4 7 9 | 8 6 5
9 5 8 | 2 1 6 | 4 7 3
7 6 4 | 8 3 5 | 2 9 1
- = -   - = -   - = - 23    0:01:19.822566
```

Add custom creation

Let's prevent the creation of invalid gene sequences in the first place. Maybe that will resolve the stall.

```
67    def fnCreate():
68        return random.sample(geneset * 9, 81)
69
70    def fnMutate(genes):
```

```
73    best = genetic.get_best(fnGetFitness, None, optimalValue, None,
74                            fnDisplay, fnMutate, fnCreate, maxAge=5000)
```

With that change we can simplify the implementation of the mutation function and just perform swaps.

```
42 def mutate(genes, geneIndexes):
43     indexA, indexB = random.sample(geneIndexes, 2)
44     genes[indexA], genes[indexB] = genes[indexB], genes[indexA]
```

Then update the test harness to match the parameter change.

```
62      geneIndexes = [i for i in range(0, 81)]
63
64      def fnMutate(genes):
65          mutate(genes, geneIndexes)
```

Run 4

```
5 8 1 | 9 2 3 | 6 4 7
4 3 7 | 1 5 8 | 2 9 6
6 9 2 | 7 8 1 | 4 5 3
----- + ----- + -----
2 6 3 | 4 7 5 | 1 8 9
7 5 6 | 2 9 4 | 8 3 1
9 1 4 | 8 3 6 | 5 7 2
----- + ----- + -----
3 2 8 | 6 4 7 | 9 1 5
1 4 5 | 3 6 9 | 7 2 8
8 7 9 | 5 1 2 | 3 6 4
- = -   - = -   - = - 23    0:00:35.506982
```

This change removes the remaining inefficiency from the process and makes it so that we achieve a 23 fitness value 10 times out of 10. But, it still stalls. To improve further we need to think about fitness another way.

- Use a more granular fitness. (go to page 163)

- Restart from the beginning. (go to page 145)

Use custom creation

We can reduce the amount of work the engine has to do if we start with the right number of each digit. We'll do that with a permutation of 9 copies of the digits.

```python
 2 import random
 3 import unittest
```

```python
54        def fnCreate():
              return random.sample(geneset * 9, 81)
56
          best = genetic.get_best(fnGetFitness, None, optimalValue, geneset,
58                                fnDisplay, custom_create=fnCreate)
```

Run 2

This change improves the range of the fitness value to between 16 and 19 (over 10 runs) with one outlier at 23. But, it still stalls every time.

```
  .  .  .
2 5 9 | 3 1 6 | 8 4 7
6 8 4 | 9 2 7 | 5 1 3
3 1 7 | 2 5 4 | 6 8 9
----- + ----- + -----
5 9 6 | 1 3 2 | 7 4 8
8 7 6 | 2 9 3 | 1 5 4
9 3 8 | 7 6 1 | 4 2 5
----- + ----- + -----
4 2 5 | 6 7 8 | 9 3 1
7 6 1 | 8 4 5 | 3 9 2
1 4 7 | 3 8 9 | 2 5 6
- = -   - = -   - = - 19    0:00:09.601567
```

What should we do now?

- Add simulated annealing to fix the local maximum. (go to the next page)

- Add custom mutation to swap two genes. (go to page 161)

- Restart from the beginning. (go to page 145)

(Choose one of the options above)

Add simulated annealing

We seem to be hitting a local maximum. Let's see if using simulated annealing can break us out of the stall.

```
57        best = genetic.get_best(fnGetFitness, None, optimalValue, geneset,
58                               fnDisplay, custom_create=fnCreate, maxAge=5000)
```

Run 3

This improves the range of fitness values to between 19 and 23 over 10 runs, but only if we use a high maximum age. The higher the maximum age the better the fitness results, up to a point. That is a good indication that we are encountering local maximums and that they are relatively complex to resolve.

```
9 8 2 | 1 4 5 | 6 3 7
7 1 3 | 5 8 6 | 4 2 9
4 5 6 | 8 2 3 | 9 7 1
----- + ----- + -----
1 2 4 | 6 5 4 | 3 5 8
8 3 9 | 4 7 2 | 5 1 6
6 9 7 | 5 3 1 | 8 4 2
----- + ----- + -----
3 4 8 | 2 6 7 | 1 9 5
2 6 5 | 3 1 9 | 7 8 4
5 7 1 | 4 9 8 | 2 6 3
- = -   - = -   - = - 21     0:00:21.398411
```

Add custom mutation

Both custom creation and simulated annealing improved the fitness results. Since our custom creation function ensures we start with the right number of each digit, we can replace the built in mutation function with one that just swaps two genes.

```
42 def mutate(genes, geneIndexes):
       indexA, indexB = random.sample(geneIndexes, 2)
44     genes[indexA], genes[indexB] = genes[indexB], genes[indexA]

46
   class SudokuTests(unittest.TestCase):
```

```
62      geneIndexes = [i for i in range(0, 81)]

64      def fnMutate(genes):
            mutate(genes, geneIndexes)
66
        best = genetic.get_best(fnGetFitness, None, optimalValue, None,
68                               fnDisplay, fnMutate, fnCreate, maxAge=5000)
```

Run 4

```
6 3 1 | 5 7 2 | 4 8 9
5 8 7 | 4 6 9 | 3 2 1
4 9 2 | 7 5 3 | 8 1 6
----- + ----- + -----
8 7 5 | 9 1 6 | 2 3 4
1 6 3 | 2 8 4 | 9 5 7
2 4 9 | 1 3 8 | 7 6 5
----- + ----- + -----
9 1 8 | 6 2 7 | 5 4 3
7 2 6 | 3 4 5 | 1 9 8
3 5 4 | 8 9 1 | 6 7 2
- = -   - = -   - = - 23    0:00:39.616364
```

This change removes the remaining inefficiency from the process and makes it so that we achieve a 23 fitness value 10 times out of 10. But, it still stalls. To improve further we need to think about fitness another way.

- Use a more granular fitness. (go to page 163)

- Restart from the beginning. (go to page 145)

Add custom mutation

The custom creation function we added ensures that we start with the right number of each digit. This means we can replace the built in mutation function with one that just swaps two genes.

```
42  def mutate(genes, geneIndexes):
        indexA, indexB = random.sample(geneIndexes, 2)
44      genes[indexA], genes[indexB] = genes[indexB], genes[indexA]
```

```
62          geneIndexes = [i for i in range(0, 81)]

64          def fnMutate(genes):
                mutate(genes, geneIndexes)
66
            best = genetic.get_best(fnGetFitness, None, optimalValue, None,
68                                   fnDisplay, fnMutate, fnCreate)
```

Run 3

```
1 3 7 | 8 6 9 | 2 5 4
2 8 5 | 7 1 6 | 4 9 3
9 6 4 | 2 5 1 | 7 3 8
----- + ----- + -----
4 7 3 | 9 2 8 | 5 1 6
6 2 8 | 4 3 5 | 9 7 1
3 9 1 | 5 7 4 | 6 8 2
----- + ----- + -----
5 4 2 | 1 8 7 | 3 6 9
7 1 6 | 3 9 2 | 8 4 5
8 5 9 | 6 4 3 | 1 2 7
- = -   - = -   - = - 23      0:00:13.460378
```

This change enables the engine to achieve a fitness value of 22 or 23 every time, and to do so quickly most of the time. But, it still stalls.

Add simulated annealing

Let's see if using simulated annealing can break us out of what appears to be a local maximum.

```
67          best = genetic.get_best(fnGetFitness, None, optimalValue, None,
68                                   fnDisplay, fnMutate, fnCreate, maxAge=5000)
```

Run 4

This change makes it so that we achieve a 23 fitness value every time, but it still stalls. That is a good indication that we *are* encountering local maximums and that they are relatively complex to resolve.

```
6 3 8 | 1 9 4 | 7 2 5
7 4 2 | 8 3 5 | 1 6 9
9 1 5 | 7 4 2 | 8 3 6
----- + ----- + -----
3 2 4 | 9 6 8 | 5 1 7
8 7 1 | 2 5 6 | 9 4 3
5 9 6 | 3 1 7 | 2 8 4
----- + ----- + -----
4 5 7 | 6 2 1 | 3 9 8
2 8 9 | 4 7 3 | 6 5 1
1 6 3 | 5 8 9 | 4 7 2
- = -   - = -   - = - 23    0:00:09.504245
```

To improve further we need to think about fitness another way.

- Use a more granular fitness. (go on to the next page)

- Restart from the beginning. (go to page 145)

Use a more granular fitness

The root problem we're having is that we're trying to construct the whole puzzle at once. This causes us to end up in a situation where we cannot make a change without reducing the fitness because the valid rows, columns and sections are interlocked with invalid ones. The way to fix this is to build the puzzle in an organized manner row-by-row left-to-right and top-to-bottom. That will allow us to swap all we want with digits that have a higher array index in order to resolve conflicts. Once the current digit is consistent with all related digits that have a lower index, we'll advance to the next digit. However, now we need to know the point at which it becomes inconsistent. To determine that we're going to borrow the *Rule* idea from the Graph Coloring project

```
72  class Rule:
        def __init__(self, it, other):
74          if it > other:
                it, other = other, it
76          self.Index = it
            self.OtherIndex = other
78
        def __eq__(self, other):
80          return self.Index == other.Index and \
                self.OtherIndex == other.OtherIndex
82
        def __hash__(self):
84          return self.Index * 100 + self.OtherIndex

86
    if __name__ == '__main__':
```

and create back-reference rules that only enforce row, column and section uniqueness against genes with lower array indexes.

Start with a nested pair of loops where the outer loop goes through all but the last index; this will be the back-referenced index in the rule.

```
        self.assertEqual(best.Fitness, optimalValue)
70
72  def build_validation_rules():
        rules = []
74      for index in range(80):
            itsRow = index_row(index)
76          itsColumn = index_column(index)
            itsSection = row_column_section(itsRow, itsColumn)
```

The inner loop starts at the lower index plus one and iterates over the rest of the gene indexes. We then determine if the two indexes are in the same row, column and/or section, and if so, we produce a *Rule* linking them.

```
78          for index2 in range(index + 1, 81):
                otherRow = index_row(index2)
80              otherColumn = index_column(index2)
                otherSection = row_column_section(otherRow, otherColumn)
82              if itsRow == otherRow or \
                        itsColumn == otherColumn or \
84                      itsSection == otherSection:
                    rules.append(Rule(index, index2))
```

Last, we sort the rules by the upper index then the lower index so we can quickly find all the rules that affect all indexes up to the current one and do so in a consistent order.

```
87      rules.sort(key=lambda x: x.OtherIndex * 100 + x.Index)
88      return rules
```

We use the following helper functions to determine the row, column, and section from an index.

```
    def index_row(index):
92      return int(index / 9)

94
    def index_column(index):
96      return int(index % 9)

98
    def row_column_section(row, column):
100     return int(row / 3) * 3 + int(column / 3)

102
    def index_section(index):
104     return row_column_section(index_row(index), index_column(index))

106
    def section_start(index):
108     return int((index_row(index) % 9) / 3) * 27 + int(
            index_column(index) / 3) * 3
110

112 class Rule:
```

Update the test

Next, in the test harness we need to get the validation rules and pass them to the fitness and mutation functions.

```
56          validationRules = build_validation_rules()                    <==

58          def fnGetFitness(genes):
                return get_fitness(genes, validationRules)                <==
60
            def fnCreate():
62              return random.sample(geneset * 9, 81)

64          def fnMutate(genes):
                mutate(genes, validationRules)                           <==
```

Now we're in a position to use the rules in the fitness function. We'll change the fitness value to be the row and column of the index of the first square that has a digit conflict. That will make it easy for us to find the problem square in the display. It also triples the granularity of the fitness value.

Fitness

```
8  def get_fitness(genes, validationRules):
       try:
10         firstFailingRule = next(rule for rule in validationRules
                                    if genes[rule.Index] == genes[rule.OtherIndex])
12     except StopIteration:
           fitness = 100
14     else:
           fitness = (1 + index_row(firstFailingRule.OtherIndex)) * 10 \
16                   + (1 + index_column(firstFailingRule.OtherIndex))
       return fitness
```

That change means the highest broken fitness value will be 99. So, we'll make the optimal value 100.

```
44          optimalValue = 100
```

Mutate

Finally, in the mutation function we have to process the rules again to figure out which, if any, of the array indexes has a digit conflict and then swap the gene at that index with one at any higher index.

```
def mutate(genes, validationRules):
    selectedRule = next(rule for rule in validationRules
                        if genes[rule.Index] == genes[rule.OtherIndex])
    if selectedRule is None:
        return
    indexA = selectedRule.OtherIndex
    indexB = random.randrange(1 + indexA, len(genes))
    genes[indexA], genes[indexB] = genes[indexB], genes[indexA]
```

Run 5

Now when we run the test it gets stuck because all the possible values it could put at that array index have already been used in the associated row, column or section.

```
7 1 9 | 4 2 8 | 6 3 5
4 5 3 | 7 1 9 | 8 2 8
4 2 1 | 7 9 3 | 1 6 4
----- + ----- + -----
8 4 5 | 9 4 5 | 1 8 1
6 7 3 | 9 7 8 | 4 5 4
6 1 5 | 2 7 9 | 5 2 9
----- + ----- + -----
3 6 8 | 5 9 1 | 6 2 5
7 2 8 | 3 3 1 | 6 9 6
2 8 3 | 7 6 7 | 3 4 2
- = -   - = -   - = - 29     0:00:00.009169
```

The fitness value tells us the problem is at row 2 column 9. We can see above that an 8 is conflicting with another 8 in the same row. The apparent fix would be to replace it with a 1, 4, 6, or 7 but 1, 4 and 7 already appear in its row and 6 has already been used in the same section. There's nothing the mutation function can swap into that position to resolve the problem, so as a result it stays stuck.

Enable row swaps
The solution is to enable swapping with any digit on the same row as well:

```
    if selectedRule is None:
        return
    row = index_row(selectedRule.OtherIndex)
    start = row * 9
    indexA = selectedRule.OtherIndex
    indexB = random.randrange(start, len(genes))
    genes[indexA], genes[indexB] = genes[indexB], genes[indexA]
```

Run 6

Now when we run the test, 9 times out of 10 it can produce a valid Sudoku board in under a second. When it can't it looks like this:

sample output

```
9 7 1 | 4 6 2 | 8 3 5
6 2 8 | 3 5 7 | 1 4 9
3 5 4 | 9 8 1 | 6 2 7
----- + ----- + -----
7 8 5 | 6 1 3 | 2 9 4
1 4 2 | 8 9 5 | 7 6 3
3 1 1 | 4 3 9 | 2 9 1
----- + ----- + -----
2 4 6 | 5 8 6 | 5 9 8
9 8 5 | 6 4 7 | 8 2 4
7 3 3 | 7 2 7 | 5 1 6
- = -   - = -   - = - 61      0:00:00.043248
```

Now it only gets stuck on the last row of a section. When that happens swapping with another gene on the same row can't fix it because the problem is that all 9 potential digits have already been used somewhere in its row, column or section.

Final revision

The final fix is to add a small chance of shuffling the contents of all genes, starting with the first gene in the current gene's section, until all the rules up to and including those of the current gene pass.

```
38    if selectedRule is None:
          return

40
      if index_row(selectedRule.OtherIndex) % 3 == 2 \
42            and random.randint(0, 10) == 0:
          sectionStart = section_start(selectedRule.Index)
44        current = selectedRule.OtherIndex
          while selectedRule.OtherIndex == current:
46            shuffle_in_place(genes, sectionStart, 80)
              selectedRule = next(rule for rule in validationRules
48                                   if genes[rule.Index] == genes[rule.OtherIndex])
          return
50    row = index_row(selectedRule.OtherIndex)
...
```

With the shuffling function defined as:

```
def shuffle_in_place(genes, first, last):
    while first < last:
        index = random.randint(first, last)
        genes[first], genes[index] = genes[index], genes[first]
        first += 1


class SudokuTests(unittest.TestCase):
```

We can speed it up further if we reduce the maximum age for simulated annealing.

```
        best = genetic.get_best(fnGetFitness, None, optimalValue, None,
                                fnDisplay, fnMutate, fnCreate, maxAge=50)
```

Run 7

These changes resolve the final problem without a significant performance penalty.
Outstanding!

Benchmarks

Here's the benchmark function:

```
        self.assertEqual(best.Fitness, optimalValue)

    def test_benchmark(self):
        genetic.Benchmark.run(lambda: self.test())
```

Benchmark

average (seconds)	standard deviation
0.19	0.11

Summary

In this project we learned that we must be tenacious and willing to question everything about our genetic algorithm implementation in order to work around a sticking point. We also learned that approaching the problem in a controlled fashion instead of having partial solutions spread all over can result in substantial performance improvements.

Traveling Salesman Problem

Our next project involves finding an optimal or near-optimal route to visit a set of locations. This is generically known as the Traveling Salesman Problem. Route optimality can be affected by costs, priorities, etc. Variations include unequal costs to travel a route in different directions, like fuel use going up or down a hill, one-way streets, paying toll fees at certain times of the day, obstacles along the way like rivers to cross or street layouts to navigate, how much time a particular stop might require, etc. Think about how you might implement this.

Test Data

We'll start off with a data set that we can easily verify by sight - one of the solutions to the 8 Queens Puzzle (0,0 is in the bottom left corner, points are counter-clockwise starting at A):

```
. . . . A . . .
. . B . . . . .
C . . . . . . .
. . . . . . H .
. D . . . . . .
. . . . . . . G
. . . . . F . .
. . . E . . . .
4,7 2,6 0,5 1,3 3,0 5,1 7,2 6,4
```

Test and genes

As usual we'll start by defining the gene set, and in this case, a lookup table where we can get the coordinates for a given location.

tspTests.py

```python
import datetime
import unittest

import genetic


class TravelingSalesmanTests(unittest.TestCase):
    def test_8_queens(self):
        idToLocationLookup = {
            'A': [4, 7],
            'B': [2, 6],
            'C': [0, 5],
            'D': [1, 3],
            'E': [3, 0],
            'F': [5, 1],
            'G': [7, 2],
            'H': [6, 4]
        }
        optimalSequence = ['A', 'B', 'C', 'D', 'E', 'F', 'G', 'H']
        self.solve(idToLocationLookup, optimalSequence)

    def solve(self, idToLocationLookup, optimalSequence):
        geneset = [i for i in idToLocationLookup.keys()]
```

Calculating distance

To determine fitness we need to be able to calculate the distance between two locations. We are going to use Euclidean (straight line) distance.

```python
import math
import unittest
```

```python
def get_distance(locationA, locationB):
    sideA = locationA[0] - locationB[0]
    sideB = locationA[1] - locationB[1]
    sideC = math.sqrt(sideA * sideA + sideB * sideB)
    return sideC


class TravelingSalesmanTests(unittest.TestCase):
```

Fitness

Since we want to optimize for the shortest distance we'll use a custom *Fitness* object.

```python
34  class Fitness:
        def __init__(self, totalDistance):
36          self.TotalDistance = totalDistance

38      def __gt__(self, other):
            return self.TotalDistance < other.TotalDistance
40
        def __str__(self):
42          return "{:0.2f}".format(self.TotalDistance)

44
    if __name__ == '__main__':
46      unittest.main()
```

To determine the route length we're going to sum the distances for points in the route, including returning to the starting location.

```python
8   def get_fitness(genes, idToLocationLookup):
        fitness = get_distance(idToLocationLookup[genes[0]],
10                             idToLocationLookup[genes[-1]])

12      for i in range(len(genes) - 1):
            start = idToLocationLookup[genes[i]]
14          end = idToLocationLookup[genes[i + 1]]
            fitness += get_distance(start, end)
16
        return Fitness(round(fitness, 2))
18

20  def get_distance(locationA, locationB):
        sideA = locationA[0] - locationB[0]
22      sideB = locationA[1] - locationB[1]
        sideC = math.sqrt(sideA * sideA + sideB * sideB)
24      return sideC

26
    class TravelingSalesmanTests(unittest.TestCase):
```

Display

In the display function we'll simply output the route and total distance traveled.

```
20  def display(candidate, startTime):
        timeDiff = datetime.datetime.now() - startTime
22      print("{}\t{}\t{}".format(
            ' '.join(map(str, candidate.Genes)),
24          candidate.Fitness,
            timeDiff))
26

28  def get_distance(locationA, locationB):
```

The output should look like this:

```
A E F G H B C D 27.72    0:00:00.001002
```

Mutate

Since we don't want to visit any location more than once, but we do want to make sure we visit all locations, we'll borrow custom mutate

```
3  import random
4  import unittest
```

```
36  def mutate(genes, fnGetFitness):
        count = random.randint(2, len(genes))
38      initialFitness = fnGetFitness(genes)
        while count > 0:
40          count -= 1
            indexA, indexB = random.sample(range(len(genes)), 2)
42          genes[indexA], genes[indexB] = genes[indexB], genes[indexA]
            fitness = fnGetFitness(genes)
44          if fitness > initialFitness:
                return
46

48  class TravelingSalesmanTests(unittest.TestCase):
```

and custom create from the Magic Squares project.

```
64          geneset = [i for i in idToLocationLookup.keys()]
65
66          def fnCreate():
67              return random.sample(geneset, len(geneset))
```

Test

The rest of the test harness should be familiar by now:

```
70    def fnDisplay(candidate):
          display(candidate, startTime)

72    def fnGetFitness(genes):
          return get_fitness(genes, idToLocationLookup)
74
      def fnMutate(genes):
76        mutate(genes, fnGetFitness)

78    optimalFitness = fnGetFitness(optimalSequence)
      startTime = datetime.datetime.now()
80    best = genetic.get_best(fnGetFitness, None, optimalFitness, None,
                              fnDisplay, fnMutate, fnCreate)
82    self.assertTrue(not optimalFitness > best.Fitness)
```

Run

When we run this we expect the optimal solution to be some rotation of the alphabetical sequence ABCDEFGH because that's the shortest route around those 8 points. And that is exactly what we get.

sample output

```
B D C G A H F E 33.93    0:00:00
H G C D A B F E 32.39    0:00:00
F B A D C H G E 30.33    0:00:00
E B A D C H G F 28.35    0:00:00.000501
E C D A B H G F 26.48    0:00:00.000501
E C D B A H G F 23.78    0:00:00.001002
F D C B A H G E 23.73    0:00:00.002013
E D C B A H G F 20.63    0:00:00.004010
```

A larger problem

There are many commonly used data sets for this type of problem, and many more are available from a web site called TSPLIB (see: http://comopt.ifi.uni-heidelberg.de/software/TSPLIB95/). We're going to try a small variant named ulysses16. The locations in this dataset are supposedly those visited by Homer's Ulysses. The data set has 16 numbered locations that are specified by floating point x and y coordinates, and symmetric route weights.

Here's how the points appear when plotted in Microsoft Excel.

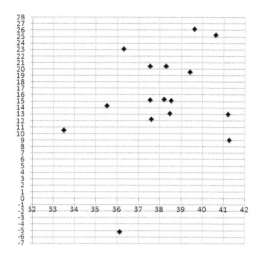

The data file is easy for parse.

```python
def load_data(localFileName):
    """ expects:
        HEADER section before DATA section, all lines start in column 0
        DATA section element all have space in column  0
            <space>1 23.45 67.89
        last line of file is: " EOF"
    """

    with open(localFileName, mode='r') as infile:
        content = infile.read().splitlines()
    idToLocationLookup = {}
    for row in content:
        if row[0] != ' ':  # HEADERS
            continue
        if row == " EOF":
            break

        id, x, y = row.split(' ')[1:4]
        idToLocationLookup[int(id)] = [float(x), float(y)]
    return idToLocationLookup


class Fitness:
```

We call the function that loads the data from the new test:

```python
    def test_ulysses16(self):
        idToLocationLookup = load_data("ulysses16.tsp")
        optimalSequence = [14, 13, 12, 16, 1, 3, 2, 4,
                           8, 15, 5, 11, 9, 10, 7, 6]
        self.solve(idToLocationLookup, optimalSequence)

    def solve(self, idToLocationLookup, optimalSequence):
```

The published optimal path for this problem treats the points as locations on Earth, which complicates the calculations with latitude, longitude, radius of the earth, etc. We're going to keep it simple and use the Euclidean distance function we already have.

The engine cannot solve this problem without simulated annealing, so we'll use that too.

```
86    best = genetic.get_best(fnGetFitness, None, optimalFitness, None,
87                            fnDisplay, fnMutate, fnCreate, maxAge=500)
```

Run

sample output

```
. . .
3 2 4 8 1 10 9 11 5 15 6 7 12 13 14 16   74.75    0:00:00.147422
3 2 4 8 1 10 9 11 5 15 6 7 14 13 12 16   74.73    0:00:00.158453
13 14 7 6 15 5 11 9 10 3 2 4 8 1 16 12   74.61    0:00:00.502374
4 8 1 13 14 15 5 11 9 10 7 6 12 16 3 2   74.28    0:00:01.036758
4 8 1 13 14 15 5 11 9 10 6 7 12 16 3 2   74.18    0:00:01.076865
7 10 9 11 5 15 1 8 4 2 3 16 12 13 14 6   74.00    0:00:04.306453
12 16 1 3 2 4 8 15 5 11 9 10 7 6 14 13   73.99    0:00:45.714639
```

It finds the optimal solution every time but overcoming the local minimum at 74.00 takes the majority of the time. In benchmarks it takes 8.69 seconds +/- 8.02 seconds, which is much too slow for us to want to use in benchmarks.

```
88         self.assertTrue(not optimalFitness > best.Fitness)
89
90    def test_benchmark(self):
91        genetic.Benchmark.run(lambda: self.test_ulysses16())
```

We're going to have to add something new.

Introducing crossover

When you read TSP research papers online the conversation invariably focuses on a genetic algorithm strategy that we haven't discussed yet - crossover. Crossover uses features from two different parents to create the new child. The idea is that the genes of each parent have part of the solution but they both may be stuck at a local minimum or maximum. So, if random parts of both are combined, it might produce a better solution to the problem.

The reason conversation focuses on crossover is because of the problem constraints and the many ways people have tried to work around them. For example, you can't just copy random genes because you might introduce duplication, which results in a worse fitness and a wasted attempt. The solution to the TSP is a cycle through all points, but the parent's genes for producing that route could start anywhere in the cycle and travel either direction along it. This means even if you use a clever method to copy genes to the new child so that you don't introduce duplication, you may be replacing clockwise-cycling genes with counter-clockwise cycling ones, which may or may not be an improvement. You may also, depending on how you select the genes that get moved, be breaking up a sequence that is already optimal. Ultimately, the point is that you will have to engineer crossover at least as much if not more than you do mutation.

Support a pool of parents

First things first. A prerequisite for crossover is two parents. Right now we only have one parent, so we're going to add the ability to set the number of parents.

❶ The community refers to this as a *pool* of parents.

genetic.py

```
34 def get_best(get_fitness, targetLen, optimalFitness, geneSet, display,
35              custom_mutate=None, custom_create=None, maxAge=None,
36              poolSize=1):
37 ...
```

Pass the pool size through to _get_improvement.

```
52     for improvement in _get_improvement(fnMutate, fnGenerateParent, maxAge,
53                                         poolSize):
```

Where we'll initialize an array of parents with the best parent.

```
60 def _get_improvement(new_child, generate_parent, maxAge, poolSize):
       bestParent = generate_parent()
62     yield bestParent
       parents = [bestParent]
64     historicalFitnesses = [bestParent.Fitness]
```

Then populate the parents array by generating new random parents. If one that has a better fitness than the best parent is found, we replace the best parent and update the list of historical best fitnesses.

```
      for _ in range(poolSize - 1):
66        parent = generate_parent()
          if parent.Fitness > bestParent.Fitness:
68            yield parent
              bestParent = parent
70            historicalFitnesses.append(parent.Fitness)
          parents.append(parent)
```

Next, since we have an array of parents, each time through the loop we'll select a different one to be the current parent.

```
72    lastParentIndex = poolSize - 1
      pindex = 1
74    while True:
          pindex = pindex - 1 if pindex > 0 else lastParentIndex
76        parent = parents[pindex]
```

The strategy we're using to curate the pool is to loop through all parents in the pool, continuously replacing parents with better children. This has the advantage of maintaining genetic diversity in the pool while keeping pool maintenance simple.

If we were to replace the parent every time then it would behave more like continuous simulated annealing. If you did the experiments when we introduced that feature, then you know that such a system would have terrible performance on pure combinatorial problems.

A much more common implementation is to have a pool of parents and a pool of children. Ways of selecting children to keep include:

- keep all children
- keep only children better than their respective parent
- keep only children better than the best child
- keep only children better than the median best child

Once the child pool is full, again there are many options for repopulating the parent pool. They include:

- The child pool replaces the parent pool as is.
- The best (user specified) N percent of the children replace the worst N percent of the parents. This is called elitism. The problem then becomes how to choose the right percentage.
- The best `sqrt(pool size)` children are combined with the best `sqrt(pool size)` parents through full crossover, every parent with every child, to produce a new parent pool.
- Pick a random number of children, then take the one with the best fitness from that group. Repeat until the pool is filled. This is known as tournament selection.
- When the fitness value is numeric, children can be given a chance of being selected to become a parent based on the ratio of their fitness to the sum of all child fitnesses. This is known as roulette wheel selection.

The remaining changes to _get_improvement involve using a parent-array index when the parent is being replaced.

```
        if random.random() < exp(-proportionSimilar):
88          parents[pindex] = child                              <==
            continue
90      bestParent.Age = 0
        parents[pindex] = bestParent                             <==
92      continue
```

```
        if not child.Fitness > parent.Fitness:
94          # same fitness
            child.Age = parent.Age + 1
96          parents[pindex] = child                              <==
            continue
98      child.Age = 0
        parents[pindex] = child                                  <==
100 ...
```

Adding only the pool to this solution, however, actually hurts performance because every item in the pool is touched before we get back around again to the one that was just improved.

tspTests.py

```
86      best = genetic.get_best(fnGetFitness, None, optimalFitness, None,
87                          fnDisplay, fnMutate, fnCreate, maxAge=500,
88                          poolSize=25)
```

Updated Benchmark

average (seconds)	standard deviation
9.45	10.83

Support crossover

Since crossover is closely linked to the genotype and project, we will not add a default implementation to the `genetic` module. It will instead be available as an optional parameter only.

We'll start with adding the optional parameter to *get_best*.

genetic.py

```
34  def get_best(get_fitness, targetLen, optimalFitness, geneSet, display,
35              custom_mutate=None, custom_create=None, maxAge=None,
36              poolSize=1, crossover=None):
37  ...
```

We don't want to use crossover *instead of* mutation but rather as a supplement. In fact, we're going to make it adaptive, so that we'll prefer whichever of the two strategies is producing the most improvements. To do that we need to track which strategy was used to create that parent. That implies a list of strategies

```
6  from enum import Enum
```

```
114  class Strategies(Enum):
         Create = 0,
116      Mutate = 1,
         Crossover = 2
118
120  class Benchmark:
```

and a *Strategy* attribute on the *Chromosome* class:

```
     class Chromosome:
108      def __init__(self, genes, fitness, strategy):
             self.Genes = genes
110          self.Fitness = fitness
             self.Strategy = strategy
112          self.Age = 0
```

Additionally, that new constructor parameter must be supplied wherever we create a
Chromosome.

```
16      return Chromosome(genes, fitness, Strategies.Create)
```

```
25      return Chromosome(childGenes, fitness, Strategies.Mutate)
```

```
32      return Chromosome(childGenes, fitness, Strategies.Mutate)
```

```
51           return Chromosome(genes, get_fitness(genes), Strategies.Create)
```

Next, we can keep a list of strategies that were used to create parents and update it
whenever _get_improvement sends it a new improvement. We also need to create
new children by selecting a random strategy from the array of successful strategies,
instead of always using mutate:

```
54    strategyLookup = {
          Strategies.Create: lambda p, i, o: fnGenerateParent(),
          Strategies.Mutate: lambda p, i, o: fnMutate(p),
56        Strategies.Crossover: lambda p, i, o:_
          crossover(p.Genes, i, o, get_fitness, crossover, fnMutate,
58                   fnGenerateParent)
      }
60
      usedStrategies = [strategyLookup[Strategies.Mutate]]
62    if crossover is not None:
          usedStrategies.append(strategyLookup[Strategies.Crossover])
64
          def fnNewChild(parent, index, parents):
66            return random.choice(usedStrategies)(parent, index, parents)
      else:
68        def fnNewChild(parent, index, parents):
              return fnMutate(parent)
70
      for improvement in _get_improvement(fnNewChild, fnGenerateParent,
72                                         maxAge, poolSize):
  ...
```

This requires a small change in _get_improvement

```
92    while True:
93        pindex = pindex - 1 if pindex > 0 else lastParentIndex
94        parent = parents[pindex]
95        child = new_child(parent, pindex, parents)                    <==
```

ⓘ Many genetic engines allow you to specify crossover and mutation *rates*. However, this puts the burden on you to experiment with the percentages to try to find values that work well for your problem. The system implemented here is to give strategies that are successful a higher chance of being used again. Since the strategy used to produce a particular *Chromosome* is included with the object, you can monitor the strategies that are used. That can help you check whether your crossover algorithm is stronger or weaker than your mutation algorithm, as we'll see later.

Finally, we need to add a convenience function for calling the crossover function.

```python
def _crossover(parentGenes, index, parents, get_fitness, crossover, mutate,
               generate_parent):
    donorIndex = random.randrange(0, len(parents))
    if donorIndex == index:
        donorIndex = (donorIndex + 1) % len(parents)
    childGenes = crossover(parentGenes, parents[donorIndex].Genes)
    if childGenes is None:
        # parent and donor are indistinguishable
        parents[donorIndex] = generate_parent()
        return mutate(parents[index])
    fitness = get_fitness(childGenes)
    return Chromosome(childGenes, fitness, Strategies.Crossover)


def get_best(get_fitness, targetLen, optimalFitness, geneSet, display,
```

That completes the infrastructural support for crossover and adaptive use of strategies in genetic.

Use crossover

Back in our test file we need to change the *solve* function to pass a crossover function to *get_best* and to request a larger pool of parents.

tspTests.py

```python
    def fnCrossover(parent, donor):                                 <==
        return crossover(parent, donor, fnGetFitness)               <==

    optimalFitness = fnGetFitness(optimalSequence)
    startTime = datetime.datetime.now()
    best = genetic.get_best(fnGetFitness, None, optimalFitness, None,
                            fnDisplay, fnMutate, fnCreate, maxAge=500,
                            poolSize=25, crossover=fnCrossover)      <==
```

Then we need to build the crossover function. It will start by constructing a lookup table of all the 2-point pairs in the donor parent's genes.

```python
48  def crossover(parentGenes, donorGenes, fnGetFitness):
        pairs = {Pair(donorGenes[0], donorGenes[-1]): 0}
50
        for i in range(len(donorGenes) - 1):
52          pairs[Pair(donorGenes[i], donorGenes[i + 1])] = 0

54
    class TravelingSalesmanTests(unittest.TestCase):
```

The *Pair* class is just a renamed copy of the *Rule* class from the Graph Coloring project. *Pair* orders the two genes so that gene pairs can be compared regardless of cycle direction.

```python
    class Pair:
138     def __init__(self, node, adjacent):
            if node < adjacent:
140             node, adjacent = adjacent, node
            self.Node = node
142         self.Adjacent = adjacent

144     def __eq__(self, other):
            return self.Node == other.Node and self.Adjacent == other.Adjacent
146
        def __hash__(self):
148         return hash(self.Node) * 397 ^ hash(self.Adjacent)

150     def __str__(self):
            return "{}{}".format(self.Node, self.Adjacent)
152

154 if __name__ == '__main__':
```

The next thing the crossover function does is make sure the first and last genes in the parent are not adjacent in the donor. If they are, then we search for a pair of adjacent points from the parent that are not adjacent in the donor. If we find one then we shift that discontinuity to the beginning of the array so that we know no sequences wrap around the end of the array.

example

```
donorGenes: ['E', 'A', 'C', 'G', 'B', 'D', 'H', 'F']
parentGenes: ['G', 'C', 'D', 'F', 'E', 'H', 'A', 'B']

pairs contains:
  EA, CA, GC, GB, DB, HD, HF, FE
```

The pair GB exists in both gene sequences. So does GC. But DC does not, so a copy of the parent genes will be shifted to the left to become:

```
tempGenes: ['D', 'F', 'E', 'H', 'A', 'B', 'G', 'C']
```

Otherwise, the parent and the donor are identical so we simply return None and let the genetic engine handle it. Continuing the crossover implementation:

```
52          pairs[Pair(donorGenes[i], donorGenes[i + 1])] = 0

54      tempGenes = parentGenes[:]
        if Pair(parentGenes[0], parentGenes[-1]) in pairs:
56          # find a discontinuity
            found = False
58          for i in range(len(parentGenes) - 1):
                if Pair(parentGenes[i], parentGenes[i + 1]) in pairs:
60                  continue
                tempGenes = parentGenes[i + 1:] + parentGenes[:i + 1]
62              found = True
                break
64          if not found:
                return None
```

Next we're going to collect all the sequences from the parent that are also in the donor. The lookup table helps us to find them regardless of the direction the parent's genes are cycling.

```
    runs = [[tempGenes[0]]]
68  for i in range(len(tempGenes) - 1):
        if Pair(tempGenes[i], tempGenes[i + 1]) in pairs:
70          runs[-1].append(tempGenes[i + 1])
            continue
72      runs.append([tempGenes[i + 1]])
```

example continued

```
common sequences:
  ['D'],
  ['F', 'E'],
  ['H'],
  ['A'],
  ['B', 'G', 'C']
```

Now we try to find a reordering of the sequences that has a better fitness than the current parent. We'll do this by swapping any pair of sequences and checking the fitness, with a chance of reversing the order.

```
74    initialFitness = fnGetFitness(parentGenes)
      count = random.randint(2, 20)
76    runIndexes = range(len(runs))
      while count > 0:
78        count -= 1
          for i in runIndexes:
80            if len(runs[i]) == 1:
                  continue
82            if random.randint(0, len(runs)) == 0:
                  runs[i] = [n for n in reversed(runs[i])]
```

If the fitness is better than that of the parent, then we return the new genetic sequence. Otherwise we repeat until we find an improvement or we complete the maximum number of attempts, at which point we give up and return what we have.

```
4  import unittest
5  from itertools import chain
```

```
84                runs[i] = [n for n in reversed(runs[i])]
          indexA, indexB = random.sample(runIndexes, 2)
86        runs[indexA], runs[indexB] = runs[indexB], runs[indexA]
          childGenes = list(chain.from_iterable(runs))
88        if fnGetFitness(childGenes) > initialFitness:
              return childGenes
90    return childGenes
```

One other change we can make is in the display function where we can output the strategy that was used to produce each improvement.

```
22 def display(candidate, startTime):
      timeDiff = datetime.datetime.now() - startTime
24    print("{}\t{}\t{}\t{}".format(
          ' '.join(map(str, candidate.Genes)),
26        candidate.Fitness,
          candidate.Strategy.name,
28        timeDiff))
```

Run

Now when we run `test_ulysses16` crossover tends to be the most commonly used strategy.

```
13 12 16 8 4 2 3 1 15 5 11 9 10 7 6 14   74.86   Crossover   0:00:01.437824
13 12 1 8 4 2 3 16 15 5 11 9 10 7 6 14   74.60   Mutate  0:00:01.468941
3 2 4 8 1 15 5 11 9 10 6 7 14 13 12 16   74.23   Crossover   0:00:02.032406
1 14 15 5 11 9 10 6 7 12 13 16 3 2 4 8   74.00   Crossover   0:00:02.170804
13 12 16 1 3 2 4 8 15 5 11 9 10 7 6 14   73.99   Crossover   0:00:02.576854
```

The algorithm also finds the optimal solution much faster on average.

Retrospective

We added two new tools, the parent pool size and crossover, that you may be able to use to improve the performance of previous projects.

For example, crossover might be used to detect the correct characters in the Password project so you can concentrate on non-matching indexes.

You might also try using crossover to exchange runs in the Sorted Numbers project.

In Graph Coloring, Linear Equations, and Knights, see how adding more parents affects the performance.

To use crossover effectively in the Knapsack project you might need to switch to a different genotype.

Updated benchmarks

Since we changed the code paths in `genetic` we'll update all the benchmarks.

project	average (seconds)	standard deviation
Guess Password	1.26	0.29
One Max	1.22	0.16
Sorted Numbers	1.18	0.63
Queens	1.56	1.31
Graph Coloring	0.73	0.25
Cards	0.01	0.01
Knights	0.70	0.72
Magic Square	0.20	0.33
Knapsack	0.66	0.45
Linear Equations	1.23	0.88
Sudoku	0.17	0.11
Traveling Salesman	1.04	0.80

Summary

In this project we added an optional pool of parents to the `genetic` module. We also added support for using crossover with adaptive strategy selection. These two powerful capabilities make our genetic engine essentially feature complete. From this point on we'll be concentrating on broadening the complexity and diversity of problems we know how to handle.

Approximating Pi

In this project we're going to use a genetic algorithm to find an approximation for Pi, a deceptively simple project. Our phenotype will be 2 integers in the range 1 to 1024 that we'll divide in order to produce a decimal value. Our genotype will be binary code. That means the gene set will only be 0 and 1. Go try it then come back to work through my implementation.

Test and genes

approximatePiTests.py

```
   import datetime
2  import unittest

4  import genetic

6
   class ApproximatePiTests(unittest.TestCase):
8      def test(self):
           geneset = [i for i in range(2)]
```

Convert bits to an integer

It takes 10 binary bits to produce integer values up to 1023. That means we need 20 bits to store the numerator and denominator that we'll be dividing to approximate Pi. We will need a utility function to convert an array of 10 bits to an integer.

```
4  import genetic

6
   def bits_to_int(bits):
8      result = 0
       for bit in bits:
10          result = (result << 1) | bit
       return result
```

It also means that the *position* of the gene changes its *value* in the phenotype:

phenotype value	genotype values			
	8	4	2	1
0	0	0	0	0
1	0	0	0	1
2	0	0	1	0
3	0	0	1	1
4	0	1	0	0
5	0	1	0	1
6	0	1	1	0
7	0	1	1	1
8	1	0	0	0
9	1	0	0	1
10	1	0	1	0

To prevent division by zero, and increase the value range to 1024, we'll add 1 to the decoded numerator and denominator.

```
14 def get_numerator(genes):
       return 1 + bits_to_int(genes[:10])
16

18 def get_denominator(genes):
       return 1 + bits_to_int(genes[10:])
```

Fitness

We want the ratio that is closest to Pi so we'll subtract the difference between the calculated value and Pi from Pi to get the fitness. This way we don't need a *Fitness* class.

```
2 import math
  import unittest
4
  import genetic
6

8 def get_fitness(genes):
      ratio = get_numerator(genes) / get_denominator(genes)
10    return math.pi - abs(math.pi - ratio)
```

Display

The display function will show the two parts of the fraction and their calculated ratio.

```python
def display(candidate, startTime):
    timeDiff = datetime.datetime.now() - startTime
    numerator = get_numerator(candidate.Genes)
    denominator = get_denominator(candidate.Genes)
    print("{}/{}\t{}\t{}".format(
        numerator,
        denominator,
        candidate.Fitness, timeDiff))
```

sample output

```
240/129 1.8604651162790697  0:00:00.001000
```

Best approximations for Pi

Next, it would be useful to know what the best approximations for Pi are in the range we're checking:

```python
    def test_find_top_10_approximations(self):
        best = {}
        for numerator in range(1, 1024):
            for denominator in range(1, 1024):
                ratio = numerator / denominator
                piDist = math.pi - abs(math.pi - ratio)
                if piDist not in best or best[piDist][0] > numerator:
                    best[piDist] = [numerator, denominator]

        bestApproximations = list(reversed(sorted(best.keys())))
        for i in range(10):
            ratio = bestApproximations[i]
            nd = best[ratio]
            print("%i / %i\t%f" % (nd[0], nd[1], ratio))


if __name__ == '__main__':
    unittest.main()
```

Top ten approximations

```
355  /  113    3.141592
732  /  233    3.141554
688  /  219    3.141553
1021 /  325    3.141538
377  /  120    3.141519
333  /  106    3.141509
776  /  247    3.141485
977  /  311    3.141479
644  /  205    3.141463
399  /  127    3.141453
```

This means we expect the engine to find 355/133 or some multiple thereof.

Optimal value

Because floating point values aren't exact in Python we'll use a value between 355/133 and 732/233 as the optimal value.

Here's the full test harness:

```python
    def test(self):
        geneset = [i for i in range(2)]
        startTime = datetime.datetime.now()

        def fnDisplay(candidate):
            display(candidate, startTime)

        def fnGetFitness(genes):
            return get_fitness(genes)

        optimalFitness = 3.14159
        best = genetic.get_best(fnGetFitness, 20, optimalFitness, geneset,
                                fnDisplay)
        self.assertTrue(optimalFitness <= best.Fitness)
```

Run

When we run it we get output like the following:
sample result

```
679/362 1.8756906077348066   0:00:00
679/361 1.8808864265927978   0:00:00
935/361 2.590027700831025    0:00:00
935/329 2.8419452887537995   0:00:00
935/321 2.912772585669782    0:00:00
943/321 2.9376947040498442   0:00:00
944/321 2.940809968847352    0:00:00
1008/321    3.1401869158878504  0:00:00
```

We can run it many times but it will rarely find the optimal solution. The problem is we can only change 1 bit at a time in either the numerator or denominator and this causes it to get stuck at a local maximum where it has individually optimized those two values as much as it can.

Modify both parts

However, we can add a custom mutation function that modifies both the numerator and denominator each time it is called:

```
 3  import random
 4  import unittest
```

```
    def mutate(genes):
40      numeratorIndex, denominatorIndex = random.randrange(0, 10), \
                                    random.randrange(10, len(genes))
42      genes[numeratorIndex] = 1 - genes[numeratorIndex]
        genes[denominatorIndex] = 1 - genes[denominatorIndex]

44

46  class ApproximatePiTests(unittest.TestCase):
```

And then use it in the test.

```
58          best = genetic.get_best(fnGetFitness, 20, optimalFitness, geneset,
59                          fnDisplay, mutate)
```

Run 2

Run the test again and it still cannot find the optimal solution.

```
924/389 2.3753213367609254   0:00:00
956/390 2.4512820512820515   0:00:00.001002
940/262 2.6953990476376015   0:00:00.001002
932/294 3.113117279968702    0:00:00.001002
931/296 3.137915036909316    0:00:00.001002
```

Since it appears that we're still hitting a local maximum, let's see if simulated annealing can fix it.

Use simulated annealing

```
58          best = genetic.get_best(fnGetFitness, 20, optimalFitness, geneset,
59                          fnDisplay, mutate, maxAge=250)
```

Run 3

Now when we run the test it can find the optimal solution every time but it can take a long time.

```
. . .
1016/324 3.1358024691358026 0:00:00.002006
1024/326 3.1411042944785277 0:00:00.006020
1021/325 3.1415384615384614 0:00:00.034090
732/233  3.1415544058920326 0:00:08.040390
355/113  3.1415923868256037 0:00:34.368389
```

We can measure how slow it is with a benchmark test:

```
62    def test_benchmark(self):
63        genetic.Benchmark.run(lambda: self.test())
64
65    def test_find_top_10_approximations(self):
```

sample results

average (seconds)	standard deviation
28.23	30.62

The issue we're having is that successive improvements don't build on the previous ones. Consider the following corner case:

```
127    [0, 1, 1, 1, 1, 1, 1, 1]
128    [1, 0, 0, 0, 0, 0, 0, 0]
```

If we needed 128 in the numerator but had 127, the genetic algorithm would have to change 8 bits. It would be very difficult for it to make that leap. Additionally, there is no slack in our genotype. There is exactly one pattern that will produce the value 355/113 for example. This is something to be aware of when choosing a genotype for a genetic algorithm.

So how can we add some slack?

Expanding the genotype

The bits in our current genotype have the following values by position:

```
[512, 256, 128, 64, 32, 16, 8, 4, 2, 1]
```

What if we simply double the number of bits we use per phenotype and then duplicate each value. Effectively:

```
[512, 512, 256, 256, 128, 128, 64, 64, 32, 32, 16, 16, 8, 8, 4, 4, 2, 2, 1, 1]
```

Let's try it.

Pass the bit values

We'll start by moving the bit values to an array,

```
50        bitValues = [512, 256, 128, 64, 32, 16, 8, 4, 2, 1]              <==

52        def fnDisplay(candidate):
              display(candidate, startTime, bitValues)                     <==
54
          def fnGetFitness(genes):
56            return get_fitness(genes, bitValues)                         <==
```

then pass the array of bit values through to the various functions that need it:

```
   def get_fitness(genes, bitValues):
10     denominator = get_denominator(genes, bitValues)                     <==
       if denominator == 0:
12         return 0

14     ratio = get_numerator(genes, bitValues) / denominator               <==
       return math.pi - math.fabs(math.pi - ratio)
```

```
18 def display(candidate, startTime, bitValues):
19     timeDiff = datetime.datetime.now() - startTime
20     numerator = get_numerator(candidate.Genes, bitValues)               <==
21     denominator = get_denominator(candidate.Genes, bitValues)           <==
22 ...
```

```
   def get_numerator(genes, bitValues):
38     return 1 + bits_to_int(genes[:10], bitValues)                       <==

40
   def get_denominator(genes, bitValues):
42     return bits_to_int(genes[10:], bitValues)                           <==
```

The final step is to use the array to decode the genes as follows:

```
24 def bits_to_int(bits, bitValues):
       result = 0
26     for i, bit in enumerate(bits):
           if bit == 0:
28             continue
           result += bitValues[i]
30     return result
```

Change the bit values

Now change the values of the bits.

```
56        bitValues = [512, 512, 256, 256, 128, 128, 64, 64, 32,
57                     32, 16, 16, 8, 8, 4, 4, 2, 2, 1, 1]
```

Since the new gene sequence length depends on the length of the bit value array, we need to update places where we reference specific indexes.

```
          def fnMutate(genes):
68            mutate(genes, len(bitValues))

70        length = 2 * len(bitValues)
          best = genetic.get_best(fnGetFitness, length, optimalFitness,
72                            geneset, fnDisplay, fnMutate, maxAge=250)
```

```
   def get_numerator(genes, bitValues):
38     return 1 + bits_to_int(genes[:len(bitValues)], bitValues)

40
   def get_denominator(genes, bitValues):
42     return bits_to_int(genes[len(bitValues):], bitValues)
```

```
45 def mutate(genes, numBits):
46     numeratorIndex, denominatorIndex \
47         = random.randrange(0, numBits), random.randrange(numBits,
48                                                          len(genes))
49 ...
```

This change substantially improves the benchmark result for this project.

sample benchmark

average (seconds)	standard deviation
0.91	0.89

This simple change resulted in a 30x speed improvement.

Exercise

Could we get more speed if none of the values were duplicates? What if we doubled the size of the array again? Do the bit values need to be ordered? What is the highest bit value we need? You should go experiment then come back.

Optimizing the bit array

What do you think it would take to find the best bit value array for this problem? It sounds exactly like something we would solve with a genetic algorithm doesn't it? Let's do it.

Since we know a poor set of values for the bit array can take a long time to run, we need to put a limit on the run time. So, let's say the goal is to find the optimal solution to the Pi project as many times as possible in 2 seconds. That means we need a way to break out of the engine after 2 seconds.

Support time constraints in the `genetic` module

We'll start by adding an optional parameter to *get_best* for the maximum number of seconds to run.

genetic.py

```
50  def get_best(get_fitness, targetLen, optimalFitness, geneSet, display,
51              custom_mutate=None, custom_create=None, maxAge=None,
52              poolSize=1, crossover=None, maxSeconds=None):
53  ...
```

Then pass that variable to _get_improvement and also handle the new additional return value that indicates that a timeout occurred.

```
86      for timedOut, improvement in \_
            get_improvement(fnNewChild, fnGenerateParent, maxAge, poolSize,
88                          maxSeconds):
            if timedOut:
90              return improvement
    ...
```

Next, at the beginning of _get_improvement we start a timer and wherever we return a result we need to include in flag for whether a timeout occurred.

```
98 def _get_improvement(new_child, generate_parent, maxAge, poolSize, maxSeconds):
       startTime = time.time()
100    bestParent = generate_parent()
       yield maxSeconds is not None and time.time() \
102        - startTime > maxSeconds, bestParent
   ...
```

We check it after each call to *generate_parent* when populating the parent pool.

```
       for _ in range(poolSize - 1):
106        parent = generate_parent()
           if maxSeconds is not None and time.time() - startTime > maxSeconds:
108            yield True, parent
           if parent.Fitness > bestParent.Fitness:
110            yield False, parent
```

We also check at the start of the while loop.

```
116    while True:
117        if maxSeconds is not None and time.time() - startTime > maxSeconds:
118            yield True, bestParent
```

We've already checked it when we find a new best parent, so we just send False.

```
144        if child.Fitness > bestParent.Fitness:
145            bestParent = child
146            yield False, bestParent
```

Optimizer

Now in the optimizer we'll see if we can make the 10-bit version run faster. We start with a gene set containing all the numbers in the range 1 to 512. And we'll give each round 2 seconds to run.

approximatePiTests.py

```
4 import time
5 import unittest
```

```
       self.assertTrue(optimalFitness <= best.Fitness)
76
   def test_optimize(self):
78     geneset = [i for i in range(1, 512 + 1)]
       length = 10
80     maxSeconds = 2
```

Next we need to write the fitness function. It will start a timer and keep a count of the number of successes.

```
82      def fnGetFitness(genes):
83          startTime = time.time()
84          count = 0
```

It will then run the Pi approximation test and count how many times it can find the optimal result. We'll also suppress its output.

```
4  import sys
5  import time
```

```
86          stdout = sys.stdout
            sys.stdout = None
88          while time.time() - startTime < maxSeconds:
                if self.test(genes, maxSeconds):
90                  count += 1
            sys.stdout = stdout
```

The fitness value will be a combination of the number of successes and a fraction. The fraction indicates how far the sum of the bit values is from 1023. This gives the engine a very granular fitness to use to find improvements.

```
92          distance = abs(sum(genes) - 1023)
93          fraction = 1 / distance if distance > 0 else distance
94          count += round(fraction, 4)
95          return count
```

Next we want a way to monitor what is happening, so we write a display function.

```
97      def fnDisplay(chromosome):
98          print("{}\t{}".format(chromosome.Genes, chromosome.Fitness))
```

For comparison we'll output the fitness of the initial sequence.

```
100         initial = [512, 256, 128, 64, 32, 16, 8, 4, 2, 1]
101         print("initial:", initial, fnGetFitness(initial))
```

Finally, we'll start the run and give it 10 minutes to try to find an improvement, with the goal being a set of bit values that can be used to find Pi 20 times in 2 seconds.

```
102        optimalFitness = 10 * maxSeconds
103        genetic.get_best(fnGetFitness, length, optimalFitness, geneset,
104                         fnDisplay, maxSeconds=600)
```

Now we need to make related changes to the test function so we can pass an array of bit values and the maximum number of seconds to run as parameters. Remember to remove the existing array definition from the function.

```
56     def test(self, bitValues=[512, 256, 128, 64, 32, 16, 8, 4, 2, 1],
57             maxSeconds=None):
```

Then pass the number of seconds through to the engine so that it knows when to stop. At the end we need to return a value indicating whether or not it found a Pi approximation at least as good as the optimal value.

```
73     best = genetic.get_best(fnGetFitness, length, optimalFitness,
74                             geneset, fnDisplay, fnMutate, maxAge=250,
75                             maxSeconds=maxSeconds)
76     return optimalFitness <= best.Fitness
```

Optimization Run

Now run it and it does find a much better bit value sequence.

sample result

```
initial: [512, 256, 128, 64, 32, 16, 8, 4, 2, 1] 0
[45, 39, 289, 407, 23, 224, 280, 240, 412, 260] 0.0008
[45, 39, 289, 407, 71, 224, 280, 240, 412, 260] 3.0008
[45, 39, 289, 407, 71, 224, 45, 240, 412, 260]  5.001
[45, 26, 289, 407, 71, 224, 45, 240, 412, 260]  6.001
[45, 26, 289, 407, 71, 82, 45, 240, 412, 260]   8.0012
[45, 26, 289, 407, 70, 82, 45, 240, 412, 260]   14.0012
```

Verify the result

Now we can use the bit value sequence it found above to verify that we get a performance improvement.

```
106    def test_benchmark(self):
107        genetic.Benchmark.run(lambda: self.test([45, 26, 289, 407, 70,
108                                   82, 45, 240, 412, 260]))
```

sample output

```
100 0.29 0.39
```

That's about 3 times better performance than we achieved by doubling the bit values. Nice!

If we allow the optimizer to run each round longer, say 4 seconds instead of 2, and run to completion it can find an even better result.

sample result

```
initial: [512, 256, 128, 64, 32, 16, 8, 4, 2, 1] 0
...
[37, 334, 38, 292, 117, 39, 50, 225, 46, 55]    3.0048
[37, 334, 38, 292, 117, 39, 50, 225, 46, 124]   5.0036
[37, 334, 38, 292, 117, 39, 50, 225, 46, 129]   8.0035
[37, 334, 38, 133, 117, 39, 50, 225, 46, 129]   11.008
[37, 334, 38, 133, 117, 39, 50, 225, 262, 129]  14.0029
[37, 334, 38, 133, 117, 39, 87, 225, 262, 129]  15.0026
[37, 334, 38, 96, 117, 39, 87, 225, 262, 129]   17.0029
[37, 334, 38, 96, 117, 39, 145, 225, 262, 129]  26.0025
[37, 334, 38, 339, 117, 39, 145, 225, 262, 129] 30.0016
[98, 334, 38, 339, 117, 39, 145, 225, 262, 129] 32.0014
[98, 334, 38, 339, 117, 39, 145, 123, 262, 129] 33.0017
[98, 334, 38, 339, 117, 39, 145, 123, 40, 129]  40.0026
```

sample benchmark

```
100 0.09 0.10
```

Wow!

Summary

In this project we learned one way to use one genetic algorithm to optimize another, that the options we have for translating values in the genotype to phenotype values can significantly impact the performance of the genetic algorithm, and that it is important to give the algorithm multiple ways to use the genes to achieve the goal.

Equation Generation

So far we've only used genes as data elements that are applied to an external problem. Our next project, equation generation, will introduce us to a new way of using genes called genetic programming. The essence of genetic programming is to overlay some kind of grammar on the genes, which may or may not include embedded data. These operation-genes can then be evaluated to produce a result.

Example

When using genetic programming it is important to understand the characteristics of both the embedded data, if any, and how we expect the operations to interact with each other and/or the environment. For example, let's say we are asked to find some combination of the numbers 1 to 7 and addition and subtraction operations that, when evaluated, produces the numeric value 29. Stop here and think about how you would implement this.

There are many ways to solve this problem. For example: 7+7+7+7+7-6

We could simply use positive and negative integers between -7 and 7 because they essentially have the addition and subtraction operations built in, but we need to learn how to evaluate operations as independent genes, so we'll make + and - separate tokens. That means the equation has 11 tokens or genes:

```
7   +   7   +   7   +   7   +   7   -   6
|   |   |   |   |   |   |   |   |   |   |
1   2   3   4   5   6   7   8   9  10  11
```

When viewed this way we can easily see the pattern, or grammar, of alternating operations and numbers. This should be easy to enforce using an odd/even check when creating and mutating chromosomes.

Next, if we visualize the equation from the point of view of the operations:

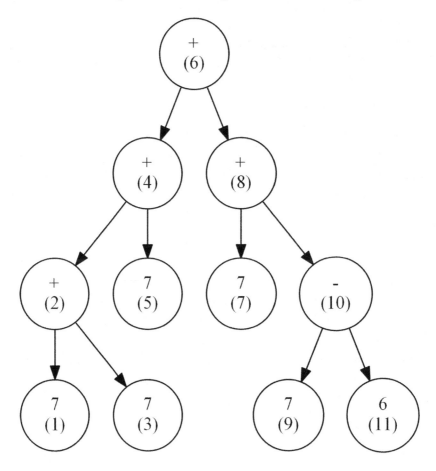

It is easy to see that each operation has 2 parameters because each acts upon 2 other genes which can be either a number or another operation.

Evaluate

The heart of a genetic programming algorithm is the function that performs evaluation. It knows how to treat the problem-specific gene sequence like a program. In this project it will apply the operation genes to the neighboring numbers, rolling up to get the final result.

equationGenerationTests.py

```python
def evaluate(genes):
    result = genes[0]
    for i in range(1, len(genes), 2):
        operation = genes[i]
        nextValue = genes[i + 1]
        if operation == '+':
            result += nextValue
        elif operation == '-':
            result -= nextValue
    return result
```

The function starts by initializing a result variable with the value of the first numeric gene. It then applies the operations, left to right, to the current result and the value-gene that follows the operation. The output of each operation is stored back in the result variable.

Test and genes

We're ready to write the rest of the genetic algorithm according to the usual pattern, starting with the gene set.

equationGenerationTests.py

```python
import datetime
import random
import unittest

import genetic


def evaluate(genes):
```

```python
    return result


class EquationGenerationTests(unittest.TestCase):
    def test(self):
        numbers = [1, 2, 3, 4, 5, 6, 7]
        operations = ['+', '-']
```

Create

Now we can immediately see that we'll need a custom gene-creation function, for two reasons. First, we don't know how many symbols we'll need to produce a particular result, and second, we need to alternate numbers and operations.

```python
def create(numbers, operations, minNumbers, maxNumbers):
    genes = [random.choice(numbers)]
    count = random.randint(minNumbers, 1 + maxNumbers)
    while count > 1:
        count -= 1
        genes.append(random.choice(operations))
        genes.append(random.choice(numbers))
    return genes


class EquationGenerationTests(unittest.TestCase):
```

This implementation prevents the creation of gene sequences that have multiple numbers or operations in a row, so we don't have to detect that situation in the fitness function.

Mutate

We also need a custom mutation function that knows how to append an operation-number pair to the gene sequence,

```python
def mutate(genes, numbers, operations, minNumbers, maxNumbers):
    numberCount = (1 + len(genes)) / 2
    adding = numberCount < maxNumbers and random.randint(0, 100) == 0
    if adding:
        genes.append(random.choice(operations))
        genes.append(random.choice(numbers))
        return
```

remove an operation-number pair,

```python
    removing = numberCount > minNumbers and random.randint(0, 20) == 0
    if removing:
        index = random.randrange(0, len(genes) - 1)
        del genes[index]
        del genes[index]
        return
```

and mutate an operation or number.

```
46    index = random.randrange(0, len(genes))
47    genes[index] = random.choice(operations) \
48        if (index & 1) == 1 else random.choice(numbers)
```

Here we use the parity of the index to determine whether we're replacing a number or an operation.

Fitness

In the fitness function we'll use the evaluation function to get the result of the equation, then compare it to the expected result. This time, instead of using a *Fitness* class we'll use a 2-stage fitness function. The first stage tracks how far the result of evaluating the genes is from the expected total. If the result is correct then the second fitness range is used. This allows us to prefer shorter gene sequences, meaning equations with fewer operations.

```
18    return result

20
def get_fitness(genes, expectedTotal):
22    result = evaluate(genes)

24    if result != expectedTotal:
          fitness = expectedTotal - abs(result - expectedTotal)
26    else:
          fitness = 1000 - len(genes)

28
      return fitness
```

Display

That just leaves the display function where we can simply write the genes separated by a space to see the equation.

```
32 def display(candidate, startTime):
       timeDiff = datetime.datetime.now() - startTime
34     print("{}\t{}\t{}".format(
           (' '.join(map(str, [i for i in candidate.Genes]))),
36         candidate.Fitness,
           timeDiff))

38

40 def create(numbers, operations, minNumbers, maxNumbers):
```

sample output

```
6 + 3 + 3 - 4 + 6 - 3 - 6 - 6 - 3 - 1    -5  0:00:00.001003
```

Test

The following full test harness should hold no surprises.

```
     def test(self):
72       numbers = [1, 2, 3, 4, 5, 6, 7]
         operations = ['+', '-']
74       expectedTotal = 29
         optimalLengthSolution = [7, '+', 7, '+', 7, '+', 7, '+', 7, '-', 6]
76       minNumbers = (1 + len(optimalLengthSolution)) / 2
         maxNumbers = 6 * minNumbers
78       startTime = datetime.datetime.now()

80       def fnDisplay(candidate):
             display(candidate, startTime)
82
         def fnGetFitness(genes):
84           return get_fitness(genes, expectedTotal)

86       def fnCreate():
             return create(numbers, operations, minNumbers, maxNumbers)
88
         def fnMutate(child):
90           mutate(child, numbers, operations, minNumbers, maxNumbers)

92       optimalFitness = fnGetFitness(optimalLengthSolution)
         best = genetic.get_best(fnGetFitness, None, optimalFitness, None,
94                       fnDisplay, fnMutate, fnCreate, maxAge=50)
         self.assertTrue(not optimalFitness > best.Fitness)
96

98 if __name__ == '__main__':
       unittest.main()
```

Run

When we run the test it finds an equivalent solution.

sample output

```
5 + 3 + 2 + 4 + 6 + 2 + 1    23  0:00:00
5 + 3 + 2 + 4 + 6 + 6 + 1    27  0:00:00
5 + 3 + 3 + 4 + 6 + 6 + 1    28  0:00:00
6 + 3 + 3 + 4 + 6 + 6 + 1    987 0:00:00
6 + 5 + 3 + 3 + 6 + 6     989 0:00:00.000998
```

Nice. But having to add 6 three times and 3 two times is boring. If we introduce a multiplication operation it might find $7 * 3 + 4 * 2$, which saves an operation, or even $7 * 4 + 1$, which saves two. Let's try it.

Support multiplication

First we have to add the multiplication token (*) to the list of operation genes.

```
73     operations = ['+', '-', '*']
```

Next we have to implement multiplication in the evaluation function. The problem is that for the math to be correct we have to perform all multiplication operations before we perform any addition or subtraction. No problem, we can just group the operations by priority.

```
73     operations = ['+', '-', '*']
74     prioritizedOperations = [['*'], ['+', '-']]
```

And update the function call to get the fitness.

```
84     def fnEvaluate(genes):
           return evaluate(genes, prioritizedOperations)
86
       def fnGetFitness(genes):
88         return get_fitness(genes, expectedTotal, fnEvaluate)
```

Then we'll evaluate all operations in priority order rather than simultaneously, which means we'll iterate over the array once for each priority group.

```
   def evaluate(genes, prioritizedOperations):
10     equation = genes[:]
       for operationSet in prioritizedOperations:
12         iOffset = 0
           for i in range(1, len(equation), 2):
14             i += iOffset
               opToken = equation[i]
16             if opToken in operationSet:
                   leftOperand = equation[i - 1]
18                 rightOperand = equation[i + 1]
                   if opToken == '+':
20                     leftOperand += rightOperand
                   elif opToken == '-':
22                     leftOperand -= rightOperand
                   elif opToken == '*':
24                     leftOperand *= rightOperand
                   equation[i - 1] = leftOperand
26                 del equation[i + 1]
                   del equation[i]
28                 iOffset -= 2
       return equation[0]
```

In the implementation above we make a copy of the genes so we can modify it each time through the loop. Each operation stores its output in the array location to its left then deletes itself and its second operand from the array. After all operations have been evaluated the result is in array index zero.

Since we changed the function to pass in the list of operations, we also need to change what we pass to the fitness function.

```
32  def get_fitness(genes, expectedTotal, fnEvaluate):
33      result = fnEvaluate(genes)
34  ...
```

Run

This code finds a solution, but not a minimal length solution, because the defined optimal length solution in the test is based on addition and subtraction. So the engine stops as soon as it beats that solution.

```
. . .
4 - 3 * 3 - 7 * 2 + 7 + 6 + 5 * 7    983 0:00:00.103305
5 + 2 - 7 * 2 + 6 + 5 + 5 * 5    985 0:00:00.115337
5 - 4 - 3 + 6 + 5 + 4 * 5    987 0:00:00.124361
5 - 4 - 3 + 6 + 5 * 5    989 0:00:00.128372
```

Extract a solve function

To fix that we need to extract a solve function so we can pass in the list of operations with the optimal solution for that set of operations.

```
    class EquationGenerationTests(unittest.TestCase):
82      def test_addition(self):
            operations = ['+', '-']
84          prioritizedOperations = [['+', '-']]
            optimalLengthSolution = [7, '+', 7, '+', 7, '+', 7, '+', 7, '-', 6]
86          self.solve(operations, prioritizedOperations, optimalLengthSolution)
```

```
88      def solve(self, operations, prioritizedOperations,
                    optimalLengthSolution):
90          numbers = [1, 2, 3, 4, 5, 6, 7]
            expectedTotal = evaluate(optimalLengthSolution,
92                                    prioritizedOperations)
            minNumbers = (1 + len(optimalLengthSolution)) / 2
```

Test multiplication

Now we can add a test for multiplication, and give it a more difficult equation to generate.

```
88    def test_multiplication(self):
          operations = ['+', '-', '*']
90        prioritizedOperations = [['*'], ['+', '-']]
          optimalLengthSolution = [6, '*', 3, '*', 3, '*', 6, '-', 7]
92        self.solve(operations, prioritizedOperations, optimalLengthSolution)

94    def solve(self, operations, prioritizedOperations,
```

Run 2

When we run that test it too can find an optimal length solution:

sample output

```
. . .
7 * 5 * 6 - 3 + 7 * 2 * 7 + 4 * 3    983 0:00:00.109255
7 * 7 * 7 - 4 * 4 - 6 - 5 + 1    985 0:00:00.141350
7 * 7 * 7 - 7 * 2 - 3 * 4    987 0:00:00.150363
5 * 7 * 7 + 6 * 2 * 6    989 0:00:00.158386
5 * 4 * 4 * 4 - 3    991 0:00:02.141662
```

Cool. When we review that solution, however, it too seems repetitive. It would be much nicer if we could reduce the equation to $5 * 4^3 - 3$. Let's do that.

Refactoring

But first, have you noticed that each time we add a new operation we have to change the evaluation function? That's an indication of a poor design that violates the Open-Closed Principal. We can fix that by extracting the operation implementations to separate functions:

```
32  def add(a, b):
        return a + b
34

36  def subtract(a, b):
        return a - b
38

40  def multiply(a, b):
        return a * b
42

44  def get_fitness(genes, expectedTotal, fnEvaluate):
```

Then make the prioritized operation list contain dictionaries where each dictionary key is the token for an operation and the value is a function that implements the operation.

```
94    def test_addition(self):
95        operations = ['+', '-']
96        prioritizedOperations = [{'+': add,
97                                  '-': subtract}]
98  ...
```

```
      def test_multiplication(self):
102       operations = ['+', '-', '*']
          prioritizedOperations = [{'*': multiply},
104                                 {'+': add,
                                     '-': subtract}]
106 ...
```

Finally, use the operation function from the dictionary in the evaluation function.

```
    def evaluate(genes, prioritizedOperations):
10      equation = genes[:]
        for operationSet in prioritizedOperations:
12          iOffset = 0
            for i in range(1, len(equation), 2):
14              i += iOffset
                opToken = equation[i]
16              if opToken in operationSet:
                    leftOperand = equation[i - 1]
18                  rightOperand = equation[i + 1]
                    equation[i - 1] = operationSet[opToken](leftOperand,
20                                                          rightOperand)
                    del equation[i + 1]
22                  del equation[i]
                    iOffset += -2
24      return equation[0]
```

Supporting Exponents

Now we can easily add support for a new operation, like exponentiation, without changing any other code:

```
104    def test_exponent(self):
           operations = ['^', '+', '-', '*']
106        prioritizedOperations = [{'^': lambda a, b: a ** b},
                                    {'*': multiply},
108                                 {'+': add,
                                     '-': subtract}]
110        optimalLengthSolution = [6, '^', 3, '*', 2, '-', 5]
           self.solve(operations, prioritizedOperations, optimalLengthSolution)
112
       def solve(self, operations, prioritizedOperations,
```

sample output

```
. . .
4 * 3 ^ 4 - 3 - 1 - 7 + 4 * 2 * 7 * 2 + 2    979 0:00:00.030079
4 * 3 ^ 4 - 2 - 7 + 4 * 2 * 7 * 2    983 0:00:00.035093
6 * 7 * 5 * 2 + 5 + 3 + 3 - 4    985 0:00:00.070215
6 * 6 * 6 * 2 + 1 - 6    989 0:00:00.083221
7 * 5 * 6 * 2 + 7    991 0:00:00.108286
6 ^ 3 * 2 - 5    993 0:00:13.129462
```

Improve performance

Since it is starting to take tens of seconds to find the solution, let's add a loop to the mutation function so that it can make a random number of changes instead of just one.

```
68  def mutate(genes, numbers, operations, minNumbers, maxNumbers, fnGetFitness):
        count = random.randint(1, 10)
70      initialFitness = fnGetFitness(genes)
        while count > 0:
72          count -= 1
            if fnGetFitness(genes) > initialFitness:
74              return                                                        <==
        numberCount = (1 + len(genes)) / 2
```

```
79              genes.append(random.choice(numbers))
80              continue                                                      <==
81
82          removing = numberCount > minNumbers and random.randint(0, 20) == 0
```

```
86              del genes[index]
87              continue                                                      <==
88
89          index = random.randrange(0, len(genes))
```

Now that we're checking the fitness in the mutation function, we also need to pass in the ability to call the fitness function:

```
140        def fnMutate(child):
141            mutate(child, numbers, operations, minNumbers, maxNumbers,
142                fnGetFitness)
```

Run

As expected, it finds the solution much faster.

sample output

```
2 + 3 ^ 4 * 5 + 3 * 6    425 0:00:00.014006
3 + 3 ^ 4 * 5 + 3 * 6    426 0:00:00.016041
4 + 3 ^ 4 * 5 + 3 * 6    989 0:00:00.024067
6 * 2 * 5 * 7 + 7   991 0:00:00.067148
2 * 6 ^ 3 - 5   993 0:00:00.567508
```

Fantastic!

Benchmarks

We'll benchmark this project with the exponent test.

```
147            self.assertTrue(not optimalFitness > best.Fitness)
148
149    def test_benchmark(self):
150        genetic.Benchmark.run(self.test_exponent)
```

Benchmark

average (seconds)	standard deviation
0.49	0.36

Summary

This project was our first introduction to genetic programming and it opened up several really interesting problems for exploration. We also learned one way to work with both data and operations in a gene sequence. This gave us experience with symbols and grammar and "program" evaluation.

The Lawnmower Problem

In this project we'll continue our exploration of genetic programming by solving John Koza's Lawnmower Problem. It asks us to provide instructions to a lawnmower to make it cut a field of grass. To make it easier for the genetic algorithm to find a solution, the initial field is toroidal, this means it wraps in all directions. So, if the mower goes off the top it ends up at the bottom and vice versa and the same side-to-side. The problem statement is that the mower begins in the middle of an 8x8 toroidal field facing south (down) and it understands two instructions, *mow* and *turn*. What is the shortest series of instructions (program) needed to make it mow the entire field?

Part I - *mow* and *turn*

The *mow* instruction tells the mower to move forward one grid square in whatever direction it is facing then cut the grass in that location. The *turn* instruction tells the mower to turn left 90 degrees in place.

So that we can visually track the mower as it moves around the field, when it mows a field location we'll replace the unmowed symbol (#) with the number of the step that mowed it, like this:

```
M^   #   #   #   #   #   #   #
11   #   #   #   #   #   #   #
10   #   #   #   #   #   #   #
 9   #   #   #   #   #   #   #
 8   #   #   #   #   #   #   #
 6   #   #   #   1   3   4   5
 #   #   #   #   #   #   #   #
 #   #   #   #   #   #   #   #
```

> **ℹ** M is the mower, < > ^ and v are used to indicate the direction the mower is facing: left, right, north or south, respectively. The gaps in the number sequence above are indicative of a *turn* instruction having been executed at steps 2 and 7.

Virtual mower infrastructure

We'll put the code that is specific to the mower and its environment into a different file than the tests.

Let's begin with the visual elements referenced above.

lawnmower.py

```python
from enum import Enum

class FieldContents(Enum):
    Grass = ' #'
    Mowed = ' .'
    Mower = 'M'

    def __str__(self):
        return self.value
```

We need a way to indicate the direction the mower is facing,

```python
class Directions(Enum):
    North = Direction(0, 0, -1, '^')
    East = Direction(1, 1, 0, '>')
    South = Direction(2, 0, 1, 'v')
    West = Direction(3, -1, 0, '<')
```

and a `Direction` object.

```python
class Direction:
    def __init__(self, index, xOffset, yOffset, symbol):
        self.Index = index
        self.XOffset = xOffset
        self.YOffset = yOffset
        self.Symbol = symbol


class Directions(Enum):
```

We'll define the *Mower* class next:

```python
class Mower:
    def __init__(self, location, direction):
        self.Location = location
        self.Direction = direction
        self.StepCount = 0
```

When the *Mower* is told to turn left, it needs to find out the new direction it should be facing.

```
34    def turn_left(self):
35        self.StepCount += 1
36        self.Direction = Directions\
37            .get_direction_after_turn_left_90_degrees(self.Direction)
```

The *Directions* class can determine that using the direction the *Mower* is currently facing.

```
      @staticmethod
28    def get_direction_after_turn_left_90_degrees(direction):
          newIndex = direction.Index - 1 \
30            if direction.Index > 0 \
              else len(Directions) - 1
32        newDirection = next(i for i in Directions
                                  if i.value.Index == newIndex)
34        return newDirection.value

36
class Mower:
```

When told to mow, the mower first asks the *Direction* object where it will end up if it moves forward from the current location. It then asks the field to translate that to a valid physical location. It also increments the move counter and updates the contents of the field in that location.

```
48    def mow(self, field):
          newLocation = self.Direction.move_from(self.Location)
50        self.Location = field.fix_location(newLocation)
          self.StepCount += 1
52        field.set(self.Location, self.StepCount
              if self.StepCount > 9
54            else " {}".format(self.StepCount))
```

That implies a *move_from* function on the *Direction* class:

```
20    def move_from(self, location, distance=1):
          return Location(location.X + distance * self.XOffset,
22                         location.Y + distance * self.YOffset)

24
class Directions(Enum):
```

Which, in turn, implies a *Location* class:

```
42    class Location:
          def __init__(self, x, y):
              self.X, self.Y = x, y
44

46    class Mower:
```

Next we need to define the field:

```
66    class Field:
          def __init__(self, width, height, initialContent):
68            self.Field = [[initialContent] * width for _ in range(height)]
              self.Width = width
70            self.Height = height
```

It knows how to change the contents of a particular grid location:

```
72        def set(self, location, symbol):
73            self.Field[location.Y][location.X] = symbol
```

It also knows how to convert a virtual location to a valid physical one. The field does not, however, know what it means to move in a particular direction from a location, so it asks the *Location* object for that, then adjusts it based on the expected virtual field behavior.

```
      def fix_location(self, location):
76        newLocation = Location(location.X, location.Y)
          if newLocation.X < 0:
78            newLocation.X += self.Width
          elif newLocation.X >= self.Width:
80            newLocation.X %= self.Width

82        if newLocation.Y < 0:
              newLocation.Y += self.Height
84        elif newLocation.Y >= self.Height:
              newLocation.Y %= self.Height
86
          return newLocation
```

This implies a *move* function on the *Location* class:

```
      def move(self, xOffset, yOffset):
46        return Location(self.X + xOffset,
                          self.Y + yOffset)
48

50    class Mower:
```

We now have the basic parts we need to support the project described: a mower starting in the middle of an 8x8 toroidal field facing south, with the ability to turn left and/or mow in a straight line.

Test class

Now we can start on the test infrastructure. Our genes for this project will have behaviors, so we'll use classes.

lawnmowerTests.py

```
class Mow:
    def __init__(self):
        pass

    @staticmethod
    def execute(mower, field):
        mower.mow(field)
```

```
class Turn:
    def __init__(self):
        pass

    @staticmethod
    def execute(mower, field):
        mower.turn_left()
```

Next we'll define a *Program* class to drive gene-instruction execution.

```
class Program:
    def __init__(self, instructions):
        self.Main = instructions

    def evaluate(self, mower, field):
        for instruction in self.Main:
            instruction.execute(mower, field)
```

Create

Next, since we don't know how many *mow* and *turn* instructions it will take for the *Mower* to mow the *field*, we need to define a custom gene creation function. It will generate a random sequence of instructions with length between the min and max given:

```python
import random

def create(geneSet, minGenes, maxGenes):
    numGenes = random.randint(minGenes, maxGenes)
    genes = [random.choice(geneSet) for _ in range(1, numGenes)]
    return genes

class Mow:
```

Test

Here's the start of the test harness.

```python
import datetime
import random
import unittest

import genetic
import lawnmower
```

```python
class LawnmowerTests(unittest.TestCase):
    def test(self):
        geneSet = [Mow(), Turn()]
        width = height = 8
        mowerStartLocation = lawnmower.Location(int(width / 2),
                                                int(height / 2))
        mowerStartDirection = lawnmower.Directions.South.value

        def fnCreate():
            return create(geneSet, 1, height)

class Mow:
```

Evaluation

In order to determine how much of the field the gene-instructions cause to be mowed, the *get_fitness* function is going command a virtual *Mower* to execute the instructions on a virtual *field.* That implies an evaluation function that will also need to be accessible to the display function.

```python
26    def fnEvaluate(instructions):
          program = Program(instructions)
28        mower = lawnmower.Mower(mowerStartLocation, mowerStartDirection)
          field = lawnmower.Field(width, height,
30                                  lawnmower.FieldContents.Grass)
          program.evaluate(mower, field)
32        return field, mower, program
```

Fitness

Now we can pass the evaluate function to *get_fitness*

```python
34    def fnGetFitness(genes):
35        return get_fitness(genes, fnEvaluate)
```

and use it to determine how many squares get mowed.

```python
6  import lawnmower

8
   def get_fitness(genes, fnEvaluate):
10     field = fnEvaluate(genes)[0]
       return Fitness(field.count_mowed(), len(genes))
```

After mowing, we need to know how much of the field was mowed, so we ask the *field*:

lawnmower.py

```python
93    def count_mowed(self):
94        return sum(1 for row in range(self.Height)
95                     for column in range(self.Width)
96                     if self.Field[row][column] != FieldContents.Grass)
```

We don't just want to mow the field, we want to do so using as few instructions as possible, so we use a *Fitness* class to manage those competing priorities.

lawnmowerTests.py

```
70 class Fitness:
       def __init__(self, totalMowed, totalInstructions):
72         self.TotalMowed = totalMowed
           self.TotalInstructions = totalInstructions
74
       def __gt__(self, other):
76         if self.TotalMowed != other.TotalMowed:
               return self.TotalMowed > other.TotalMowed
78         return self.TotalInstructions < other.TotalInstructions

80
if __name__ == '__main__':
82     unittest.main()
```

Display

Now that we can determine the fitness of a gene sequence, we'd like a way to display the state of the *field* after the gene instructions have been executed.

```
42         startTime = datetime.datetime.now()

44         def fnDisplay(candidate):
               display(candidate, startTime, fnEvaluate)
46
48 class Mow:
```

We ask the *field* to display its contents, including the location of the *Mower*. Then we print the fitness, time elapsed, and program instructions.

```
14 def display(candidate, startTime, fnEvaluate):
       field, mower, program = fnEvaluate(candidate.Genes)
16     timeDiff = datetime.datetime.now() - startTime
       field.display(mower)
18     print("{}\t{}".format(
           candidate.Fitness,
20         timeDiff))
       program.print()
22

24 def create(geneSet, minGenes, maxGenes):
```

When asked to print its contents, the *field* loops through the array and writes the contents.

lawnmower.py

```
98      def display(self, mower):
            for rowIndex in range(self.Height):
100             if rowIndex != mower.Location.Y:
                    row = ' '.join(map(str, self.Field[rowIndex]))
102             else:
                    r = self.Field[rowIndex][:]
104                 r[mower.Location.X] = "{}{}".format(
                        FieldContents.Mower, mower.Direction.Symbol)
106                 row = ' '.join(map(str, r))
                print(row)
```

The instructions also need a __str__ implementation so that the display function can print the gene contents.

lawnmowerTests.py

```
66      def __str__(self):
            return "mow"
68

70 class Turn:
```

```
78      def __str__(self):
            return "turn"
80

82 class Program:
```

The display function asks *Fitness* to stringify itself:

```
        def __str__(self):
102         return "{} mowed with {} instructions".format(
                self.TotalMowed, self.TotalInstructions)
104

106 if __name__ == '__main__':
```

and asks the *Program* to print itself:

lawnmowerTests.py

```
90      def print(self):
            print(' '.join(map(str, self.Main)))
92

94 class Fitness:
```

Mutate

Since we don't know how many instructions will be required to mow the field, we also need a custom mutation function that tries to add, remove, and change instructions.

lawnmowerTests.py

```
24 def mutate(genes, geneSet, minGenes, maxGenes, fnGetFitness, maxRounds):
       count = random.randint(1, maxRounds)
26     initialFitness = fnGetFitness(genes)
       while count > 0:
28         count -= 1
           if fnGetFitness(genes) > initialFitness:
30             return
           adding = len(genes) == 0 or \
32                 (len(genes) < maxGenes and random.randint(0, 5) == 0)
           if adding:
34             genes.append(random.choice(geneSet))
               continue
36
           removing = len(genes) > minGenes and random.randint(0, 50) == 0
38         if removing:
               index = random.randrange(0, len(genes))
40             del genes[index]
               continue
42
           index = random.randrange(0, len(genes))
44         genes[index] = random.choice(geneSet)
46
   def create(geneSet, minGenes, maxGenes):
```

Next we need to define a glue function in the test so we can provide the additional required parameters.

Since *mow* can only affect one field position at a time, we can set a lower bound on the number of instructions required to mow the entire field. We'll set the maximum number of instructions to 1.5 times that value.

```
80         minGenes = width * height
           maxGenes = int(1.5 * minGenes)
82         maxMutationRounds = 3
84         def fnMutate(child):
               mutate(child, geneSet, minGenes, maxGenes, fnGetFitness,
86                     maxMutationRounds)
88
   class Mow:
```

Optimal fitness

To determine the optimal fitness, we need to figure out how many *turn* instructions would be required. Since the field is toroidal, for calculation purposes we can shift the start location to the southwest corner, pointed south, without affecting the calculations.

```
 .  .   .   .   .   .   .   .
 .  .   .   .   .   .   .   .
 .  .   .   .   .   .   .   .
 .  .   .   .   .   .   .   .
 .  .   .   .   .   .   .   .
 .  .   .   .   .   .   .   .
 .  .   .   .   .   .   .   .
Mv  .   .   .   .   .   .   .
```

In an optimal solution the mower will only turn when it encounters a square that has already been mowed, so that it doesn't waste an instruction. This results in a spiral mowing pattern.

```
1  28 27 26 25 24 23 22
2  29 48 47 46 45 44 21
3  30 49 60 59 58 43 20
4  31 50 61 64 57 42 19
5  32 51 62 63 56 41 18
6  33 52 53 54 55 40 17
7  34 35 36 37 38 39 16
8* 9  10 11 12 13 14 15     * starting location
```

From this we can determine that the optimal gene sequence will have 1 *mow* for each square of the field plus width + height - 2 *turn* instructions, or 78 total instructions.

```
88        expectedNumberOfInstructions = 78
          optimalFitness = Fitness(width * height,
90                                 expectedNumberOfInstructions)

92
       class Mow:
```

Crossover

We're also going to apply crossover to this problem.

```
def crossover(parent, otherParent):
    childGenes = parent[:]
    if len(parent) <= 2 or len(otherParent) < 2:
        return childGenes
    length = random.randint(1, len(parent) - 2)
    start = random.randrange(0, len(parent) - length)
    childGenes[start:start + length] = otherParent[start:start + length]
    return childGenes


class LawnmowerTests(unittest.TestCase):
```

This implementation overwrites a random contiguous sequence of genes in the child with those from the donor parent.

Test

Lastly we need to call the engine from the test.

```
        best = genetic.get_best(fnGetFitness, None, optimalFitness, None,
                                fnDisplay, fnMutate, fnCreate, maxAge=None,
                                poolSize=10, crossover=crossover)
        self.assertTrue(not optimalFitness > best.Fitness)


class Mow:
```

Run

With all the necessary pieces defined we're ready to run the test. As expected, the result is an inward spiral:

```
M^ 67 48 21  4 35 58 73
76 66 47 20  5 36 59 74
63 64 46 19  6 37 60 62
42 43 44 18  7 38 40 41
13 14 15 16  8 10 11 12
28 27 26 24  1 31 30 29
53 52 50 23  2 33 55 54
70 68 49 22  3 34 57 71
64 mowed with 78 instructions    0:00:09.541468
mow mow mow mow mow mow mow mow turn mow mow mow mow mow mow mow turn mow mow mow mow
    mow mow mow turn mow mow mow mow mow mow turn mow mow mow mow mow mow turn mow
    mow mow mow mow turn mow mow mow mow mow turn mow mow mow mow turn mow mow mow
    mow turn mow mow mow turn mow mow mow turn mow mow turn mow mow turn mow turn mow
```

Unfortunately, with the current instruction set that is the only result we *can* get.

Part II - Jump

To make the project more interesting we're going to add a new instruction. Following John Koza's problem definition again, the new instruction is *jump*. It causes the mower to jump forward and to the right a specified number of squares and cut the grass in the square where it lands. *jump* will have 2 non-negative integer parameters for how far to move forward and right, respectively.

For example, if the mower is facing south at the start location (4,4)

```
.   .   .   .   .   .  .  .
.   .   .   .   .   .  .  .
.   .   .   .   .   .  .  .
.   .   .   .   .   .  .  .
.   .   .   . Mv .   .  .
.   .   .   .   .   .  .  .
.   .   .   .   .   .  .  .
.   .   .   .   .   .  .  .
```

and is told to jump (2,3) it will end up at (1,6) (numbered from the top left), still facing south.

```
.   .   .   .   .   .  .  .
.   .   .   .   .   .  .  .
.   .   .   .   .   .  .  .
.   .   .   .   .   .  .  .
.   .   .   . .* .   .  .      * - previous location
.   .   .   .   .   .  .  .
. Mv .   .   .   .  .  .
.   .   .   .   .   .  .  .
```

Implementation

To implement this we'll start with adding a *jump* instruction. The forward and right distances will be random values supplied to the constructor and limited by the size of the field.

```
     class Jump:
132      def __init__(self, forward, right):
             self.Forward = forward
134          self.Right = right

136
     class Program:
```

It will also need an execution function to do the work.

```
136    def execute(self, mower, field):
137        mower.jump(field, self.Forward, self.Right)
```

and `__str__` for the display function to use:

```
139    def __str__(self):
140        return "jump({},{})".format(self.Forward, self.Right)
```

Update the mower

The implementation of *jump* in the *Mower* is interesting because *forward* and *right* result in different x and y offsets depending on the direction the *Mower* is facing.

lawnmower.py

```
    def jump(self, field, forward, right):
70        newForwardLocation = self.Direction.move_from(self.Location,
                                                        forward)
72        rightDirection = Directions\
            .get_direction_after_turn_right_90_degrees(self.Direction)
74        newLocation = rightDirection.move_from(newForwardLocation, right)
        self.Location = field.fix_location(newLocation)
76        self.StepCount += 1
        field.set(self.Location, self.StepCount
78            if self.StepCount > 9
            else " {}".format(self.StepCount))
80

82 class Field:
```

This requires a new function on the *Directions* class:

```
40    @staticmethod
    def get_direction_after_turn_right_90_degrees(direction):
42        newIndex = direction.Index + 1 \
            if direction.Index < len(Directions) - 1 \
44            else 0
        newDirection = next(i for i in Directions
46                            if i.value.Index == newIndex)
        return newDirection.value
48

50 class Location:
```

Use lambdas to create genes

jump requires parameters and the parameters should be random, so we can't simply create one and put it in our instructions list anymore. This means we must convert the list of instructions to a list of lambda-that-returns-an-instruction.

Before we do that, we need to extract some of the variable configuration values from the test so that we can have one test that continues to use only *mow* and *turn* while adding a new test that uses those and adds *jump*.

lawnmowerTests.py

```
class LawnmowerTests(unittest.TestCase):
    def test_mow_turn(self):
        width = height = 8
        geneSet = [lambda: Mow(),
                   lambda: Turn()]
        minGenes = width * height
        maxGenes = int(1.5 * minGenes)
        maxMutationRounds = 3
        expectedNumberOfInstructions = 78
        self.run_with(geneSet, width, height, minGenes, maxGenes,
                      expectedNumberOfInstructions, maxMutationRounds)
```

```
    def run_with(self, geneSet, width, height, minGenes, maxGenes,
                 expectedNumberOfInstructions, maxMutationRounds):
        mowerStartLocation = lawnmower.Location(int(width / 2),
                                                int(height / 2))
        mowerStartDirection = lawnmower.Directions.South.value

        def fnCreate():
```

Also remove the definitions of *minGenes*, *maxGenes*, *maxMutationRounds*, and *expectedNumberOfInstructions* from the helper function since they are now parameters.

Now we can add the new test function with *jump* included in the gene set.

```
    def test_mow_turn_jump(self):
        width = height = 8
        geneSet = [lambda: Mow(),
                   lambda: Turn(),
                   lambda: Jump(random.randint(0, min(width, height)),
                                random.randint(0, min(width, height)))]
        minGenes = width * height
        maxGenes = int(1.5 * minGenes)
        maxMutationRounds = 1
        expectedNumberOfInstructions = 64
        self.run_with(geneSet, width, height, minGenes, maxGenes,
                      expectedNumberOfInstructions, maxMutationRounds)

    def run_with(self, geneSet, width, height, minGenes, maxGenes,
```

Note that the expected number of instructions has been reduced to 64. This is because *jump* also causes a *mow* to occur and it has the ability to jump anywhere in the field, so it should be possible to reach to every location using only *jump* instructions, thus 64 instructions for an 8 by 8 field.

Also, since the gene set now contains lambdas, we need to execute them wherever we were simply using the value before in *create*:

```
47 def create(geneSet, minGenes, maxGenes):
48     numGenes = random.randint(minGenes, maxGenes)
49     genes = [random.choice(geneSet)() for _ in range(1, numGenes)]        <==
50     return genes
```

and in the *add* and *change* sections of the mutation function:

```
33         if adding:
34             genes.append(random.choice(geneSet)())
35             continue
```

```
43         index = random.randrange(0, len(genes))
44         genes[index] = random.choice(geneSet)()
```

Run

When we run the new test we get a result like the following:
sample output

```
51 36 45 31   4 Mv  9 19
52 37 46 32   5 58 10 20
13 38 47 33   6 59 11 21
14 39 48 34 61 60 12 22
15 40 49 35 62 27 54 23
16 41 56 63  1 28 55 24
53 42 57 29  2 25  7 17
50 43 44 30  3 26  8 18
64 mowed with 64 instructions    0:00:19.720286
mow mow mow mow mow mow jump(4,6) mow mow mow jump(1,0) mow jump(7,6) mow mow mow
    jump(1,1) mow mow mow mow mow mow mow jump(1,2) mow jump(5,0) mow jump(1,2) mow
    mow mow mow mow mow jump(4,2) mow mow mow mow mow mow mow jump(8,7) mow mow mow
    mow mow jump(3,2) mow mow jump(5,8) jump(6,2) mow jump(8,4) mow jump(3,5) mow mow
    jump(8,1) mow jump(1,1) jump(3,6)
```

Above, we see that the genetic algorithm has completely abandoned the *turn* instruction in favor of the more powerful *jump* instruction because this results in a shorter program. However, that's only true on a toroidal field.

Try a validating field

What if we were to use a field that did not let the mower go beyond the edge? It would have to check the legality of the move before making it. We implement that by defining a validating field class that inherits from the current *Field* class.

lawnmower.py

```
131  class ValidatingField(Field):
132      def __init__(self, width, height, initialContent):
133          super().__init__(width, height, initialContent)
```

The function it uses to fix the location will check to see if the given location is outside the bounds of the field array. If so, it will return False indicating that the move is invalid, otherwise True, along with the location.

```
     def fix_location(self, location):
136      if location.X >= self.Width or \
                     location.X < 0 or \
138                  location.Y >= self.Height or \
                     location.Y < 0:
140          return None, False
         return location, True
```

This requires a similar change in the toroidal field. First we need to define the toroidal field class to hold the function implementation specific to that kind of field and make it inherit from the *Field* class too.

lawnmower.py

```
144  class ToroidField(Field):
145      def __init__(self, width, height, initialContent):
146          super().__init__(width, height, initialContent)
```

Then we'll **move** the original location correction function from *Field* to it. This function will always return `True` because moves on a toroidal field wrap around the edges of the field.

```
134    def fix_location(self, location):
           newLocation = Location(location.X, location.Y)
136        if newLocation.X < 0:
               newLocation.X += self.Width
138        elif newLocation.X >= self.Width:
               newLocation.X %= self.Width
140
           if newLocation.Y < 0:
142            newLocation.Y += self.Height
           elif newLocation.Y >= self.Height:
144            newLocation.Y %= self.Height

146        return newLocation, True
```

Then in the mower we have to check the Boolean value that was returned before updating its location.

```
70    def mow(self, field):
          newLocation = self.Direction.move_from(self.Location)
72        newLocation, isValid = field.fix_location(newLocation)
          if isValid:                                                    <==
74            self.Location = newLocation
              self.StepCount += 1
76            field.set(self.Location, self.StepCount
                  if self.StepCount > 9
78                else " {}".format(self.StepCount))
```

```
80    def jump(self, field, forward, right):
          newLocation = self.Direction.move_from(self.Location, forward)
82        rightDirection = Directions\
              .get_direction_after_turn_right_90_degrees(self.Direction)
84        newLocation = rightDirection.move_from(newLocation, right)
          newLocation, isValid = field.fix_location(newLocation)
86        if isValid:                                                    <==
              self.Location = newLocation
88            self.StepCount += 1
              field.set(self.Location, self.StepCount
90                if self.StepCount > 9
                  else " {}".format(self.StepCount))
```

Next we need to update the tests. Because each is going to use a different field type we'll define a function that creates the field, then pass it to the helper function.

lawnmowerTests.py

```
72    expectedNumberOfInstructions = 78

74    def fnCreateField():
          return lawnmower.ToroidField(width, height,
76                                     lawnmower.FieldContents.Grass)

78    self.run_with(geneSet, width, height, minGenes, maxGenes,
                    expectedNumberOfInstructions, maxMutationRounds,
                    fnCreateField)
```

```
90    expectedNumberOfInstructions = 64

92    def fnCreateField():
          return lawnmower.ToroidField(width, height,
94                                     lawnmower.FieldContents.Grass)

96    self.run_with(geneSet, width, height, minGenes, maxGenes,
                    expectedNumberOfInstructions, maxMutationRounds,
98                  fnCreateField)
```

Now add the function to be executed to the helper function's parameters and use it.

```
100   def run_with(self, geneSet, width, height, minGenes, maxGenes,
101                expectedNumberOfInstructions, maxMutationRounds,
102                fnCreateField):
```

```
110   def fnEvaluate(instructions):
          program = Program(instructions)
112       mower = lawnmower.Mower(mowerStartLocation, mowerStartDirection)
          field = fnCreateField()
114       program.evaluate(mower, field)
          return field, mower, program
```

Using a validating field makes the *jump* test significantly more complex because once the mower moves to the right the only way to get back to the unmowed squares on the left side is to *turn*. The best solution that includes a *jump* would be for the *Mower* to jump to the southwest corner, turn, and then do a spiral around the field. That would take 1 extra move at the beginning to set up the spiral, so 79 instructions.

Make a copy of the *jump* test then change it to use a validating field and to expect 79 instructions.

```
100     def test_mow_turn_jump_validating(self):
101 ...
```

```
        expectedNumberOfInstructions = 79
110
        def fnCreateField():
112         return lawnmower.ValidatingField(width, height,
                                        lawnmower.FieldContents.Grass)
114 ...
```

Run

When we run the test with a validating field it always hits a local maximum.

```
#  #  #  #  #  # 18 M^
#  #  #  # 16  # 17  #
#  #  # 14 15  #  #  #
#  #  # 13  #  #  #  #
1  #  # 12  #  #  #  #
2  #  # 11  #  #  #  #
3  5  6 10  #  #  #  #
#  #  7  9  #  #  #  #
17 mowed with 19 instructions    0:00:06.782601
jump(0,4) mow mow turn mow mow jump(0,1) turn jump(0,1) mow mow mow mow mow jump(0,1)
        mow jump(0,2) mow jump(0,1)
```

We can work around that by increasing the maximum number of mutation rounds in this test.

```
108         maxMutationRounds = 3
```

Run 2

With that change it *can* find the optimal solution but it can take several minutes to do so. It still uses all 3 instructions but *jump* no longer dominates.

```
27 26 25 24 23 22 21 19
29 52 51 50 49 48 46 18
30 54 66 65 64 62 45 17
31 55 57 58 59 61 44 16
32 34 35 36 37 38 43 15
 1 M< 78 77 76 74 42 14
 2 68 70 71 72 39 40 13
 3  5  6  7  8  9 10 11
64 mowed with 79 instructions    0:04:21.840003
jump(1,4) mow mow turn mow mow mow mow mow mow mow turn mow mow mow mow mow mow mow
    turn mow mow mow mow mow mow mow turn mow mow mow mow turn mow mow mow mow mow
    jump(0,2) mow turn mow mow mow mow mow turn mow mow mow mow mow turn mow mow turn
     mow mow mow turn jump(0,1) mow turn mow mow mow turn jump(4,1) turn mow mow mow
     turn jump(1,1) turn mow mow mow mow
```

This would run much faster if the mutation function was engineered to select only from *jump* or *mow* destinations that are unmowed, and otherwise *turn* and try again. But that optimization is about to become completely unnecessary because we're now in a position to explore Koza's purpose for this project.

As interesting as the solutions have been so far, the sequence of instructions generated by the engine is completely different from the solution a human would use. Think about how you'd instruct a person to mow a field when they have never mowed. You wouldn't give them detailed instructions for every step, right? You'd break it down into a set of repeatable sequences. In a toroidal field you might simply say, mow in a straight line until you encounter an area that has already been mowed, then turn left and do it again, repeat until you've mowed the whole field.

In a non-toroidal field you might say something like: start at the corner of the field and mow a strip along the edge of the field all the way to the other side.

```
#  #  #  #  #  #  #  #
#  #  #  #  #  #  #  #
#  #  #  #  #  #  #  #
#  #  #  #  #  #  #  #
#  #  #  #  #  #  #  #
#  #  #  #  #  #  #  #
#  #  #  #  #  #  #  #
.  .  .  .  .  .  . M>
```

Then turn the mower back the other direction and mow the strip right next to the one you just completed until you get back to where you started.

```
# # # # # # # #
# # # # # # # #
# # # # # # # #
# # # # # # # #
# # # # # # # #
# # # # # # # #
M<  .   .   .   .   .   .   .
    .   .   .   .   .   .   .   .
```

Turn around again and repeat the process on the next unmowed strip until you've mowed the whole field.

See how we automatically combine squares into strips and trips across-and-back into a repeatable pattern. How do we do that with the unmanned mower?

The best result we've generated so far requires 64 *jump* and *mow* instructions, one for each grid square, to tell the mower how to cut the grass in the field. Can you imagine having to poke those in via a dip-switch interface on the mower? I'd probably make an error part way through and have to start over. It would be much nicer to enter a short sequence of instructions like those we'd give a human. To do that we have to introduce the ability to repeat a sequence of instructions.

Part III - Repeat

The next instruction we're going to add is *repeat*. Like *jump* it will have 2 non-negative integer parameters. The first indicates how many of the instructions that follow it in the gene sequence are to be repeated, and the second tells how many times to repeat them.

lawnmowerTests.py

```
190         return "jump({},{})".format(self.Forward, self.Right)

192 class Repeat:
        def __init__(self, opCount, times):
194         self.OpCount = opCount
            self.Times = times
196         self.Ops = []
```

A variable will contain the instructions to be repeated. When the execution function is called it will execute that list of instructions the number of times requested.

```
198     def execute(self, mower, field):
199         for i in range(self.Times):
200             for op in self.Ops:
201                 op.execute(mower, field)
```

Lastly, we need to provide a textual representation for the display function to use. If the operations property is populated we'll combine the instructions' string representations into a string and return it, otherwise we'll use the step counter.

```python
    def __str__(self):
        return "repeat({},{})".format(
            ' '.join(map(str, self.Ops))
            if len(self.Ops) > 0
            else self.OpCount,
            self.Times)
```

Update Program

The *program* constructor will collect the instructions that the *repeat* instruction is going to repeat.

```python
class Program:
    def __init__(self, instructions):
        temp = instructions[:]
        for index in reversed(range(len(temp))):
            if type(temp[index]) is Repeat:
                start = index + 1
                end = min(index + temp[index].OpCount + 1, len(temp))
                temp[index].Ops = temp[start:end]
                del temp[start:end]
        self.Main = temp
```

New Test

```python
    def test_mow_turn_repeat(self):
        width = height = 8
        geneSet = [lambda: Mow(),
                   lambda: Turn(),
                   lambda: Repeat(random.randint(0, 8),
                                  random.randint(0, 8))]
        minGenes = 3
        maxGenes = 20
        maxMutationRounds = 3
        expectedNumberOfInstructions = 7

        def fnCreateField():
            return lawnmower.ToroidField(width, height, lawnmower.FieldContents.Grass
                )

        self.run_with(geneSet, width, height, minGenes, maxGenes,
                      expectedNumberOfInstructions, maxMutationRounds,
                      fnCreateField)
```

Run

When we run that test we witness the power of repetition:

```
193 167 75 76 77 189 191 192
142 166 139 27 26 50 159 143
163 164 138 46 47 48 160 162
114 113 137 110 230 229 228 226
133 134 135 109 Mv 18 19 225
197 85 84 108 217 201 200 224
196 104 105 106 218 220 221 222
195 168 56 55 79 188 172 171
64 mowed with 7 instructions      0:00:02.690764
repeat(turn repeat(mow mow turn mow,7),8)
```

Wow! We can mow the field with only 7 instructions! However, there are a couple of issues to be resolved. The output of the display function is now messy because the step count has gone to 3 digits. It has never been that high before. Also, occasionally the engine builds a very deep set of repeats that causes a RecursionError to be thrown. When that happens we can simply catch the error and move on, trusting the genetic engine to eliminate that gene sequence.

```
     def fnEvaluate(instructions):
148      program = Program(instructions)
         mower = lawnmower.Mower(mowerStartLocation, mowerStartDirection)
150      field = fnCreateField()
         try:
152          program.evaluate(mower, field)
         except RecursionError:
154          pass
         return field, mower, program
```

Optimizing for fuel efficiency

Another issue is fuel efficiency. If the *Mower* used fuel for each step, the set of instructions above would cost us almost 4 times as much as the hard coded but optimal solution. To fix this we're going to change the *Fitness* class to prefer fewer steps to fewer instructions.

Start by adding the step count to the *Fitness* class.

```
class Fitness:
252     def __init__(self, totalMowed, totalInstructions, stepCount):
            self.TotalMowed = totalMowed
254         self.TotalInstructions = totalInstructions
            self.StepCount = stepCount
```

Then update its comparison function

```
      def __gt__(self, other):
258       if self.TotalMowed != other.TotalMowed:
              return self.TotalMowed > other.TotalMowed
260       if self.StepCount != other.StepCount:
              return self.StepCount < other.StepCount
262       return self.TotalInstructions < other.TotalInstructions
```

and add the step count to the data that gets displayed.

```
264   def __str__(self):
265       return "{} mowed with {} instructions and {} steps".format(
266           self.TotalMowed, self.TotalInstructions, self.StepCount)
```

Next we need to provide the value when we create the *Fitness* object in *get_fitness*,

```
 9 def get_fitness(genes, fnEvaluate):
10     field, mower, _ = fnEvaluate(genes)
11     return Fitness(field.count_mowed(), len(genes), mower.StepCount)
```

and when we create the optimal fitness value in the helper function.

```
137   def run_with(self, geneSet, width, height, minGenes, maxGenes,
138               expectedNumberOfInstructions, maxMutationRounds,
139               fnCreateField, expectedNumberOfSteps):
```

```
169       optimalFitness = Fitness(width * height,
170                                expectedNumberOfInstructions,
171                                expectedNumberOfSteps)
```

That requires compensating changes in the tests to send the new parameter. Starting with the turn test:

```
77        self.run_with(geneSet, width, height, minGenes, maxGenes,
78                      expectedNumberOfInstructions, maxMutationRounds,
79                      fnCreateField, expectedNumberOfInstructions)
```

Jump test:

```
96        self.run_with(geneSet, width, height, minGenes, maxGenes,
97                      expectedNumberOfInstructions, maxMutationRounds,
98                      fnCreateField, expectedNumberOfInstructions)
```

Validating jump test:

```
115        self.run_with(geneSet, width, height, minGenes, maxGenes,
116                       expectedNumberOfInstructions, maxMutationRounds,
117                       fnCreateField, expectedNumberOfInstructions)
```

And the repeat test gets two changes:

```
128        expectedNumberOfInstructions = 9
129        expectedNumberOfSteps = 88
```

```
134        self.run_with(geneSet, width, height, minGenes, maxGenes,
135                       expectedNumberOfInstructions, maxMutationRounds,
136                       fnCreateField, expectedNumberOfSteps)
```

Run

Now when we run the test it takes longer but produces a more fuel efficient yet still quite short set of instructions.

```
59 58 57 55 63 62 61 60
50 51 52 53 65 47 48 49
81 80 79 77 85 84 83 82
72 73 74 75 87 69 70 71
15 14 13 11 Mv 18 17 16
 6  7  8  9 21  3  4  5
37 36 35 33 41 40 39 38
28 29 30 31 43 25 26 27
64 mowed with 9 instructions and 88 steps    0:18:21.102552
repeat(repeat(mow turn repeat(mow,7) turn,2) mow mow,4)
```

Not bad.

Part IV - Automatically defined functions

We've seen how powerful *repeat* is but it is a special case of grouping instructions together for reuse. What if we were to let the engine build its own function instead? This is a commonly used strategy and such functions are referred to as automatically defined functions or ADFs. ADFs are like *repeat* in that when called they execute a set of instructions randomly put there by the algorithm, but they are different in that they only execute the instructions once for each time the function is called.

The Func instruction

To support ADFs we'll introduce a Func instruction. It is similar to *repeat* in that it performs some number of instructions but instead of claiming a specific number of instructions that follow it, it simply marks the start of the ADF.

```
234  class Func:
         def __init__(self):
236          self.Ops = []

238      def execute(self, mower, field):
             for op in self.Ops:
240              op.execute(mower, field)

242      def __str__(self):
             return "func: {}".format(' '.join(map(str, self.Ops))) \
244              if len(self.Ops) > 0 else "call-func"

246
     class Program:
```

The Func instruction will take ownership of all instructions that come after it in the gene sequence. We're only going to do that for the first Func instruction we encounter:

```
     class Program:
248      Func = None
         Main = None
250
         def __init__(self, instructions):
252          temp = instructions[:]
             func = None
254  ...
```

```
                     del temp[start:end]
260                  continue

262              if type(temp[index]) is Func:
                     if func is not None:
264                      temp[index].Ops = []
                         continue
266                  start = index + 1
                     end = len(temp)
268                  temp[index].Ops = [i for i in temp[start:end]
                                        if type(i) is not Repeat or
270                                     type(i) is Repeat and len(i.Ops) > 0
                                        ]
272                  func = temp[index]
                     del temp[index:end]
274
             self.Main = temp
276          self.Func = func
```

At the end of the constructor we store the function's instructions separate from those of the main program so we can easily access them.

Next, if we encounter a Func instruction in the evaluation function we call the execution function on the one we set aside.

```
278    def evaluate(self, mower, field):
           for i, instruction in enumerate(self.Main):
280            if type(instruction) is Func:
                   self.Func.execute(mower, field)
282                continue
               instruction.execute(mower, field)
284
       def print(self):
```

Also add the Func instructions to what gets displayed when the program is asked to display itself.

```
285    def print(self):
286        if self.Func is not None:
287            print(self.Func)
288        print(' '.join(map(str, self.Main)))
```

Finally, we need a test. So, we'll duplicate the test we added for the *repeat* instruction. Then create a Func instead of a *repeat* instruction when building its gene set. We also have to increase the expected number of instructions because Func isn't quite as powerful as *repeat*.

```
138    def test_mow_turn_jump_func(self):
           width = height = 8
140        geneSet = [lambda: Mow(),
                      lambda: Turn(),
142                   lambda: Jump(random.randint(0, min(width, height)),
                                   random.randint(0, min(width, height))),
144                   lambda: Func()]                                          <==
           minGenes = 3
146        maxGenes = 20
           maxMutationRounds = 3
148        expectedNumberOfInstructions = 18                                   <==
           expectedNumberOfSteps = 65                                         <==
150    ...
```

Run

It runs much faster than the *repeat* version and still produces a reasonably short program like the following.

sample result

```
36  46  48  58    4  14  16  26
37  47  49  59    5  15  17  27
38  40  50  60    6   8  18  28
39  41  51  61    7   9  19  29
32  42  52  62  M> 10  20  30
33  43  53  63    1  11  21  31
34  44  54  56    2  12  22  24
35  45  55  57    3  13  23  25
64 mowed with 18 instructions and 65 steps  0:00:04.805489
func: mow mow mow  mow mow mow  mow jump(7,7)
call-func call-func call-func call-func call-func call-func call-func call-func turn
```

Multiple ADFs

One limitation of our current method of building the automatically defined function is that we can only have one ADF. Studying the generated main function above, we can see where we could shorten the program if we had a second function whose instructions were:

```
mow  mow  mow
```

or even:

```
call-func call-func call-func call-func
```

To support this capability we need to add an explicit *call* instruction that has the id (index) of the Func it should call as a parameter.

```
class Call:
    def __init__(self, funcId=None):
        self.FuncId = funcId
        self.Funcs = None


class Program:
```

We also need to add an `Id` attribute to `Func` and, in order to keep the previous test working, we need to add a parameter to its constructor.

```
254  class Func:
         def __init__(self, expectCall=False):
256          self.Ops = []
             self.ExpectCall = expectCall
258          self.Id = None
```

We'll also use the presence of an `Id` to tell whether the gene set includes a *call* instruction and change the `str` output accordingly:

```
264      def __str__(self):
265          return "func{1}: {0}".format(
266              ' '.join(map(str, self.Ops)),
267                  self.Id if self.Id is not None else '')
```

Next, we have to update the *Program* class to support *call* and multiple functions. We'll start by renaming its `Func` attribute to `Funcs` and initialize it to an empty array:

```
276  class Program:
         def __init__(self, genes):
278          temp = genes[:]
             funcs = []
280          for index in reversed(range(len(temp))):
```

```
             end = min(index + temp[index].OpCount + 1, len(temp))
284          temp[index].Ops = [i for i in temp[start:end]
                                 if type(i) is not Repeat or
286                              type(i) is Repeat and len(i.Ops) > 0
                                 ]
288          del temp[start:end]
             continue
```

Then in the loop, when we encounter a *call* instruction, we need to give it a reference to the array of functions.

```
291              if type(temp[index]) is Call:
292                  temp[index].Funcs = funcs
293              if type(temp[index]) is Func:
```

And for backwards compatibility when we find an Nth `Func` instruction when the gene set does not contain a *call* instruction, we're going to convert it to a *call*.

```
        if type(temp[index]) is Func:
294         if len(funcs) > 0 and not temp[index].ExpectCall:
                temp[index] = Call()
296             temp[index].Funcs = funcs
                continue
```

Otherwise, if we're expecting *call* instructions, we'll assign it an id (for display purposes)

```
            end = len(temp)
300         func = Func()
            if temp[index].ExpectCall:
302             func.Id = len(funcs)
            func.Ops = [i for i in temp[start:end]]
```

and add it to the function array after populating its operations attribute.

```
307         funcs.append(func)
308         del temp[index:end]
```

After processing all instructions, we're going to do some cleanup of the function contents, removing any *call* instructions that reference a function index that doesn't exist and any `Func` that has an empty list of instructions to execute.

```
308         del temp[index:end]

310     for func in funcs:
            for index in reversed(range(len(func.Ops))):
312             if type(func.Ops[index]) is Call:
                    func_id = func.Ops[index].FuncId
314                 if func_id is None:
                        continue
316                 if func_id >= len(funcs) or \
                                    len(funcs[func_id].Ops) == 0:
318                     del func.Ops[index]
```

Then we'll perform that same optimization on *call* instructions in the main program before assigning the functions and main to their respective attributes.

```
318                         del func.Ops[index]

320         for index in reversed(range(len(temp))):
                if type(temp[index]) is Call:
322                 func_id = temp[index].FuncId
                    if func_id is None:
324                     continue
                    if func_id >= len(funcs) or \
326                             len(funcs[func_id].Ops) == 0:
                        del temp[index]
```

```
329         self.Main = temp
330         self.Funcs = funcs
```

We can now move the *call* specific code from the evaluation function

```
332     def evaluate(self, mower, field):
333         for i, instruction in enumerate(self.Main):
334             instruction.execute(mower, field)
```

into *call* and update it to call the appropriate function, again with backward compatibility.

```
        def execute(self, mower, field):
276         funcId = 0 if self.FuncId is None else self.FuncId
            if len(self.Funcs) > funcId:
278             self.Funcs[funcId].execute(mower, field)

280
    class Program:
```

The final change to the *Program* class is to handle multiple functions when `print` is called.

```
        def print(self):
342         if self.Funcs is not None:
                for func in self.Funcs:
344                 if func.Id is not None and len(func.Ops) == 0:
                        continue
346                 print(func)
            print(' '.join(map(str, self.Main)))
```

We also need to support `__str__` in *call* for display purposes.

```python
280     def __str__(self):
            return "call-{}".format(
282             self.FuncId
                if self.FuncId is not None
284             else 'func')

286
class Program:
```

Lastly, for a test we can make a copy of the jump test then add *call* and update the Func constructor.

```python
158     def test_mow_turn_jump_call(self):
            width = height = 8
160         geneSet = [lambda: Mow(),
                    lambda: Turn(),
162                 lambda: Jump(random.randint(0, min(width, height)),
                            random.randint(0, min(width, height))),
164                 lambda: Func(expectCall=True),
                    lambda: Call(random.randint(0, 5))]
166         minGenes = 3
            maxGenes = 20
168         maxMutationRounds = 3
            expectedNumberOfInstructions = 18
170         expectedNumberOfSteps = 65
    ...
```

Run

It starts off building highly recursive programs that take thousands of steps to mow the field

sample output

```
1248 1241 1234 1227 1284 1269 1262 1255
1249 1242 1235 1228 1277 1270 1263 1256
1250 1243 1236 1285 1278 1271 1264 1257
1251 1244 1229 1286 1279 1272 1265 1258
1252 1237 1230 1287 1280 1273 1266 1259
1245 1238 1231 1288 1281 1274 1267 1260
1246 1239 1232 Mv 1282 1275 1268 1253
1247 1240 1233 1226 1283 1276 1261 1254
64 mowed with 16 instructions and 1288 steps     0:00:46.505430
func0: mow call-2
func1: mow mow mow jump(2,1) mow mow mow call-0
func2: call-1
call-0 mow
```

It eventually discovers that eliminating the recursion reduces the number of steps but that can take *hours*.

sample output

```
79 78 77 75 57 56 55 53
81 62 40 74 38 37 36 52
82 63 42 73 17 16 14 51
83 64 43 72 46 47 48 49
101 100 99 98 97 95 12 31
103 66 68 69 21 94 11 30
104 88 89 90 91 92 10 29
Mv   3   4   5 23 25 26 27
64 mowed with 30 instructions and 105 steps   10:00:47.530544
func0: jump(3,0)
func1: jump(3,4)
func2: call-4
func3: mow mow turn mow mow mow mow
func4: call-3 call-3 mow turn jump(3,7) call-3 call-3
call-1 call-2 call-4 call-4 call-4
```

The fix is to prevent recursion in the first place.

Exercise

Recursion can be easily prevented if we change the implementation so that a *call* is only valid if it references a Func that has a higher (or lower if you prefer) index than the function the *call* is in, excluding the main function. You can do that in the cleanup step when constructing the *Program*. Make this change and you'll be able to see the power of ADFs.

Summary

In this project we surveyed some of the control structures used in genetic programming instructions, ultimately ending with automatically defined functions. This gave us insight into how they might be useful in other projects. It also greatly expanded the realm of projects to which we can apply genetic algorithms. Welcome to genetic programming!

Logic Circuits

Logic gates are the basic building blocks of logic circuits. In this project we're going to use a genetic algorithm to combine logic gates into circuits that can do work.

Circuit infrastructure

As in the Lawnmower project, it makes sense that our phenotype should have behaviors, so we'll use objects. Also like that project we'll build the infrastructure in a separate file. We'll start with providing built-in gates for NOT and AND.

NOT and AND gates

The NOT gate takes one Boolean input and returns its opposite, so True if the input is False, otherwise False.

input	output
0	1
1	0

Since our input will not be a bare Boolean value but an upstream gate in the circuit, when asked for its output the NOT gate will first ask the upstream gate for its value, then return the opposite.

circuits.py

```
class Not:
    def __init__(self, input):
        self._input = input

    def get_output(self):
        return not self._input.get_output()
```

247

The AND gate takes two Boolean inputs, A and B, and returns True if they are both True, otherwise False.

inputs		output
A	B	
0	0	0
0	1	0
1	0	0
1	1	1

Like the NOT gate, the AND gate must ask the gates that feed into it for their values before it can provide its output.

```
class And:
10    def __init__(self, inputA, inputB):
          self._inputA = inputA
12        self._inputB = inputB

14    def get_output(self):
          aValue = self._inputA.get_output()
16        bValue = self._inputB.get_output()
          return aValue and bValue
```

In addition to logic gates, the circuit will also contain references to the actual A and B source inputs we're testing. We need to be able to change the source values to check the fitness of the circuit, so we'll give it a reference to a container whose contents we can modify externally.

```
20 class Source:
      def __init__(self, sourceId, sourceContainer):
22        self._sourceId = sourceId
          self._sourceContainer = sourceContainer

24
      def get_output(self):
26        return self._sourceContainer[self._sourceId]
```

We'll use a new structure for the genotype, a tree node that contains the type of gate and indexes to 2 child tree nodes (potential inputs).

circuitTests.py

```
class Node:
    def __init__(self, createGate, indexA=None, indexB=None):
        self.CreateGate = createGate
        self.IndexA = indexA
        self.IndexB = indexB


if __name__ == '__main__':
    unittest.main()
```

Nodes to circuit

Now we'll write the function that builds the circuit.

```
def nodes_to_circuit(nodes):
    circuit = []
```

It loops through all the nodes starting with the leaf nodes and moves toward the root while connecting the logic gates together.

```
    for i, node in enumerate(nodes):
```

Using what we learned in the last project we can prevent recursion by design with the convention that child indexes are only valid if they are lower than the node index.

```
        inputA = circuit[node.IndexA] if node.IndexA is not None \
                                    and i > node.IndexA else None
        inputB = circuit[node.IndexB] if node.IndexB is not None \
                                    and i > node.IndexB else None
```

Lastly, we update the circuit by creating the gate. The circuit we'll use ends up fully connected and in the last index of the array. There may be latent circuits in the array as well when we're done.

```
        circuit.append(node.CreateGate(inputA, inputB))
    return circuit[-1]


class Node:
```

Note that since the A and B inputs can both be None it can cause NOT and AND gates to be instantiated with None inputs, so we need to handle that situation. A None input makes the gate output invalid so we'll make it return None when that happens.

circuits.py

```
14    def get_output(self):
          if self._inputA is None or self._inputB is None:
16            return None
          aValue = self._inputA.get_output()
18        bValue = self._inputB.get_output()
          return aValue and bValue
```

```
5     def get_output(self):
6         if self._input is None:
7             return None
8         return not self._input.get_output()
```

That change forces us to also handle the possibility that the input gate is not None but returns None:

```
8         value = self._input.get_output()
9         if value is None:
10            return None
11        return not value
```

```
      def get_output(self):
20        if self._inputA is None or self._inputB is None:
              return None
22        aValue = self._inputA.get_output()
          if aValue is None:
24            return None
          bValue = self._inputB.get_output()
26        if bValue is None:
              return None
28        return aValue and bValue
```

Now we have what we need to build a circuit, provide inputs to a circuit, and check the output. We're ready to test.

Generate OR

For the first test we're going to use a genetic algorithm to generate a circuit that behaves like an OR gate. An OR gate takes two Boolean inputs and returns True if either is True otherwise False. We can use the following truth table to see the expected output for each combination of inputs.

inputs		output
A	B	
0	0	0
0	1	1
1	0	1
1	1	1

In our test function we convert the table to an array of rules that can be used to evaluate a circuit's fitness.

circuitTests.py

```python
import datetime
import random
import unittest

import circuits
import genetic


class CircuitTests(unittest.TestCase):
    def test_generate_OR(self):
        rules = [[[False, False], False],
                 [[False, True], True],
                 [[True, False], True],
                 [[True, True], True]]

        optimalLength = 6
        self.find_circuit(rules, optimalLength)


def nodes_to_circuit(nodes):
```

If we could negate the first row we'd have a circuit that works for all four rules. NOT A anded with NOT B would get False. If we NOT that we get a circuit that works for all four rules, like this:

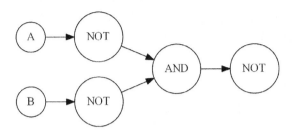

We used the node count in that circuit to limit the number of nodes we use.

That implies find_circuit in the test class

```
        def find_circuit(self, rules, expectedLength):
20          def fnGetFitness(genes):
                return get_fitness(genes, rules, self.inputs)
22

24  def nodes_to_circuit(nodes):
```

and a property to hold the inputs, which is created before the first test runs.

```
 9  class CircuitTests(unittest.TestCase):
10      @classmethod
11      def setUpClass(cls):
12          cls.inputs = dict()
```

Now we have what we need to build the fitness function.

Fitness

To calculate the fitness we need to build the circuit from the nodes then use each rule's inputs to test the circuit and count how many rules the circuit can satisfy.

```
     def get_fitness(genes, rules, inputs):
10       circuit = nodes_to_circuit(genes)
         sourceLabels = "AB"
12       rulesPassed = 0
         for rule in rules:
14           inputs.clear()
             inputs.update(zip(sourceLabels, rule[0]))
16           if circuit.get_output() == rule[1]:
                 rulesPassed += 1
18       return rulesPassed

20
     class CircuitTests(unittest.TestCase):
```

Display

We want to output the matching circuit, so we need to add `__str__` functions to the source and gate classes. If the gate has invalid inputs then we'll show a question mark.

circuits.py

```
     def __str__(self):
14       if self._input is None:
             return "Not(?)"
16       return "Not({})".format(self._input)

18
 class And:
```

```
     def __str__(self):
36       if self._inputA is None or self._inputB is None:
             return "And(?)"
38       return "And({} {})".format(self._inputA, self._inputB)

40
 class Source:
```

```
49   def __str__(self):
50       return self._sourceId
```

This will produce output like the following:
sample output

```
Not(And(Not(B) And(Not(A) Not(B))))
```

Now we will bring it all together in the display function:

circuitTests.py

```
22    def display(candidate, startTime):
          circuit = nodes_to_circuit(candidate.Genes)
          timeDiff = datetime.datetime.now() - startTime
24        print("{}\t{}\t{}".format(
              circuit,
26            candidate.Fitness,
              timeDiff))

28

30  class CircuitTests(unittest.TestCase):
```

```
44        def find_circuit(self, rules, expectedLength):
              startTime = datetime.datetime.now()
46
              def fnDisplay(candidate):
48                display(candidate, startTime)
```

Create

Our gene objects are complex, so we'll use a special function to create them.

```
          def fnCreateGene(index):
54            return create_gene(index, self.geneset)

56
    def nodes_to_circuit(nodes):
```

Now we can complete the test harness by populating the gene set.

```
30  class CircuitTests(unittest.TestCase):
        @classmethod
32      def setUpClass(cls):
            cls.inputs = dict()
34          cls.geneset = [[circuits.And, circuits.And],
                           [lambda i1, i2: circuits.Not(i1), circuits.Not],
36                         [lambda i1, i2: circuits.Source('A', cls.inputs),
                            circuits.Source],
38                         [lambda i1, i2: circuits.Source('B', cls.inputs),
                            circuits.Source]]
```

It will pick child index values relative to the index where the node will be inserted so they're more likely to be valid when converted to a circuit. We'll also try to make the input indexes different so we can reduce the waste from gates like And(A A).

```python
30 def create_gene(index, geneset):
       gateType = random.choice(geneset)
32     indexA = indexB = None
       if gateType[1].input_count() > 0:
34         indexA = random.randint(0, index)
       if gateType[1].input_count() > 1:
36         indexB = random.randint(0, index) if index > 1 else 0
           if indexB == indexA:
38             indexB = random.randint(0, index)
       return Node(gateType[0], indexA, indexB)
40


42 class CircuitTests(unittest.TestCase):
```

That implies the addition of a function that counts inputs to the source class

circuits.py

```python
60     @staticmethod
61     def input_count():
62         return 0
```

Not gate

```python
18     @staticmethod
       def input_count():
20         return 1

22
class And:
```

and And gate.

```python
44     @staticmethod
       def input_count():
46         return 2

48
class Source:
```

Mutate

Next we'll add a custom mutation function.

circuitTests.py

```
74      def fnMutate(genes):
            mutate(genes, fnCreateGene)
76

78 def nodes_to_circuit(genes):
```

To be efficient in the mutation function, we only want to change the nodes that we actually use in the circuit. We can accumulate those while we're building the circuit. The change in the function that builds the circuit is to add a tracking array where each element contains the set of node indexes that are used to build the corresponding circuit.

```
78 def nodes_to_circuit(genes):
       circuit = []
80     usedIndexes = []                                               <==
       for i, node in enumerate(genes):
82         used = {i}                                                 <==
           inputA = inputB = None
84         if node.IndexA is not None and i > node.IndexA:
               inputA = circuit[node.IndexA]
86             used.update(usedIndexes[node.IndexA])                  <==
               if node.IndexB is not None and i > node.IndexB:
88                 inputB = circuit[node.IndexB]
                   used.update(usedIndexes[node.IndexB])              <==
90         circuit.append(node.CreateGate(inputA, inputB))
           usedIndexes.append(used)                                   <==
92     return circuit[-1], usedIndexes[-1]                            <==
```

That requires a corresponding change to the fitness function

```
 9 def get_fitness(genes, rules, inputs):
10     circuit = nodes_to_circuit(genes)[0]
```

and display function.

```
21 def display(candidate, startTime):
22     circuit = nodes_to_circuit(candidate.Genes)[0]
```

Now we can call the circuit builder to get the list of node indexes to use as mutation candidates.

```python
42 def mutate(childGenes, fnCreateGene):
       count = random.randint(1, 5)
44     while count > 0:
           count -= 1
46         indexesUsed = [i for i in nodes_to_circuit(childGenes)[1]]
           index = random.choice(indexesUsed)
48         childGenes[index] = fnCreateGene(index)

50
   class CircuitTests(unittest.TestCase):
```

Create

We also need a custom creation function. It is simple enough to be added inline.

```python
84             mutate(genes, fnCreateGene)

86         maxLength = expectedLength

88         def fnCreate():
               return [fnCreateGene(i) for i in range(maxLength)]
```

Finally we call the genetic engine.

```python
           best = genetic.get_best(fnGetFitness, None, len(rules), None,
92                             fnDisplay, fnMutate, fnCreate, poolSize=3)
           self.assertTrue(best.Fitness == len(rules))
94         self.assertFalse(len(nodes_to_circuit(best.Genes)[1])
                       > expectedLength)

96
98 def nodes_to_circuit(genes):
```

Run

When we run the test it finds the optimal solution every time.

```
Not(And(?)) 0   0:00:00
Not(B)  1    0:00:00
And(B B)    3   0:00:00.001004
Not(And(Not(A) Not(B))) 4   0:00:09.581228
```

Generate XOR

Now let's see if we can generate a circuit that behaves like an XOR (exclusive-or) gate. An XOR gate returns True if the inputs are different, otherwise False.

	inputs		output
	A	B	
	0	0	0
	0	1	1
	1	0	1
	1	1	0

We'll start by building a new test with those rules.

```
    def test_generate_XOR(self):
72      rules = [[[False, False], False],
                [[False, True], True],
74              [[True, False], True],
                [[True, True], False]]
```

By comparing the XOR gate truth table with that of the OR gate we notice that the only difference is the last rule. This means that in order to determine the optimal solution for the XOR gate we can start with the circuit for the OR gate, Not(And(Not(A) Not(B))) (circles below), and AND that with the opposite of a circuit that produces the fourth rule, Not(And(A B)). Here's a visual representation:

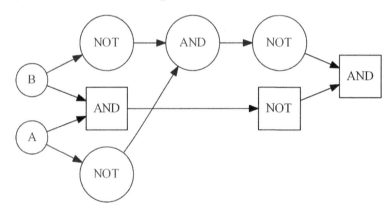

The strict number of nodes in the circuit is 9, or 11 if we double count the source (A and B) nodes. That lets us finish writing the XOR test:

```
76      self.find_circuit(rules, 9)
77
78  def find_circuit(self, rules, expectedLength):
```

Run

Run the test and it almost always stalls.

```
And(B And(B B)) 2    0:00:00.001003
Not(And(B A))    3    0:00:00.014127
And(Not(And(Not(A) Not(B))) Not(And(A B)))  4   0:09:44.378545
```

Can you think of any ways in which we can take advantage of our knowledge of the problem space to improve the performance of the genetic algorithm? Before reading further take about half an hour to experiment.

Performance improvement

The following is one of the easiest improvements to implement. Notice that the sources take up 2 of the 4 slots in the gene set. This means that on average they end up taking half the slots in the *Chromosome*, which makes it very difficult for the engine to build a complex circuit. The solution is to separate the sources from the gates and use only one copy of each of the sources because they can be referenced by index from any node with a higher index.

```
     class CircuitTests(unittest.TestCase):
52       @classmethod
         def setUpClass(cls):
54           cls.inputs = dict()
             cls.gates = [[circuits.And, circuits.And],
56                        [lambda i1, i2: circuits.Not(i1), circuits.Not]]
             cls.sources = [[lambda i1, i2: circuits.Source('A', cls.inputs),
58                          circuits.Source],
                            [lambda i1, i2: circuits.Source('B', cls.inputs),
60                          circuits.Source]]
```

Then pass both to the function that creates genes:

```
87       def fnCreateGene(index):
88           return create_gene(index, self.gates, self.sources)
```

Next change that function so that sources are only added at the start of the node array, leaving the rest of the indexes for gates.

```
30 def create_gene(index, gates, sources):
       if index < len(sources):                                    <==
32         gateType = sources[index]
       else:
34         gateType = random.choice(gates)
```

```
38      if gateType[1].input_count() > 1:
39          indexB = random.randint(0, index) \
40              if index > 1 and index >= len(sources) else 0        <==
41          if indexB == indexA:
```

We can also use our knowledge of the source locations in the gene sequence to reduce waste by preventing the mutation function from touching those nodes.

```
94          def fnMutate(genes):
95              mutate(genes, fnCreateGene, fnGetFitness, len(self.sources))
```

We'll also check the fitness and return early if we find an improvement.

```
46  def mutate(childGenes, fnCreateGene, fnGetFitness, sourceCount):
        count = random.randint(1, 5)
48      initialFitness = fnGetFitness(childGenes)                      <==
        while count > 0:
50          count -= 1
            indexesUsed = [i for i in nodes_to_circuit(childGenes)[1]  <==
52                         if i >= sourceCount]
            if len(indexesUsed) == 0:
54              return
            index = random.choice(indexesUsed)
56          childGenes[index] = fnCreateGene(index)
            if fnGetFitness(childGenes) > initialFitness:             <==
58              return
```

These changes make it possible for the engine to find the solution every time.

```
And(?)  0    0:00:00.001005
Not(And(B Not(B)))  2    0:00:00.001005
And(Not(B) Not(Not(A)))  3    0:00:00.004011
And(Not(And(Not(B) Not(A))) Not(And(B A)))  4    0:00:02.235138
```

Very good!

Generate A XOR B XOR C

We've seen that the genetic algorithm can generate a circuit that passes the 4 rules required for 2 sources. Let's try a circuit that uses 3 sources. This means it will have 2^3 (8) rules. The circuit we'll try to reproduce is A XOR B XOR C.

inputs			output
A	B	C	
0	0	0	0
0	0	1	1
0	1	0	1
0	1	1	0
1	0	0	1
1	0	1	0
1	1	0	0
1	1	1	1

Given that information, we can start writing the test.

```
88  def test_generate_AxBxC(self):
        rules = [[[False, False, False], False],
90              [[False, False, True], True],
                [[False, True, False], True],
92              [[False, True, True], False],
                [[True, False, False], True],
94              [[True, False, True], False],
                [[True, True, False], False],
96              [[True, True, True], True]]
        self.sources.append(
98          [lambda l, r: circuits.Source('C', self.inputs),
            circuits.Source])
```

That means we need to add c to the source labels in the fitness function too:

```
9  def get_fitness(genes, rules, inputs):
10     circuit = nodes_to_circuit(genes)[0]
11     sourceLabels = "ABC"
```

Since we know we can build OR from AND and NOT we'll add OR to the gates so we can use it to help keep the final circuit relatively short.

```
99           circuits.Source])
100      self.gates.append([circuits.Or, circuits.Or])
```

The OR gate implementation would be almost identical to that of the AND gate, so let's extract a base class.

circuits.py

```
   class GateWith2Inputs:
24     def __init__(self, inputA, inputB, label, fnTest):
           self._inputA = inputA
26         self._inputB = inputB
           self._label = label
28         self._fnTest = fnTest

30     def get_output(self):
           if self._inputA is None or self._inputB is None:
32             return None
           aValue = self._inputA.get_output()
34         if aValue is None:
               return None
36         bValue = self._inputB.get_output()
           if bValue is None:
38             return None
           return self._fnTest(aValue, bValue)

40
       def __str__(self):
42         if self._inputA is None or self._inputB is None:
               return "{}(?)".format(self._label)
44         return "{}({} {})".format(self._label, self._inputA, self._inputB)

46     @staticmethod
       def input_count():
48         return 2


50
   class And:
```

That simplifies the AND gate implementation to:

```
51 class And(GateWith2Inputs):
52     def __init__(self, inputA, inputB):
53         super().__init__(inputA, inputB, type(self).__name__,
54                          lambda a, b: a and b)
```

The OR gate implementation is just as easy:

```
   class Or(GateWith2Inputs):
58     def __init__(self, inputA, inputB):
           super().__init__(inputA, inputB, type(self).__name__,
60                          lambda a, b: a or b)

62
   class Source:
```

Next we need to solve the problem of figuring out what the optimal solution is. We could use a Karnaugh Map to reduce those 8 rules to a minimal circuit but doing so for circuits with *many* inputs becomes messy. So, let's find another way. Historically we've used a variable length gene sequence when we didn't know how many genes were needed, but as you may have observed, using tree nodes already makes the length adaptive if we give it enough indexes to work with. So we're going to take this opportunity to introduce a new machine learning technique.

Hill climbing

> Hill climbing is a popular problem space exploration technique where one feature of the *Chromosome* is incrementally adjusted until a better solution is found or a local minimum or maximum is detected, at which point the process repeats with a different feature. Some variants change any feature as long as it only affects a single piece of data, which may be smaller than a gene. An example from our current project would be to only change the gate type or just one of the indexes in a node rather than replacing the entire node as we're doing now. Be aware that hill climbing doesn't always find the optimal solution so it may need to be supplemented with simulated annealing.

We'll implement hill climbing in the `genetic` module so that it is reusable. Starting with the function definition, it includes the optimization function it will call, a function to test whether an improvement has been found, a function to test whether the improvement is optimal so we can stop, a function that gets the next feature value, a display function, and the initial value of the feature we're trying to optimize.

genetic.py

```
150  def hill_climbing(optimizationFunction, is_improvement, is_optimal,
151                    get_next_feature_value, display, initialFeatureValue):
```

We get the initial result. Then, to keep it from being chatty, we redirect the output just like we do when benchmarking, and only restore it for calls to the display function.

```
152      best = optimizationFunction(initialFeatureValue)
153      stdout = sys.stdout
154      sys.stdout = None
```

Once we have a result we're going to enter a loop where we keep getting new results until we find an optimal one.

```
155    while not is_optimal(best):
156        featureValue = get_next_feature_value(best)
157        child = optimizationFunction(featureValue)
```

When we find an improvement it becomes the new best value and we display it.

```
158        if is_improvement(best, child):
               best = child
160            sys.stdout = stdout
               display(best, featureValue)
162            sys.stdout = None
```

If we find the optimal solution we return it.

```
       sys.stdout = stdout
164    return best

166
class Chromosome:
```

Add hill climbing to the test harness

Now we need to build the inputs we're going to pass to the hill climbing function. We'll start by wrapping the current call to *get_best* in a new function. This will be the optimization function. We'll give it a maximum of 50 gates to work with and see what it finds.

circuitTests.py

```
       maxLength = 50
118
       def fnCreate():
120        return [fnCreateGene(i) for i in range(maxLength)]

122    def fnOptimizationFunction(variableLength):
           nonlocal maxLength
124        maxLength = variableLength
           return genetic.get_best(fnGetFitness, None, len(rules), None,
126                                 fnDisplay, fnMutate, fnCreate,
                                    poolSize=3, maxSeconds=30)
```

I gave it 30 seconds to try to find an improvement, but you might be able to use a lower value. The feature we're optimizing is the number of nodes in the circuit. We need to get that to the gene-creation function. We'll do that by transferring it to the existing maximum length variable that is already passed to that function.

Next we need a function that can tell whether the new result is better than the current best. We return `True` if all the rules pass and the number of gates used in the new result if less than that of the current best result, otherwise `False`.

```
129    def fnIsImprovement(currentBest, child):
130        return child.Fitness == len(rules) and \
131            len(nodes_to_circuit(child.Genes)[1]) < \
132            len(nodes_to_circuit(currentBest.Genes)[1])
```

We also need a function that can tell whether we've found the known optimal solution. Note that if we don't know the optimal value we could simply use an impossibly low value and let it run until we're ready to stop it.

```
134    def fnIsOptimal(child):
           return child.Fitness == len(rules) and \
136            len(nodes_to_circuit(child.Genes)[1]) <= expectedLength

138    best = genetic.get_best(fnGetFitness, None, len(rules), None,
```

As for display, we can simply add an optional parameter to the existing display function for the feature value. When it is set we show the number of nodes used in the new best circuit.

```
       def fnDisplay(candidate, length=None):
           if length is not None:
106            print("-- distinct nodes in circuit:",
108                len(nodes_to_circuit(candidate.Genes)[1]))
           display(candidate, startTime)
```

When an improvement is found we'll make the number of nodes in that circuit the new value to beat.

```
141    def fnGetNextFeatureValue(currentBest):
142        return len(nodes_to_circuit(currentBest.Genes)[1])
```

At the end we call the hill climbing function.

```
144    best = genetic.hill_climbing(fnOptimizationFunction,
                                    fnIsImprovement, fnIsOptimal,
146                                 fnGetNextFeatureValue, fnDisplay,
                                    maxLength)
148    self.assertTrue(best.Fitness == len(rules))
       self.assertFalse(len(nodes_to_circuit(best.Genes)[1])
150                        > expectedLength)

152
def nodes_to_circuit(genes):
```

Now we're finally able to finish the test implementation.

```
100        self.gates.append([circuits.Or, circuits.Or])
101        self.find_circuit(rules, 12)
```

Run

Let's first verify that the OR and XOR tests work.

sample OR test result

```
And(And(And(And(?) Not(And(?))) Not(Not(And(?)))) And(Not(And(?)) Not(And(?)))) 0
    0:00:00
Not(Not(B)) 3    0:00:00.004012
Not(And(Not(And(Not(A) B)) And(Not(Not(Not(Not(A))))) Not(B)))) 4
    0:00:00.013128
-- distinct nodes in circuit: 8
Not(And(Not(B) And(Not(B) Not(A)))) 4    0:00:00.021112
-- distinct nodes in circuit: 6
Not(And(Not(A) Not(B))) 4    0:00:00.080303
```

sample XOR test result

```
Not(And(?)) 0    0:00:00.001003
Not(And(And(Not(And(A B)) And(Not(Not(And(A B))) Not(And(A B)))) A))    2
    0:00:00.003008
And(Not(And(A And(A B))) Not(Not(Not(And(A B)))))    3    0:00:00.007047
And(Not(And(Not(A) Not(B))) Not(And(And(And(B And(B A)) And(B A)) Not(Not(And(B A)))
    )) 4    0:00:00.287776
-- distinct nodes in circuit: 9
And(Not(And(B A)) Not(And(Not(B) Not(A)))) 4    0:00:02.833747
```

Now let's see how it does on A XOR B XOR C.

```
And(Or(?) Not(Not(C))) 0    0:00:00.001001
And(And(Not(C) And(And(Not(A) B) Not(Not(Not(C))))) Not(A)) 5    0:00:00.006120
And(And(Not(And(B Or(A C))) Not(A)) Not(And(Not(C) Not(Or(B And(B Or(A C)))))))) 6
    0:00:00.470108
And(Or(Not(Or(And(A And(A C)) And(Or(A C) B))) And(And(And(And(A C) Or(A C)) B) And(
    Not(Not(Or(And(A And(A C)) And(Or(A C) B)))) And(Or(A C) B)))) Or(And(Or(A C) Not
    (Or(And(A And(A C)) And(Or(A C) B)))) B)) 8    0:00:02.133227
-- distinct nodes in circuit: 13
And(Not(And(Or(B C) And(A Or(Not(C) Not(B))))) Or(A And(Or(Not(C) Not(B)) Or(B C))))
    8    0:00:50.958561
-- distinct nodes in circuit: 12
Or(And(Or(A C) Not(Or(And(A C) B))) And(B Or(And(A C) Not(Or(A C))))) 8
    0:01:04.648605
```

Excellent!

If it takes an excessively long time to find the result on your box, you may need to increase the number of seconds you let it run on each optimization pass.

Generate a 2-bit adder

Now for something more interesting, a 2-bit adder. A 2-bit adder can add two numbers in the range 0..3 to get a result in the range 0..6. This means we need 4 sources, A and B for the first number, and C and D for the second. We also need 3 result bits for the 4's, 2's and 1's result bits. 4 source-inputs means we'll have 2^4 (16) rules. Here's the truth table.

input 1		input 2		outputs			meaning
A (2's)	B (1's)	C (2's)	D (1's)	4's	2's	1's	
0	0	0	0	0	0	0	0 + 0 = 0
0	0	0	1	0	0	1	0 + 1 = 1
0	0	1	0	0	1	0	0 + 2 = 2
0	0	1	1	0	1	1	0 + 3 = 3
0	1	0	0	0	0	1	1 + 0 = 1
0	1	0	1	0	1	0	1 + 1 = 2
0	1	1	0	0	1	1	1 + 2 = 3
0	1	1	1	1	0	0	1 + 3 = 4
1	0	0	0	0	1	0	2 + 0 = 2
1	0	0	1	0	1	1	2 + 1 = 3
1	0	1	0	1	0	0	2 + 2 = 4
1	0	1	1	1	0	1	2 + 3 = 5
1	1	0	0	0	1	1	3 + 0 = 3
1	1	0	1	1	0	0	3 + 1 = 4
1	1	1	0	1	0	1	3 + 2 = 5
1	1	1	1	1	1	0	3 + 3 = 6

We could change the code to work with N-result bits, essentially N-circuits, but we can get the same result without that complexity by searching for each result bit's circuit in a separate test and sharing the setup code between them. We can build the setup function from the truth table above.

```python
    def get_2_bit_adder_rules_for_bit(self, bit):
        rules = [[[0, 0, 0, 0], [0, 0, 0]],   # 0 + 0 = 0
                 [[0, 0, 0, 1], [0, 0, 1]],   # 0 + 1 = 1
                 [[0, 0, 1, 0], [0, 1, 0]],   # 0 + 2 = 2
                 [[0, 0, 1, 1], [0, 1, 1]],   # 0 + 3 = 3
                 [[0, 1, 0, 0], [0, 0, 1]],   # 1 + 0 = 1
                 [[0, 1, 0, 1], [0, 1, 0]],   # 1 + 1 = 2
                 [[0, 1, 1, 0], [0, 1, 1]],   # 1 + 2 = 3
                 [[0, 1, 1, 1], [1, 0, 0]],   # 1 + 3 = 4
                 [[1, 0, 0, 0], [0, 1, 0]],   # 2 + 0 = 2
                 [[1, 0, 0, 1], [0, 1, 1]],   # 2 + 1 = 3
                 [[1, 0, 1, 0], [1, 0, 0]],   # 2 + 2 = 4
                 [[1, 0, 1, 1], [1, 0, 1]],   # 2 + 3 = 5
                 [[1, 1, 0, 0], [0, 1, 1]],   # 3 + 0 = 3
                 [[1, 1, 0, 1], [1, 0, 0]],   # 3 + 1 = 4
                 [[1, 1, 1, 0], [1, 0, 1]],   # 3 + 2 = 5
                 [[1, 1, 1, 1], [1, 1, 0]]]   # 3 + 3 = 6
        bitNRules = [[rule[0], rule[1][2 - bit]] for rule in rules]
```

Here we take advantage of a Python feature that equates 0 with `False` and 1 with `True` to simplify the implementation. We also need to add c and d to the sources, and to keep the results short we'll use both an OR gate and an XOR gate.

```
122    self.gates.append([circuits.Or, circuits.Or])
       self.gates.append([circuits.Xor, circuits.Xor])
124    self.sources.append([lambda l, r: circuits.Source('C', self.inputs),
                            circuits.Source])
126    self.sources.append([lambda l, r: circuits.Source('D', self.inputs),
                            circuits.Source])
       return bitNRules
```

Next add D to the source labels in the fitness function.

```
 9  def get_fitness(genes, rules, inputs):
10      circuit = nodes_to_circuit(genes)[0]
11      sourceLabels = "ABCD"
```

Here's the implementation of the XOR gate.

circuits.py

```
class Xor(GateWith2Inputs):
64    def __init__(self, inputA, inputB):
         super().__init__(inputA, inputB, type(self).__name__,
66                        lambda a, b: a != b)

68
class Source:
```

Tests

Now we're ready to add the tests that find the circuit for each bit.

circuitTests.py

```
129    def test_2_bit_adder_1s_bit(self):
130        rules = self.get_2_bit_adder_rules_for_bit(0)
131        self.find_circuit(rules, 3)
```

```
133    def test_2_bit_adder_2s_bit(self):
134        rules = self.get_2_bit_adder_rules_for_bit(1)
135        self.find_circuit(rules, 7)
```

```
137    def test_2_bit_adder_4s_bit(self):
138        rules = self.get_2_bit_adder_rules_for_bit(2)
139        self.find_circuit(rules, 9)
```

Run

It can quickly generate the optimal solution for the 1's bit

sample solution for 1's bit

```
Not(Or(And(?) C))    0    0:00:00.001003
Not(Or(Or(A C) C))   8    0:00:00.002006
And(Not(And(Xor(D Not(Not(Or(And(B D)) C)))) And(A D))) Not(Not(Xor(D And(A And(B D)))
    ))))   9    0:00:00.007068
And(Not(Xor(Xor(Xor(D And(A And(B D))) A) Or(Xor(And(B D) Xor(D And(A And(B D)))) Not
    (Or(And(B D) C))))) Not(Not(Xor(D And(A And(B D))))))  10   0:00:00.009073
And(Not(Xor(Xor(Xor(D Xor(And(A D) B)) A) Or(Not(A) Not(Or(And(B D) C))))) Not(Not(
    Xor(D Xor(And(A D) B)))))    11   0:00:00.014086
Or(Xor(D B) Xor(And(Xor(D B) Not(D)) A))     12   0:00:00.032165
Or(Xor(D B) And(Not(D) Xor(D B)))   16   0:00:00.035143
-- distinct nodes in circuit: 3
Xor(D B)    16   0:00:00.036146
```

the 2's bit

sample output for 2's bit

```
. . .
Xor(Xor(Xor(And(B D) A) And(Xor(Not(C) C) B)) Xor(Xor(B Not(C)) Or(Xor(Not(C) C) Xor(
    And(B D) A)))) 16   0:00:00.338064
-- distinct nodes in circuit: 8
Xor(And(B And(D B)) Xor(A C))    16   0:00:00.431277
-- distinct nodes in circuit: 7
Xor(Xor(And(D B) C) A)   16   0:00:30.907710
```

and the 4's bit.

sample solution for 4's bit

```
. . .
And(And(Or(D And(C A)) Or(Not(Or(A Xor(Not(B) C))) Or(C And(Not(And(A Not(B))) B))))
    Or(A Xor(Not(B) C)))    16   0:00:11.065914
-- distinct nodes in circuit: 13
And(Or(And(A C) And(Not(Not(D)) B)) Or(Xor(And(Not(Not(D)) A) Not(D)) C))    16
    0:00:15.089580
-- distinct nodes in circuit: 10
Or(And(C A) And(And(B D) Or(Xor(A C) A)))    16   0:00:28.089024
-- distinct nodes in circuit: 9
And(Or(C And(D B)) Or(And(C And(D B)) A))    16   0:01:15.223721
```

Outstanding!

Retrospective

Tree nodes are often used instead of arrays in genetic programming because it is much easier to inject new functionality between two nodes. You should be able to adapt the way tree nodes are used in this project to the Lawnmower Problem. One way would be for all nodes to use the first child node to point to the next instruction. Then each `func` instruction could define its instructions on the second child node, making it easier for the genetic algorithm to modify the contents of the function.

You might also implement NAND and NOR gates to see if they improve upon the optimal solutions we found in this project.

Summary

This project showed how tree nodes can be used in a genetic algorithm for both fixed- and variable-length genotypes. It also introduced hill climbing, a very useful but potentially time consuming optimization technique.

Regular Expressions

The next project is to build a genetic algorithm that can evolve a regular expression (regex) that matches all items in a set of wanted strings without matching any items in a set of unwanted strings.

As you probably know, meta characters in regular expressions have special meanings, for example * means repeat zero or more times, + means repeat at least once, etc. Go experiment with some simple sequences then come back.

Test

The base gene set for the genetic algorithm will include four of these, which will be defined in global variables within the genetic algorithm file.

regexTests.py

```python
import datetime
import random
import unittest

import genetic

repeatMetas = {'?', '*', '+'}
startMetas = {'|'}
allMetas = repeatMetas | startMetas
```

Next, the strings the generated regex should match, and those it should not match, are defined in a test. The genetic algorithm is also given a specific regex length to achieve. This keeps it from simply using the | (or) meta character to concatenate all the wanted strings.

```python
class RegexTests(unittest.TestCase):
    def test_two_digits(self):
        wanted = {"01", "11", "10"}
        unwanted = {"00", ""}
        self.find_regex(wanted, unwanted, 7)
```

Fitness

The fitness function first compiles the regex to see if it is valid or not. If not it returns a comparably low fitness value.

```
3  import re
4  import unittest
```

```
10  allMetas = repeatMetas | startMetas

12
    def get_fitness(genes, wanted, unwanted):
14      pattern = ''.join(genes)
        length = len(pattern)

16
        try:
18          re.compile(pattern)
        except re.error:
20          return Fitness(0, len(wanted), len(unwanted), length)
```

Otherwise, it determines the fitness of the generated regex by counting the number of wanted and unwanted strings the regex matches exactly.

```
22      numWantedMatched = sum(1 for i in wanted if re.fullmatch(pattern, i))
23      numUnwantedMatched = sum(1 for i in unwanted if re.fullmatch(pattern, i))
24      return Fitness(numWantedMatched, len(wanted), numUnwantedMatched, length)
```

As usual the fitness function has a related helper function in the test harness:

```
33      def find_regex(self, wanted, unwanted, expectedLength):
34          def fnGetFitness(genes):
35              return get_fitness(genes, wanted, unwanted)
```

This genetic algorithm uses a *Fitness* object because there are multiple objectives. They are:

- to maximize the number of wanted strings that match,

- to minimize the number of unwanted strings that match, and

- to minimize the length of the regex

```
   class Fitness:
38     def __init__(self, numWantedMatched, totalWanted, numUnwantedMatched,
                    length):
40         self.NumWantedMatched = numWantedMatched
           self._totalWanted = totalWanted
42         self.NumUnwantedMatched = numUnwantedMatched
           self.Length = length
```

The comparison function first combines the number of wanted strings that were not matched with the number of unwanted strings that were matched. When that value differs, the algorithm should keep the chromosome with the smallest total. That achieves the first two objectives while allowing the matched wanted and unwanted counts to vary.

```
       def __gt__(self, other):
46         combined = (self._totalWanted - self.NumWantedMatched) \
                    + self.NumUnwantedMatched
48         otherCombined = (other._totalWanted - other.NumWantedMatched) \
                    + other.NumUnwantedMatched
50         if combined != otherCombined:
               return combined < otherCombined
```

When the regex fails to match one or more wanted strings, or matches one or more unwanted strings, the algorithm should keep the newer one. This should prevent the algorithm from hanging on a particularly bad chromosome.

```
52         success = combined == 0
           otherSuccess = otherCombined == 0
54         if success != otherSuccess:
               return success
56         if not success:
               return False
```

Otherwise the shortest regex is chosen.

```
58         return self.Length < other.Length
```

The output of the `__str__` function makes the values easy to read when displayed.

```
60    def __str__(self):
          return "matches: {} wanted, {} unwanted, len {}".format(
62            "all" if self._totalWanted == self.NumWantedMatched else self.
                  NumWantedMatched,
              self.NumUnwantedMatched,
64            self.Length)

66
   if __name__ == '__main__':
68     unittest.main()
```

Display

```
27 def display(candidate, startTime):
28     timeDiff = datetime.datetime.now() - startTime
29     print("{}\t{}\t{}".format(
30         ''.join(candidate.Genes), candidate.Fitness, timeDiff))
```

expected output

```
|| 01|11?*+    matches 0 wanted 2 unwanted, len 8  0:00:00                    ||
```

Next is the helper function for the test harness.

```
    def find_regex(self, wanted, unwanted, expectedLength):
40      startTime = datetime.datetime.now()

42      def fnDisplay(candidate):
            display(candidate, startTime)
```

Mutation

Since the genetic algorithm needs to be able to change the length of the regex, a custom mutation function is used. The mutation function has a loop that breaks early if it produces a gene sequence with an improved fitness.

```
33 def mutate(genes, fnGetFitness, mutationOperators, mutationRoundCounts):
34     initialFitness = fnGetFitness(genes)
```

The number of times the loop executes is adaptive based on previously successful loop counts.

```
35      count = random.choice(mutationRoundCounts)
36      for i in range(1, count + 2):
```

The mutation function receives an array of operators that can be used to modify the gene sequence. Each time through the loop it makes a temporary copy of the operators then picks one and uses it to try to modify the gene sequence. The operator returns a Boolean value indicating whether it was able to make a change or not. If not, that operator is removed from the temporary copy so it will not be tried again in that round.

```
            copy = mutationOperators[:]
38          func = random.choice(copy)
            while not func(genes):
40              copy.remove(func)
                func = random.choice(copy)
```

When an operator does make a change, the fitness of the changed genes is compared with the initial fitness. If the fitness improves then the adaptive loop count is updated and the loop halts.

```
42          if fnGetFitness(genes) > initialFitness:
                mutationRoundCounts.append(i)
44              return

46
class RegexTests(unittest.TestCase):
```

Mutation Operators

The default mutation operators are: add, remove, replace, swap and move.

```
33 def mutate_add(genes, geneset):
34      index = random.randrange(0, len(genes) + 1) if len(genes) > 0 else 0
35      genes[index:index] = [random.choice(geneset)]
36      return True
```

```
def mutate_remove(genes):
40      if len(genes) < 1:
            return False
42      del genes[random.randrange(0, len(genes))]
        if len(genes) > 1 and random.randint(0, 1) == 1:
44          del genes[random.randrange(0, len(genes))]
        return True
```

```
48 def mutate_replace(genes, geneset):
       if len(genes) < 1:
50         return False
       index = random.randrange(0, len(genes))
52     genes[index] = random.choice(geneset)
       return True
```

```
56 def mutate_swap(genes):
       if len(genes) < 2:
58         return False
       indexA, indexB = random.sample(range(len(genes)), 2)
60     genes[indexA], genes[indexB] = genes[indexB], genes[indexA]
       return True
```

```
64 def mutate_move(genes):
       if len(genes) < 3:
66         return False
       start = random.choice(range(len(genes)))
68     stop = start + random.randint(1, 2)
       toMove = genes[start:stop]
70     genes[start:stop] = []
       index = random.choice(range(len(genes)))
72     if index >= start:
           index += 1
74     genes[index:index] = toMove
       return True
76
78 def mutate(genes, fnGetFitness, mutationOperators, mutationRoundCounts):
```

Notice that two of the functions have multiple parameters but the mutation function only calls them with one variable. The function-specific parameters, if any, are provided when the list of mutation operators is created in the test harness, through the use of the partial function.

> partial gives us the ability to pre-fill or lock function parameters. This is useful when you know the parameters will not change. When the partial version of that function is called you only need to supply the remaining parameters, if any.

```
4 import unittest
5 from functools import partial
```

```
108       mutationRoundCounts = [1]

110       mutationOperators = [
              partial(mutate_add, geneset=fullGeneset),
112           partial(mutate_replace, geneset=fullGeneset),
              mutate_remove,
114           mutate_swap,
              mutate_move,
116       ]

118       def fnMutate(genes):
              mutate(genes, fnGetFitness, mutationOperators,
120                  mutationRoundCounts)

122
   class Fitness:
```

Test Harness

The test harness starts by adding the unique letters from each of the wanted strings, as well as the wanted strings themselves, to the set of gene tokens the algorithm can use to build the regex. That way the algorithm doesn't have to struggle to reassemble long sequences or words.

```
100       startTime = datetime.datetime.now()
101       textGenes = wanted | set(c for w in wanted for c in w)
102       fullGeneset = [i for i in allMetas | textGenes]
```

Next come the helper functions, given previously, and finally the call to run the engine.

```
124       optimalFitness = Fitness(len(wanted), len(wanted), 0, expectedLength)

126       best = genetic.get_best(fnGetFitness,
                               max(len(i) for i in textGenes),
128                            optimalFitness, fullGeneset, fnDisplay,
                               fnMutate, poolSize=10)
130       self.assertTrue(not optimalFitness > best.Fitness)

132
   class Fitness:
```

Run

sample result

```
+10 matches: 0 wanted, 2 unwanted, len 3    0:00:00.001003
111 matches: 0 wanted, 0 unwanted, len 3    0:00:00.001003
10  matches: 1 wanted, 0 unwanted, len 2    0:00:00.001003
10?1?   matches: 2 wanted, 0 unwanted, len 5    0:00:00.017079
11|10|01    matches: all wanted, 0 unwanted, len 8  0:00:00.317880
1*0?10* matches: all wanted, 0 unwanted, len 7  0:00:01.137309
```

It worked! It found a successful regex in a fraction of a second but then struggled for a comparatively long time to reduce it to the requested length. A benchmark function will show long it takes on average.

```
132     def test_benchmark(self):
            genetic.Benchmark.run(self.test_two_digits)
134

136 class Fitness:
```

sample benchmark

average (seconds)	standard deviation
0.70	1.02

Performance improvement

Improving the performance of this genetic algorithm requires revisiting the `try..` `except` block in the fitness function, the one that detects invalid regular expressions. The following temporary code change will make it possible to measure how often that happens.

```
11 allMetas = repeatMetas | startMetas
12
13 total = invalid = 0
```

```
16 def get_fitness(genes, wanted, unwanted):
17     global total
18     total += 1
```

```
24    except re.error:
25        global invalid
26        invalid += 1
```

```
136        self.assertTrue(not optimalFitness > best.Fitness)
137        print("{}% of {} generated regexes were invalid".format(
138            int(100 * invalid / total), total
139        ))
```

Running the test a few times gets results like the following:

sample results

```
18% of 82018 generated regexes were invalid
21% of 57325 generated regexes were invalid
23% of 212732 generated regexes were invalid
25% of 216453 generated regexes were invalid
29% of 24124 generated regexes were invalid
34% of 2734 generated regexes were invalid
```

Ouch. A lot of opportunities to find an improvement are lost due to the generated regex being invalid. What could make the regex invalid? To find out, replace the measurement code with code that captures the details of the error in a global variable, with preference for the shortest example of the given error.

```
regexErrorsSeen = {}
14
16 def get_fitness(genes, wanted, unwanted):
       pattern = ''.join(genes)
18     length = len(pattern)

20     try:
           re.compile(pattern)
22     except re.error as e:
           key = str(e)
24         key = key[:key.index("at position")]
           info = [str(e),
26                 "genes = ['{}']".format("', '".join(genes)),
                   "regex: " + pattern]
28         if key not in regexErrorsSeen or len(info[1]) < len(
                   regexErrorsSeen[key][1]):
30             regexErrorsSeen[key] = info
       return Fitness(0, len(wanted), len(unwanted), length)
```

Then print all the errors at the end of the test harness.

```
140        self.assertTrue(not optimalFitness > best.Fitness)
           for info in regexErrorsSeen.values():
142            print("")
               print(info[0])
144            print(info[1])
               print(info[2])
```

Now run the test to get the error samples:

sample errors

```
nothing to repeat at position 0
genes = ['?']
regex: ?

multiple repeat at position 2
genes = ['0', '?', '*']
regex: 0?*
```

Run the test a few times to see variations. There are two situations: The first is when the regex has a repeat-type meta character with no text before it. The other is when two repeat-type meta characters are adjacent. One solution is to repair the regex.

Regex repair

```
16 def get_fitness(genes, wanted, unwanted):
17     pattern = repair_regex(genes)
18     length = len(pattern)
```

The repair function can be built iteratively by running the test and adding code that detects and corrects the errors found. Eventually all the regexes can be repaired. Here's one possible implementation:

```
16 def repair_regex(genes):
       result = []
18     f = repair_ignore_repeat_metas
       for token in genes:
20         f = f(token, result)
       return ''.join(result)
```

```
24 def repair_ignore_repeat_metas(token, result):
       if token in repeatMetas:
26         return repair_ignore_repeat_metas
       result.append(token)
28     return repair_ignore_repeat_metas_following_repeat_or_start_metas
```

```
   def repair_ignore_repeat_metas_following_repeat_or_start_metas(token, result):
32     last = result[-1]
       if token not in repeatMetas:
34         result.append(token)
       elif last in startMetas:
36         pass
       elif token == '?' and last == '?' and len(result) > 2 and \
38                     result[-2] in repeatMetas:
           pass
40     elif last in repeatMetas:
           pass
42     else:
           result.append(token)
44     return repair_ignore_repeat_metas_following_repeat_or_start_metas

46
   def get_fitness(genes, wanted, unwanted):
```

Because the regex repair function does not change the original genes it must also be called from the display function.

```
69 def display(candidate, startTime):
70     timeDiff = datetime.datetime.now() - startTime
71     print("{}\t{}\t{}".format(
72         repair_regex(candidate.Genes), candidate.Fitness, timeDiff))
```

The genetic algorithm now finds the solution much faster on average.

average (seconds)	standard deviation
0.30	0.63

A side effect of repairing the regex is the genes that are removed during the repair become latent. They can be activated if a mutation operator affects the gene to their left. This unexpectedly gives the genetic algorithm an additional tool.

Groups

The second test regex will require the use of the group-type meta characters (and) so support for those must be added.

```
10 startMetas = {'|', '('}
11 endMetas = {')'}
12 allMetas = repeatMetas | startMetas | endMetas
```

Repair

Now running *test_two_digits* produces examples of the next set of regex issues to repair:

sample errors

```
missing ), unterminated subpattern at position 0
genes = ['(']
regex: (

unbalanced parenthesis at position 0
genes = [')']
regex: )
```

The first issue can be solved by appending missing end-group) meta characters to the final regex.

```
def repair_regex(genes):
    result = []
    finals = []                                             <==
    f = repair_ignore_repeat_metas
    for token in genes:
        f = f(token, result, finals)                        <==
    result.extend(reversed(finals))                         <==
    return ''.join(result)
```

```
def repair_ignore_repeat_metas(token, result, finals):
    if token in repeatMetas or token in endMetas:
        return repair_ignore_repeat_metas
    if token == '(':                                        <==
        finals.append(')')
    result.append(token)
    return repair_ignore_repeat_metas_following_repeat_or_start_metas
```

The second issue can be resolved by prefixing the final regex with the missing start-group (meta character.

```
36 def repair_ignore_repeat_metas_following_repeat_or_start_metas(token, result, finals)
       :
       last = result[-1]
38     if token not in repeatMetas:
           if token == '(':                                              <==
40             finals.append(')')
           elif token == ')':
42             match = ''.join(finals).rfind(')')
               if match != -1:
44                 del finals[match]
               else:
46                 result[0:0] = ['(']                                    <==
           result.append(token)
48     elif last in startMetas:
    ...
```

New test

Now that the regex problems have been repaired, the new test can be added and run.

```
    def test_grouping(self):
154     wanted = {"01", "0101", "010101"}
        unwanted = {"0011", ""}
156     self.find_regex(wanted, unwanted, 5)

158 def find_regex(self, wanted, unwanted, expectedLength):
```

sample result

```
01010101|0101() matches: 1 wanted, 0 unwanted, len 15   0:00:00
(0101)|01+  matches: 2 wanted, 0 unwanted, len 10   0:00:00.003005
(01??11?|010101)+   matches: all wanted, 0 unwanted, len 17 0:00:00.106251
(01|)+01    matches: all wanted, 0 unwanted, len 8  0:00:00.108257
(01)+    matches: all wanted, 0 unwanted, len 5  0:00:00.130313
```

Nice!

Character-sets

The next test regex will require the use of the character-set-type meta characters [and]. To support those first add them to the meta global variables.

```
10 startMetas = {'|', '(', '['}
11 endMetas = {')', ']'}
```

As before, next run the existing tests to produce error samples.

sample errors

```
missing ), unterminated subpattern at position 0
genes = ['[', '*', ')', ']', '*', '0']
regex: ([)]*0

unbalanced parenthesis at position 5
genes = ['[', '(', ']', '*', '0']
regex: [(]*0)

unterminated character set at position 0
genes = ['[']
regex: [
```

The first two are caused by the group completion code added in the previous section completing groups that begin or end inside a character-set.

Repair

```
     def repair_regex(genes):
18       result = []
         finals = []
20       f = repair_ignore_repeat_metas
         for token in genes:
22           f = f(token, result, finals)
         if ']' in finals and result[-1] == '[':          <==
24           del result[-1]                                <==
         result.extend(reversed(finals))
26       return ''.join(result)
```

```
     def repair_ignore_repeat_metas(token, result, finals):
30       if token in repeatMetas or token in endMetas:
             return repair_ignore_repeat_metas
32       if token == '(':
             finals.append(')')
34       result.append(token)
         if token == '[':                                 <==
36           finals.append(']')                           <==
             return repair_in_character_set               <==
38       return repair_ignore_repeat_metas_following_repeat_or_start_metas
```

```
     def repair_ignore_repeat_metas_following_repeat_or_start_metas(token, result, finals)
         :
42       last = result[-1]
         if token not in repeatMetas:
44           if token == '[':                                          <==
                 result.append(token)                                  <==
46               finals.append(']')                                    <==
                 return repair_in_character_set                        <==
48           if token == '(':
```

```
     def repair_in_character_set(token, result, finals):
70       if token == ']':
             if result[-1] == '[':
72               del result[-1]
             result.append(token)
74           match = ''.join(finals).rfind(']')
             if match != -1:
76               del finals[match]
             return repair_ignore_repeat_metas_following_repeat_or_start_metas
78       elif token == '[':
             pass
80       elif token == '|' and result[-1] == '|':
             pass  # suppresses FutureWarning about ||
82       else:
             result.append(token)
84       return repair_in_character_set

86
     def get_fitness(genes, wanted, unwanted):
```

New test

```
     def test_state_codes(self):
186      wanted = {"NE", "NV", "NH", "NJ", "NM", "NY", "NC", "ND"}
         unwanted = {"N" + l for l in "ABCDEFGHIJKLMNOPQRSTUVWXYZ"
188                  if "N" + l not in wanted}
         self.find_regex(wanted, unwanted, 11)
190
     def find_regex(self, wanted, unwanted, expectedLength):
```

sample result

```
NM|NC|NV|ND|NJ|NE|NY|NH matches: all wanted, 0 unwanted, len 23 0:00:08.716123
NY|NE|NC|NH|NV?J*D*M*   matches: all wanted, 0 unwanted, len 21 0:00:15.928484
NH|NE|NV|NC*D?J*Y?M?    matches: all wanted, 0 unwanted, len 20 0:00:52.029423
N[D(ECYM??JVYHJD]   matches: all wanted, 0 unwanted, len 17 0:01:51.952601
N[D(ECYM?JVHYJD]    matches: all wanted, 0 unwanted, len 16 0:01:51.957615
N[DECYM?JJVHYD] matches: all wanted, 0 unwanted, len 15 0:01:51.987693
N[VJYM?HDCYED]  matches: all wanted, 0 unwanted, len 14 0:01:52.168333
N[VMCDJYCHED]   matches: all wanted, 0 unwanted, len 13 0:01:52.249548
N[VMCJYHED] matches: all wanted, 0 unwanted, len 11 0:01:52.254562
```

The genetic algorithm succeeds but it can take a long time to discover the character-set solution if it has already found a successful regex. That is because removing repeated items from a character-set, or moving wanted items into a character-set, usually only negatively impact the fitness at this stage. Conversely, those actions may not affect the fitness at all before a working solution is found. That means introducing a character-set that improves the fitness requires multiple sequential steps, that's not something genetic algorithms do well. They are much more successful when they can find ways to make incremental improvements. It would be much more likely to succeed if it had access to a character-set specific operator. That kind of mutation operator might only be useful to particular regexes.

Supporting custom operators

First add an optional parameter to the *find* function and append its contents to the array of mutation operators.

```
191    def find_regex(self, wanted, unwanted, expectedLength,
192                   customOperators=None):
```

```
211        ]
212        if customOperators is not None:
213            mutationOperators.extend(customOperators)
```

Then define the character-set operator.

```
160 def mutate_to_character_set_left(genes, wanted):
        if len(genes) < 4:
162         return False
        ors = [i for i in range(-1, len(genes) - 3)
164             if (i == -1 or genes[i] in startMetas) and
                len(genes[i + 1]) == 2 and
166             genes[i + 1] in wanted and
                (len(genes) == i + 1 or genes[i + 2] == '|' or
168              genes[i + 2] in endMetas)]
        if len(ors) == 0:
170         return False
        lookup = {}
172     for i in ors:
            lookup.setdefault(genes[i + 1][0], []).append(i)
174     min2 = [i for i in lookup.values() if len(i) > 1]
        if len(min2) == 0:
176         return False
```

It finds all the two-character *wanted* strings that have a | meta character, or end-of-array, on both sides. If there are at least two that have the same first character, for example MA| and |ME| then they become candidates to be replaced with a character-set, i.e. M[AE]. Pick a candidate, add the character-set and remove the parts from the regex.

```
        choice = random.choice(min2)
178     characterSet = ['|', genes[choice[0] + 1][0], '[']
        characterSet.extend([genes[i + 1][1] for i in choice])
180     characterSet.append(']')
        for i in reversed(choice):
182         if i >= 0:
                genes[i:i + 2] = []
184     genes.extend(characterSet)
        return True
186

188 def mutate(genes, fnGetFitness, mutationOperators, mutationRoundCounts):
```

Next use the new operator in the test.

```
    def test_state_codes(self):
214     wanted = {"NE", "NV", "NH", "NJ", "NM", "NY", "NC", "ND"}
        unwanted = {"N" + l for l in "ABCDEFGHIJKLMNOPQRSTUVWXYZ"
216             if "N" + l not in wanted}
        customOperators = [                                          <==
218         partial(mutate_to_character_set_left, wanted=wanted),    <==
        ]                                                            <==
220     self.find_regex(wanted, unwanted, 11, customOperators)       <==
```

Now run the test again and it can usually find the regex in a few seconds. Additionally, the situation where it first finds the solution that does not use a character-set becomes rare, and when it does occur the genetic algorithm can easily find the character-set solution.

sample result

```
NY|NM|NH*(V*(J|C*D*|E)) matches: all wanted, 0 unwanted, len 23 0:00:07.173342
NY|NM|NH*V*(J|C*D*|E)   matches: all wanted, 0 unwanted, len 21 0:00:07.252551
N[)EJ+YMCVDH+VV]    matches: all wanted, 0 unwanted, len 16 0:00:08.928685
N[)VYMCV)EVHJD] matches: all wanted, 0 unwanted, len 15 0:00:08.997869
N[VMVC)HEJYD]    matches: all wanted, 0 unwanted, len 13 0:00:09.035971
N[VJVCHEMYD]     matches: all wanted, 0 unwanted, len 12 0:00:09.053016
N[JVCEHDMY] matches: all wanted, 0 unwanted, len 11 0:00:09.183363
```

Repetition

The next regex will use a repetition-type meta token like {2} or {2,}. First add them to the meta global variable.

```
9  repeatMetas = {'?', '*', '+', '{2}', '{2,}'}
```

Run the existing tests and there should be no errors to correct.

New test

```
222    def test_even_length(self):
           wanted = {"00", "01", "10", "11", "0000", "0001", "0010", "0011",
224                   "0100", "0101", "0110", "0111", "1000", "1001", "1010",
                      "1011", "1100", "1101", "1110", "1111"}
226        unwanted = {"0", "1", "000", "001", "010", "011", "100", "101",
                      "110", "111", ""}
228        self.find_regex(wanted, unwanted, 10)

230    def find_regex(self, wanted, unwanted, expectedLength,
```

sample result

```
. . .
([1110]{2})?[10]{2} matches: all wanted, 0 unwanted, len 19 0:00:13.188051
([10]{2})?[10]{2}   matches: all wanted, 0 unwanted, len 17 0:00:15.622529
([1101]{2}|11)+ matches: all wanted, 0 unwanted, len 15 0:00:24.155222
([110101]{2})+  matches: all wanted, 0 unwanted, len 14 0:00:26.304940
([01]{2})+  matches: all wanted, 0 unwanted, len 10 0:00:26.494444
```

The genetic algorithm is slow to find this regex and it can also stall if it finds this particular solution:

```
(00|10|01|11)+  matches: all wanted, 0 unwanted, len 14 0:00:12.010740
```

The following custom mutation operator resolves the problem. It finds all the cases where a | meta character has non-meta characters on both sides. If any are found it picks one and replaces the three genes with a character-set containing only the unique characters from the two non-meta character genes.

Example: `['00', '|', '01']` becomes `['[', '0', '1', ']']`.

```
160  def mutate_to_character_set(genes):
         if len(genes) < 3:
162          return False
         ors = [i for i in range(1, len(genes) - 1)
164              if genes[i] == '|' and
                 genes[i - 1] not in allMetas and
166              genes[i + 1] not in allMetas]
         if len(ors) == 0:
168          return False
         shorter = [i for i in ors
170              if sum(len(w) for w in genes[i - 1:i + 2:2]) >
                 len(set(c for w in genes[i - 1:i + 2:2] for c in w))]
172      if len(shorter) == 0:
             return False
174      index = random.choice(ors)
         distinct = set(c for w in genes[index - 1:index + 2:2] for c in w)
176      sequence = ['['] + [i for i in distinct] + [']']
         genes[index - 1:index + 2] = sequence
178      return True


180

     def mutate_to_character_set_left(genes, wanted):
```

Then change the test to use the new mutation operator.

```
249          customOperators = [
250              mutate_to_character_set,
251          ]
252          self.find_regex(wanted, unwanted, 10, customOperators)
```

Run the test now and it can find the solution every time.

sample result

```
. . .
([0*1000]{2})+  matches: all wanted, 0 unwanted, len 14 0:00:05.221497
([1000]{2})+     matches: all wanted, 0 unwanted, len 12 0:00:05.379950
([01][10])+ matches: all wanted, 0 unwanted, len 11 0:00:05.519291
([01]{2})+  matches: all wanted, 0 unwanted, len 10 0:00:06.595626
```

State codes

The final regex test in this project is to find a reasonably short regex for all 50 U.S. state codes.

```
254   def test_50_state_codes(self):
          wanted = {"AL", "AK", "AZ", "AR", "CA",
256                  "CO", "CT", "DE", "FL", "GA",
                     "HI", "ID", "IL", "IN", "IA",
258                  "KS", "KY", "LA", "ME", "MD",
                     "MA", "MI", "MN", "MS", "MO",
260                  "MT", "NE", "NV", "NH", "NJ",
                     "NM", "NY", "NC", "ND", "OH",
262                  "OK", "OR", "PA", "RI", "SC",
                     "SD", "TN", "TX", "UT", "VT",
264                  "VA", "WA", "WV", "WI", "WY"}
          unwanted = {a + b for a in "ABCDEFGHIJKLMNOPQRSTUVWXYZ"
266                         for b in "ABCDEFGHIJKLMNOPQRSTUVWXYZ"
                            if a + b not in wanted} | \
268                  set(i for i in "ABCDEFGHIJKLMNOPQRSTUVWXYZ")
          customOperators = [
270               partial(mutate_to_character_set_left, wanted=wanted),
                  mutate_to_character_set,
272           ]
          self.find_regex(wanted, unwanted, 120, customOperators)
274
      def find_regex(self, wanted, unwanted, expectedLength,
```

sample result

```
RI|DE|VA|CO|SC|CA|PA|LA|SD|TX|WY|GA|WI|HI|M[IASDETNO]|N[CMDJYMEVH]|VT+|CT|TN|UT|WA|WV
    |FL|A[RLZK]|K[YS]|O[RHK]|I[LNDA]   matches: all wanted, 0 unwanted, len 117
    2:44:17.252814
```

It produces a good result but doing so can take hours.

Now add the following custom mutation operator.

```
    def mutate_add_wanted(genes, wanted):
210     index = random.randrange(0, len(genes) + 1) if len(genes) > 0 else 0
        genes[index:index] = ['|'] + [random.choice(wanted)]
212     return True

214
    def mutate(genes, fnGetFitness, mutationOperators, mutationRoundCounts):
```

It shortcuts the process of getting all the wanted sequences into the regex by inserting a | meta character followed by a random wanted string. That allows the algorithm to quickly switch its focus to reducing the length of the regex.

```
276         customOperators = [
                partial(mutate_to_character_set_left, wanted=wanted),
                mutate_to_character_set,
278             partial(mutate_add_wanted, wanted=[i for i in wanted]),
            ]
280         self.find_regex(wanted, unwanted, 120, customOperators)
```

Run 2

Now the genetic algorithm can find a successful regex in a couple of minutes, but the new mutation operator makes it grow faster than it can be reduced. This results in very long regexes like the one below that then have to be reduced after the fact, a much slower process that can take tens of minutes.

```
|ILKYORNV|||RI|WA|[|AK{2,}{2}MTSLCNV]]LCTDEVA|ME||VA|AK|UT|HI|LA|[FNJ]LANV|MO|AZ|FL|
    TX|||GA|MA[SNCM]|AR||MA|MDLANVAZ|TN|MD|NE[HMSTN)SLD]X|PAN|SCI][NH||RIN|NEVHNV]VT|
    GA[J|CAJI]||MNUWY|CA|NC|WIVDENH]NC|WV|ME|MS|NE|VT|MT|ILLDE|IA|LAWILNV|WY|VA|PA|KY
    |UT|IL|WVTW|PCAMNNC|ID|||AL|VAOK[UV]|NJ|MI|CT|OK|]|NJ|IN||CO[D|UI|MDA]ME]|UTMNC|
    NV|KS|NY|CO|WI|CAMT[LNCNNKSHA|OH|||OWGA]CT+ND|SD|OHSDAAL|K]ARVTMAWICA[
    NYWVWIWYCOOHO|WIZLM|RINH*]ANDILMSN?TN||INAMSWV|MN|WVNJ[OICM][|AVFL]WIMDI]A|N[
    CMEEDEH]]|SC|DE|O[HR]   matches: all wanted, 0 unwanted, len 493     0:02:41.872429
```

The growth of the regex can be controlled through the introduction of a static configuration setting on the *Fitness* class.

```
327 class Fitness:
328     UseRegexLength = False
```

Then update the comparison function.

```
348         if not success:
349             return self.Length <= other.Length if Fitness.UseRegexLength else False
350         return self.Length < other.Length
```

This works by controlling when the engine switches to a new genetic line. When the setting is True then, all other things being equal, the engine will only switch if the other regex is longer.

Finally, enable the setting in the test.

```
260     def test_50_state_codes(self):
261         Fitness.UseGeneLength = True
```

Now the genetic algorithm can find the final regex in just a few minutes.

sample result

```
FL||LA|GA|HI|UT|CT|DE|OK|RI|A[LKRZ]|O[RH]|S[DC]|K[YS]|]|I[NL]|PA|V[AT]|C[OA]|I[AD]|M[
    SETNODIA]|W[VIAY]|T[XN]|N[VCYJEMDH]    matches: all wanted, 0 unwanted, len 120
    0:03:13.662164
```

Excellent! Unsurprisingly *test_state_codes* benefits from the use of this setting too.

Exercise

Notice in the final regex above that there are still characters that could be removed, for example in |K[YS]|]|. Also, CT could be merged into C[OA]. Those would eventually be discovered by the genetic algorithm if a shorter goal length was used. However, there are other potential savings that it is unlikely to find. For example, LA, GA, and PA could be combined if there was a mutation operator for creating character-sets with a common ending letter. Try adding one.

This is a great project for experimentation and there are many more regex meta characters to play with.

Summary

This project introduced three new concepts. The first is the idea of repairing the chromosome, which is useful when some phenotype values are incompatible. The second is latent genes, or genes that are ignored in invalid combinations but used in valid ones, thus giving the algorithm another tool. The third concept is using the change in the number of genes to control chromosome growth.

Tic-tac-toe

The final project is to build a genetic algorithm that produces human-readable rules for playing Tic-tac-toe without losing.

A Tic-tac-toe game board has 9 squares in a 3 by 3 grid. In this project they are numbered as follows:

```
1  2  3
4  5  6
7  8  9
```

All the squares start empty. The players take turns placing a marker (X for the first player to move, O for the opponent) on an empty square with the goal of getting three of their own markers in a single row, column, or diagonal before their opponent does.

That should be enough information to build the game portion. If you've worked through the previous projects you know what comes next so I'm not going to go over every line of code. Instead, I'm going to point out a couple of new things. If you get stuck, or just want to start with working code, check the code sample for this project.

Genes

The goal is to end up with a relatively short list of rules that a child could use to play the game. That's why the rules need to be human-readable. That also eliminates index specific rules like *index 1 is EMPTY and index 3 has an OPPONENT piece*. That is not the way we teach children to play this game.

There are two gene categories: location and content.

Location genes select a move based on the location of the empty square. For example: is it a corner, edge, the center, in the top/middle/bottom row, left/middle/right column, in a diagonal, etc.

Content rules look at the content of the row/column/diagonal containing the empty square. Examples might resemble the following, depending on how much time you want to spend on grammar:

```
its ROW has 2 OPPONENT pieces
its COLUMN has 1 EMPTY square
its DIAGONAL has NONE of MY pieces
```

Move selection should work like this: The engine passes the current set of empty squares to the first rule, or more precisely filter, in the gene sequence. If a rule eliminates all the remaining empty board positions, skip it. Otherwise use its output as the input for the next filter in the gene sequence. Evaluation stops when there are no more rules, or a rule reduces the set of empty squares to one. When only one square remains, that is where the genetic algorithm's piece should be placed.

Fitness

Calculate the fitness by playing all possible games given 1) the genetic algorithm makes the first move, and 2) the opponent makes the first move. Whenever it is the opponent's turn, all possible moves should be played out unless there is a winning move for the opponent, in which case it wins. This can be done depth-first or breadth-first as you prefer. If at any point there are empty squares and the genetic algorithm cannot provide a move, it loses that game.

Count the number of times the genetic algorithm wins, loses, and ties. Then use those counts in a Fitness comparison function like the following:

ticTacToeTests.py

```
624    def __gt__(self, other):
           if self.PercentLosses != other.PercentLosses:
626            return self.PercentLosses < other.PercentLosses

628        if self.Losses > 0:
               return False
630
           if self.Ties != other.Ties:
632            return self.Ties < other.Ties
           return self.GeneCount < other.GeneCount
```

Using the *percentage* instead of the *absolute number* of losses allows the number of games played to vary. You should try the other way too so you can see how the behavior changes.

Mutation and Crossover

Use adaptive mutation rules similar to the ones in the previous project.

For crossover, combine the first half of the parent, with the last half of the donor, then call mutate. Calling mutate afterward is very important. It helps to prevent the pool from converging to a single gene sequence.

```
         def fnCrossover(parent, donor):
238          child = parent[0:int(len(parent) / 2)] + \
                 donor[int(len(donor) / 2):]
240          fnMutate(child)
             return child
```

Results

It takes between 10 and 30 minutes for my implementation to produce a set of rules that never lose and there is a lot of duplication in that first success:

```
its ROW has 2 MINE
its DIAGONAL has 2 MINE
its ROW has 2 OPPONENT
is in CENTER
its DIAGONAL has 2 OPPONENT
its COLUMN has 2 OPPONENT
its COLUMN has 0 OPPONENT
is in DIAGONAL
its ROW has 2 MINE
its ROW has 0 MINE
its DIAGONAL has 1 OPPONENT
is a CORNER
its ROW has 1 OPPONENT
its ROW has 2 OPPONENT
its COLUMN has 1 OPPONENT
is in RIGHT COLUMN
is in BOTTOM ROW
its ROW has 0 MINE
its DIAGONAL has 0 OPPONENT
its DIAGONAL has 1 OPPONENT
is in BOTTOM ROW
0.0% Losses (0), 35.6% Ties (289), 64.4% Wins (522), 21 rules
0:21:41.420539
```

The final set of rules, however, has no duplication and not only guarantees we never lose, it also helps to avoid tie games when the opponent is experienced. It generally takes 1-2 hours to plateau at 14 rules and 135 ties.

```
its DIAGONAL has 2 MINE          <==
its ROW has 2 MINE               <==
its COLUMN has 2 MINE            <==
its COLUMN has 2 OPPONENT        <==
its ROW has 2 OPPONENT           <==
its DIAGONAL has 0 MINE
its COLUMN has 0 MINE
its ROW has 0 OPPONENT
is in MIDDLE COLUMN
is in TOP ROW
its DIAGONAL has 1 OPPONENT
its COLUMN has 1 OPPONENT
is a CORNER
is in LEFT COLUMN
0.0% Losses (0), 21.3% Ties (135), 78.7% Wins (498), 14 rules
2:07:36.146149
```

Rules 1, 2 and 3 detect the winning move for us. Rules 4 and 5 handle blocking the opponent from winning. The rest of the rules work to minimize the number of tie games.

There's nothing clever about these rules and they perform well. They are not the only generic rules possible however. For example, adding rules that check for row-, column- and diagonal-opposites of the empty square enables the genetic algorithm to find a set of rules that result in even fewer ties. A row-opposite for a square is the square at the other end of the row and a column-opposite is the square at the other end of the column.

```
its ROW has 2 MINE               <==
its DIAGONAL has 2 MINE          <==
its COLUMN has 2 MINE            <==
its ROW has 2 OPPONENT           <==
its COLUMN has 2 OPPONENT        <==
is in CENTER                     <==
its ROW has 0 OPPONENT
its DIAGONAL has 0 MINE
ROW-OPPOSITE is OPPONENT
is in BOTTOM ROW
its DIAGONAL has 1 OPPONENT
is a CORNER
its COLUMN has 1 MINE
its COLUMN has 1 OPPONENT
is in LEFT COLUMN
0.0% Losses (0), 19.6% Ties (127), 80.4% Wins (522), 15 rules
```

As before, rules 1, 2 and 3 detect the winning move for us. Rules 4 and 5 handle blocking the opponent from winning. That means the center (rule 6) is the most valuable square on the board, as many of us learned as children.

Tournament selection

Tic-tac-toe is a simple enough game that we have the ability play out every possible game in order to evolve an optimal solution. Many other games have so many potential moves that playing all possible games is not an option. That means we need a way to get a good set of rules with partial knowledge. One way to do that is through tournament selection.

In tournament selection a generation of gene sequences (rules in this problem) is created. Each is then tested against every other gene sequence in that generation to get a fitness value. The gene sequences are then ranked by their fitness value and those with the best fitness values become the parents used to populate the next generation through crossover and mutation. Their children form about 90 percent of the next generation. The remainder could be copies of the parents (this is called *elitism*), mutated parents, randomly generated, or some combination thereof.

Because successive generations are based on the previous one, the pool can rapidly lose diversity. This can cause the genetic algorithm to become stuck at a local minimum or maximum. That makes it doubly important to mutate the children produced through crossover. A small number of randomly generated gene sequences can be added to the pool each generation as well but this is less effective as a random sequence is unlikely to compete well against a highly evolved one.

Implementation

The tournament implementation will be added to the genetic module to make it available for other projects.

First add an `enum` that can be used like an integer for array indexes.

genetic.py

```
7 from enum import IntEnum                                        <==
8 from math import exp
```

genetic.py

```
168 class CompetitionResult(IntEnum):
        Loss = 0,
170     Tie = 1,
        Win = 2,
172

174 class Chromosome:
```

The tournament function first populates the parent pool and creates a convenience function for getting a parent's sort key.

```
166 def tournament(generate_parent, crossover, compete, display, sort_key,
                   numParents=10, max_generations=100):
168     pool = [[generate_parent(), [0, 0, 0]]
                for _ in range(1 + numParents * numParents)]
170     best, bestScore = pool[0]

172     def getSortKey(x):
            return sort_key(x[0], x[1][CompetitionResult.Win],
174                         x[1][CompetitionResult.Tie],
                            x[1][CompetitionResult.Loss])
```

Next, each gene sequence plays against every other gene sequence both as first-to-move and as the opponent, keeping track of wins, losses and ties.

```
        generation = 0
178     while generation < max_generations:
            generation += 1
180         for i in range(0, len(pool)):
                for j in range(0, len(pool)):
182                 if i == j:
                        continue
184                 playera, scorea = pool[i]
                    playerb, scoreb = pool[j]
186                 result = compete(playera, playerb)
                    scorea[result] += 1
188                 scoreb[2 - result] += 1
```

The gene sequences are then sorted and the display function is called if an improvement is found.

```
190         pool.sort(key=getSortKey, reverse=True)
            if getSortKey(pool[0]) > getSortKey([best, bestScore]):
192             best, bestScore = pool[0]
                display(best, bestScore[CompetitionResult.Win],
194                     bestScore[CompetitionResult.Tie],
                        bestScore[CompetitionResult.Loss], generation)
```

Finally, a new generation is created by crossbreeding the best N gene sequences. They are also included in the new generation along with 1 additional randomly generated gene sequence. When the maximum number of generations have completed, the function returns the best gene sequence that was seen.

```
196        parents = [pool[i][0] for i in range(numParents)]
           pool = [[crossover(parents[i], parents[j]), [0, 0, 0]]
198              for i in range(len(parents))
                 for j in range(len(parents))
200              if i != j]
           pool.extend([parent, [0, 0, 0]] for parent in parents)
202        pool.append([generate_parent(), [0, 0, 0]])
       return best
```

There's nothing special about the usage of this function so I won't repeat it here - see test_tournament in the code for this project.

It takes a little over a minute to produce a set of rules that never loses *against the other rules in its generation.* That's the main caveat, the result is only as good as the sample size. The result improves if more parents are used since $O(n^4)$ games are played in each generation but that can take quite a while.

sample result with 13 parents and 100 generations

```
-- generation 73 --
    its ROW has 2 OPPONENT
    its COLUMN has 2 OPPONENT
    its COLUMN has 2 MINE
    its ROW has 2 MINE
    its DIAGONAL has 0 OPPONENT
    is in MIDDLE COLUMN
    its COLUMN has 0 OPPONENT
    is in LEFT COLUMN
    is a CORNER
    is in TOP ROW
0.0% Losses (0), 45.0% Ties (152), 55.0% Wins (186), 10 rules
0:16:18.756137
```

Summary

This project introduced a new method of sampling and recombining gene sequences to find a good combination. One potential usage is to quickly find a starting place for a slower, more comprehensive survey of the problem space.

Afterword

This book has given you a solid introduction to genetic algorithms. There is still a lot more to learn on this topic but you now know enough to teach yourself, and that will lead to true mastery. For your next step you have several options, they include:

- use the module from this book to explore problems in your field of expertise,

- switch to a different Python-based module and repeat some of the experiments in order to spin up your knowledge of that module,

- learn about another machine learning tool like decision trees or neural networks.

Other projects you could explore:

- Optimize a neural network https://t.co/tZammOHeSk

- Evolve wheeled vehicles https://youtu.be/uxourrlPlf8

- Create optimal sorting networks https://t.co/jvqma9M8Zs

- Reproduce pictures https://youtu.be/SJEoyMsG_qM

- and much more...

If you found this book to be valuable then please take some time to write a review or mention it on social media or ask your school or local public library to order a copy for their collection.

Good luck!

Clinton Sheppard

Other books by Clinton Sheppard

Get a hands-on introduction to building and using decision trees and random forests. Tree-based machine learning algorithms are used to categorize data by known outcomes in order to facilitate predicting outcomes in new situations.

You will learn not only how to use decision trees and random forests for classification and regression, and their respective limitations, but also how the algorithms that build them work. Each project introduces a new data concern and then walks you through modifying the code, thus building the engine just-in-time. Along the way you will gain experience making decision trees and random forests work for you.

https://www.amazon.com/dp/B0756FGJCP/

https://www.amazon.com/dp/1975860977/

Learn to read more than 100 essential Chinese characters with lessons that build your vocabulary one character at a time and include more than 1,650 practice sentences and phrases.

The characters in this book were selected to expose you to a variety of grammar patterns and common words. When you finish this book you will know a little more than 28 percent of the characters you will encounter in any given text on average.

https://www.amazon.com/dp/1732029814

Final code from each project

Chapter 1: Hello World!

guessPasswordTests.py

```python
# File: guessPasswordTests.py
#    from chapter 1 of _Genetic Algorithms with Python_
#
# Author: Clinton Sheppard <fluentcoder@gmail.com>
# Copyright (c) 2016 Clinton Sheppard
#
# Licensed under the Apache License, Version 2.0 (the "License").
# You may not use this file except in compliance with the License.
# You may obtain a copy of the License at
#    http://www.apache.org/licenses/LICENSE-2.0
#
# Unless required by applicable law or agreed to in writing, software
# distributed under the License is distributed on an "AS IS" BASIS,
# WITHOUT WARRANTIES OR CONDITIONS OF ANY KIND, either express or
# implied.  See the License for the specific language governing
# permissions and limitations under the License.

import datetime
import random
import unittest

import genetic


def get_fitness(guess, target):
    return sum(1 for expected, actual in zip(target, guess)
               if expected == actual)


def display(candidate, startTime):
    timeDiff = datetime.datetime.now() - startTime
    print("{}\t{}\t{}".format(
        candidate.Genes, candidate.Fitness, timeDiff))


class GuessPasswordTests(unittest.TestCase):
    geneset = " abcdefghijklmnopqrstuvwxyzABCDEFGHIJKLMNOPQRSTUVWXYZ!.,"
```

```python
    def test_Hello_World(self):
        target = "Hello World!"
        self.guess_password(target)

    def test_For_I_am_fearfully_and_wonderfully_made(self):
        target = "For I am fearfully and wonderfully made."
        self.guess_password(target)

    def guess_password(self, target):
        startTime = datetime.datetime.now()

        def fnGetFitness(genes):
            return get_fitness(genes, target)

        def fnDisplay(candidate):
            display(candidate, startTime)

        optimalFitness = len(target)
        best = genetic.get_best(fnGetFitness, len(target), optimalFitness,
                                self.geneset, fnDisplay)
        self.assertEqual(best.Genes, target)

    def test_Random(self):
        length = 150
        target = ''.join(random.choice(self.geneset)
                         for _ in range(length))

        self.guess_password(target)

    def test_benchmark(self):
        genetic.Benchmark.run(self.test_Random)


if __name__ == '__main__':
    unittest.main()
```

genetic.py

```python
# File: genetic.py
#     from chapter 1 of _Genetic Algorithms with Python_
#
# Author: Clinton Sheppard <fluentcoder@gmail.com>
# Copyright (c) 2016 Clinton Sheppard
#
# Licensed under the Apache License, Version 2.0 (the "License").
# You may not use this file except in compliance with the License.
# You may obtain a copy of the License at
#   http://www.apache.org/licenses/LICENSE-2.0
#
# Unless required by applicable law or agreed to in writing, software
# distributed under the License is distributed on an "AS IS" BASIS,
# WITHOUT WARRANTIES OR CONDITIONS OF ANY KIND, either express or
```

```python
# implied.  See the License for the specific language governing
# permissions and limitations under the License.

import random
import statistics
import sys
import time


def _generate_parent(length, geneSet, get_fitness):
    genes = []
    while len(genes) < length:
        sampleSize = min(length - len(genes), len(geneSet))
        genes.extend(random.sample(geneSet, sampleSize))
    genes = ''.join(genes)
    fitness = get_fitness(genes)
    return Chromosome(genes, fitness)


def _mutate(parent, geneSet, get_fitness):
    index = random.randrange(0, len(parent.Genes))
    childGenes = list(parent.Genes)
    newGene, alternate = random.sample(geneSet, 2)
    childGenes[index] = alternate if newGene == childGenes[index] else newGene
    genes = ''.join(childGenes)
    fitness = get_fitness(genes)
    return Chromosome(genes, fitness)


def get_best(get_fitness, targetLen, optimalFitness, geneSet, display):
    random.seed()
    bestParent = _generate_parent(targetLen, geneSet, get_fitness)
    display(bestParent)
    if bestParent.Fitness >= optimalFitness:
        return bestParent
    while True:
        child = _mutate(bestParent, geneSet, get_fitness)
        if bestParent.Fitness >= child.Fitness:
            continue
        display(child)
        if child.Fitness >= optimalFitness:
            return child
        bestParent = child


class Chromosome:
    def __init__(self, genes, fitness):
        self.Genes = genes
        self.Fitness = fitness


class Benchmark:
    @staticmethod
```

```python
def run(function):
    timings = []
    stdout = sys.stdout
    for i in range(100):
        sys.stdout = None
        startTime = time.time()
        function()
        seconds = time.time() - startTime
        sys.stdout = stdout
        timings.append(seconds)
        mean = statistics.mean(timings)
        if i < 10 or i % 10 == 9:
            print("{} {:3.2f} {:3.2f}".format(
                1 + i, mean,
                statistics.stdev(timings, mean) if i > 1 else 0))
```

Chapter 2: One Max Problem

oneMaxTests.py

```python
# File: oneMaxTests.py
#    from chapter 2 of _Genetic Algorithms with Python_
#
# Author: Clinton Sheppard <fluentcoder@gmail.com>
# Copyright (c) 2016 Clinton Sheppard
#
# Licensed under the Apache License, Version 2.0 (the "License").
# You may not use this file except in compliance with the License.
# You may obtain a copy of the License at
#    http://www.apache.org/licenses/LICENSE-2.0
#
# Unless required by applicable law or agreed to in writing, software
# distributed under the License is distributed on an "AS IS" BASIS,
# WITHOUT WARRANTIES OR CONDITIONS OF ANY KIND, either express or
# implied.  See the License for the specific language governing
# permissions and limitations under the License.

import datetime
import unittest

import genetic


def get_fitness(genes):
    return genes.count(1)


def display(candidate, startTime):
    timeDiff = datetime.datetime.now() - startTime
    print("{}...{}\t{:3.2f}\t{}".format(
        ''.join(map(str, candidate.Genes[:15])),
```

```
            ''.join(map(str, candidate.Genes[-15:])),
        candidate.Fitness,
        timeDiff))


class OneMaxTests(unittest.TestCase):
    def test(self, length=100):
        geneset = [0, 1]
        startTime = datetime.datetime.now()

        def fnDisplay(candidate):
            display(candidate, startTime)

        def fnGetFitness(genes):
            return get_fitness(genes)

        optimalFitness = length
        best = genetic.get_best(fnGetFitness, length, optimalFitness,
                                geneset, fnDisplay)
        self.assertEqual(best.Fitness, optimalFitness)

    def test_benchmark(self):
        genetic.Benchmark.run(lambda: self.test(4000))


if __name__ == '__main__':
    unittest.main()
```

genetic.py

```
# File: genetic.py
#     from chapter 2 of _Genetic Algorithms with Python_
#
# Author: Clinton Sheppard <fluentcoder@gmail.com>
# Copyright (c) 2016 Clinton Sheppard
#
# Licensed under the Apache License, Version 2.0 (the "License").
# You may not use this file except in compliance with the License.
# You may obtain a copy of the License at
#   http://www.apache.org/licenses/LICENSE-2.0
#
# Unless required by applicable law or agreed to in writing, software
# distributed under the License is distributed on an "AS IS" BASIS,
# WITHOUT WARRANTIES OR CONDITIONS OF ANY KIND, either express or
# implied.  See the License for the specific language governing
# permissions and limitations under the License.

import random
import statistics
import sys
import time
```

```python
def _generate_parent(length, geneSet, get_fitness):
    genes = []
    while len(genes) < length:
        sampleSize = min(length - len(genes), len(geneSet))
        genes.extend(random.sample(geneSet, sampleSize))
    fitness = get_fitness(genes)
    return Chromosome(genes, fitness)


def _mutate(parent, geneSet, get_fitness):
    childGenes = parent.Genes[:]
    index = random.randrange(0, len(parent.Genes))
    newGene, alternate = random.sample(geneSet, 2)
    childGenes[index] = alternate if newGene == childGenes[index] else newGene
    fitness = get_fitness(childGenes)
    return Chromosome(childGenes, fitness)


def get_best(get_fitness, targetLen, optimalFitness, geneSet, display):
    random.seed()
    bestParent = _generate_parent(targetLen, geneSet, get_fitness)
    display(bestParent)
    if bestParent.Fitness >= optimalFitness:
        return bestParent
    while True:
        child = _mutate(bestParent, geneSet, get_fitness)
        if bestParent.Fitness >= child.Fitness:
            continue
        display(child)
        if child.Fitness >= optimalFitness:
            return child
        bestParent = child


class Chromosome:
    def __init__(self, genes, fitness):
        self.Genes = genes
        self.Fitness = fitness


class Benchmark:
    @staticmethod
    def run(function):
        timings = []
        stdout = sys.stdout
        for i in range(100):
            sys.stdout = None
            startTime = time.time()
            function()
            seconds = time.time() - startTime
            sys.stdout = stdout
            timings.append(seconds)
```

```
                    mean = statistics.mean(timings)
                    if i < 10 or i % 10 == 9:
                        print("{} {:3.2f} {:3.2f}".format(
                            1 + i, mean,
                            statistics.stdev(timings, mean) if i > 1 else 0))
```

guessPasswordTests.py

```
# File: guessPasswordTests.py
#    from chapter 2 of _Genetic Algorithms with Python_
#
# Author: Clinton Sheppard <fluentcoder@gmail.com>
# Copyright (c) 2016 Clinton Sheppard
#
# Licensed under the Apache License, Version 2.0 (the "License").
# You may not use this file except in compliance with the License.
# You may obtain a copy of the License at
#    http://www.apache.org/licenses/LICENSE-2.0
#
# Unless required by applicable law or agreed to in writing, software
# distributed under the License is distributed on an "AS IS" BASIS,
# WITHOUT WARRANTIES OR CONDITIONS OF ANY KIND, either express or
# implied.  See the License for the specific language governing
# permissions and limitations under the License.

import datetime
import random
import unittest

import genetic


def get_fitness(guess, target):
    return sum(1 for expected, actual in zip(target, guess)
              if expected == actual)


def display(candidate, startTime):
    timeDiff = datetime.datetime.now() - startTime
    print("{}\t{}\t{}".format(
        ''.join(candidate.Genes),
        candidate.Fitness,
        timeDiff))


class GuessPasswordTests(unittest.TestCase):
    geneset = " abcdefghijklmnopqrstuvwxyzABCDEFGHIJKLMNOPQRSTUVWXYZ!.,"

    def test_Hello_World(self):
        target = "Hello World!"
        self.guess_password(target)
```

```python
    def test_For_I_am_fearfully_and_wonderfully_made(self):
        target = "For I am fearfully and wonderfully made."
        self.guess_password(target)

    def guess_password(self, target):
        startTime = datetime.datetime.now()

        def fnGetFitness(genes):
            return get_fitness(genes, target)

        def fnDisplay(candidate):
            display(candidate, startTime)

        optimalFitness = len(target)
        best = genetic.get_best(fnGetFitness, len(target), optimalFitness,
                                self.geneset, fnDisplay)
        self.assertEqual(''.join(best.Genes), target)

    def test_Random(self):
        length = 150
        target = ''.join(random.choice(self.geneset)
                         for _ in range(length))

        self.guess_password(target)

    def test_benchmark(self):
        genetic.Benchmark.run(self.test_Random)


if __name__ == '__main__':
    unittest.main()
```

Chapter 3: Sorted Numbers

sortedNumbersTests.py

```python
# File: sortedNumbersTests.py
#    from chapter 3 of _Genetic Algorithms with Python_
#
# Author: Clinton Sheppard <fluentcoder@gmail.com>
# Copyright (c) 2016 Clinton Sheppard
#
# Licensed under the Apache License, Version 2.0 (the "License").
# You may not use this file except in compliance with the License.
# You may obtain a copy of the License at
#    http://www.apache.org/licenses/LICENSE-2.0
#
# Unless required by applicable law or agreed to in writing, software
# distributed under the License is distributed on an "AS IS" BASIS,
# WITHOUT WARRANTIES OR CONDITIONS OF ANY KIND, either express or
# implied.  See the License for the specific language governing
# permissions and limitations under the License.


import datetime
import unittest

import genetic


def get_fitness(genes):
    fitness = 1
    gap = 0

    for i in range(1, len(genes)):
        if genes[i] > genes[i - 1]:
            fitness += 1
        else:
            gap += genes[i - 1] - genes[i]
    return Fitness(fitness, gap)


def display(candidate, startTime):
    timeDiff = datetime.datetime.now() - startTime
    print("{}\t=> {}\t{}".format(
        ', '.join(map(str, candidate.Genes)),
        candidate.Fitness,
        timeDiff))


class SortedNumbersTests(unittest.TestCase):
    def test_sort_10_numbers(self):
        self.sort_numbers(10)

    def sort_numbers(self, totalNumbers):
```

```python
        geneset = [i for i in range(100)]
        startTime = datetime.datetime.now()

        def fnDisplay(candidate):
            display(candidate, startTime)

        def fnGetFitness(genes):
            return get_fitness(genes)

        optimalFitness = Fitness(totalNumbers, 0)
        best = genetic.get_best(fnGetFitness, totalNumbers, optimalFitness,
                                geneset, fnDisplay)
        self.assertTrue(not optimalFitness > best.Fitness)

    def test_benchmark(self):
        genetic.Benchmark.run(lambda: self.sort_numbers(40))


class Fitness:
    def __init__(self, numbersInSequenceCount, totalGap):
        self.NumbersInSequenceCount = numbersInSequenceCount
        self.TotalGap = totalGap

    def __gt__(self, other):
        if self.NumbersInSequenceCount != other.NumbersInSequenceCount:
            return self.NumbersInSequenceCount > other.NumbersInSequenceCount
        return self.TotalGap < other.TotalGap

    def __str__(self):
        return "{} Sequential, {} Total Gap".format(
            self.NumbersInSequenceCount,
            self.TotalGap)


if __name__ == '__main__':
    unittest.main()
```

genetic.py

```python
# File: genetic.py
#    from chapter 3 of _Genetic Algorithms with Python_
#
# Author: Clinton Sheppard <fluentcoder@gmail.com>
# Copyright (c) 2016 Clinton Sheppard
#
# Licensed under the Apache License, Version 2.0 (the "License").
# You may not use this file except in compliance with the License.
# You may obtain a copy of the License at
#    http://www.apache.org/licenses/LICENSE-2.0
#
# Unless required by applicable law or agreed to in writing, software
# distributed under the License is distributed on an "AS IS" BASIS,
```

```
# WITHOUT WARRANTIES OR CONDITIONS OF ANY KIND, either express or
# implied.  See the License for the specific language governing
# permissions and limitations under the License.

import random
import statistics
import sys
import time


def _generate_parent(length, geneSet, get_fitness):
    genes = []
    while len(genes) < length:
        sampleSize = min(length - len(genes), len(geneSet))
        genes.extend(random.sample(geneSet, sampleSize))
    fitness = get_fitness(genes)
    return Chromosome(genes, fitness)


def _mutate(parent, geneSet, get_fitness):
    childGenes = parent.Genes[:]
    index = random.randrange(0, len(parent.Genes))
    newGene, alternate = random.sample(geneSet, 2)
    childGenes[index] = alternate if newGene == childGenes[index] else newGene
    fitness = get_fitness(childGenes)
    return Chromosome(childGenes, fitness)


def get_best(get_fitness, targetLen, optimalFitness, geneSet, display):
    random.seed()

    def fnMutate(parent):
        return _mutate(parent, geneSet, get_fitness)

    def fnGenerateParent():
        return _generate_parent(targetLen, geneSet, get_fitness)

    for improvement in _get_improvement(fnMutate, fnGenerateParent):
        display(improvement)
        if not optimalFitness > improvement.Fitness:
            return improvement


def _get_improvement(new_child, generate_parent):
    bestParent = generate_parent()
    yield bestParent
    while True:
        child = new_child(bestParent)
        if bestParent.Fitness > child.Fitness:
            continue
        if not child.Fitness > bestParent.Fitness:
            bestParent = child
            continue
```

```
            yield child
            bestParent = child


class Chromosome:
    def __init__(self, genes, fitness):
        self.Genes = genes
        self.Fitness = fitness


class Benchmark:
    @staticmethod
    def run(function):
        timings = []
        stdout = sys.stdout
        for i in range(100):
            sys.stdout = None
            startTime = time.time()
            function()
            seconds = time.time() - startTime
            sys.stdout = stdout
            timings.append(seconds)
            mean = statistics.mean(timings)
            if i < 10 or i % 10 == 9:
                print("{} {:3.2f} {:3.2f}".format(
                    1 + i, mean,
                    statistics.stdev(timings, mean) if i > 1 else 0))
```

Chapter 4: the 8 Queens Puzzle

8queensTests.py

```
# File: 8queensTests.py
#     from chapter 4 of _Genetic Algorithms with Python_
#
# Author: Clinton Sheppard <fluentcoder@gmail.com>
# Copyright (c) 2016 Clinton Sheppard
#
# Licensed under the Apache License, Version 2.0 (the "License").
# You may not use this file except in compliance with the License.
# You may obtain a copy of the License at
#    http://www.apache.org/licenses/LICENSE-2.0
#
# Unless required by applicable law or agreed to in writing, software
# distributed under the License is distributed on an "AS IS" BASIS,
# WITHOUT WARRANTIES OR CONDITIONS OF ANY KIND, either express or
# implied.  See the License for the specific language governing
# permissions and limitations under the License.


import datetime
import unittest
```

```python
import genetic


def get_fitness(genes, size):
    board = Board(genes, size)
    rowsWithQueens = set()
    colsWithQueens = set()
    northEastDiagonalsWithQueens = set()
    southEastDiagonalsWithQueens = set()
    for row in range(size):
        for col in range(size):
            if board.get(row, col) == 'Q':
                rowsWithQueens.add(row)
                colsWithQueens.add(col)
                northEastDiagonalsWithQueens.add(row + col)
                southEastDiagonalsWithQueens.add(size - 1 - row + col)
    total = size - len(rowsWithQueens) \
            + size - len(colsWithQueens) \
            + size - len(northEastDiagonalsWithQueens) \
            + size - len(southEastDiagonalsWithQueens)
    return Fitness(total)


def display(candidate, startTime, size):
    timeDiff = datetime.datetime.now() - startTime
    board = Board(candidate.Genes, size)
    board.print()
    print("{}\t- {}\t{}".format(
        ' '.join(map(str, candidate.Genes)),
        candidate.Fitness,
        timeDiff))


class EightQueensTests(unittest.TestCase):
    def test(self, size=8):
        geneset = [i for i in range(size)]
        startTime = datetime.datetime.now()

        def fnDisplay(candidate):
            display(candidate, startTime, size)

        def fnGetFitness(genes):
            return get_fitness(genes, size)

        optimalFitness = Fitness(0)
        best = genetic.get_best(fnGetFitness, 2 * size, optimalFitness,
                                geneset, fnDisplay)
        self.assertTrue(not optimalFitness > best.Fitness)

    def test_benchmark(self):
        genetic.Benchmark.run(lambda: self.test(20))
```

```python
class Board:
    def __init__(self, genes, size):
        board = [['.'] * size for _ in range(size)]
        for index in range(0, len(genes), 2):
            row = genes[index]
            column = genes[index + 1]
            board[column][row] = 'Q'
        self._board = board

    def get(self, row, column):
        return self._board[column][row]

    def print(self):
        # 0,0 prints in bottom left corner
        for i in reversed(range(len(self._board))):
            print(' '.join(self._board[i]))


class Fitness:
    def __init__(self, total):
        self.Total = total

    def __gt__(self, other):
        return self.Total < other.Total

    def __str__(self):
        return "{}".format(self.Total)


if __name__ == '__main__':
    unittest.main()
```

Chapter 5: Graph Coloring

graphColoringTests.py

```python
# File: graphColoringTests.py
#    from chapter 5 of _Genetic Algorithms with Python_
#
# Author: Clinton Sheppard <fluentcoder@gmail.com>
# Copyright (c) 2016 Clinton Sheppard
#
# Licensed under the Apache License, Version 2.0 (the "License").
# You may not use this file except in compliance with the License.
# You may obtain a copy of the License at
#    http://www.apache.org/licenses/LICENSE-2.0
#
# Unless required by applicable law or agreed to in writing, software
# distributed under the License is distributed on an "AS IS" BASIS,
# WITHOUT WARRANTIES OR CONDITIONS OF ANY KIND, either express or
```

```python
# implied.  See the License for the specific language governing
# permissions and limitations under the License.

import datetime
import unittest

import genetic


def load_data(localFileName):
    """ expects: T D1 [D2 ... DN]
        where T is the record type
        and D1 .. DN are record-type appropriate data elements
    """
    rules = set()
    nodes = set()
    with open(localFileName, mode='r') as infile:
        content = infile.read().splitlines()
    for row in content:
        if row[0] == 'e':  # e aa bb, aa and bb are node ids
            nodeIds = row.split(' ')[1:3]
            rules.add(Rule(nodeIds[0], nodeIds[1]))
            nodes.add(nodeIds[0])
            nodes.add(nodeIds[1])
            continue
        if row[0] == 'n':  # n aa ww, aa is a node id, ww is a weight
            nodeIds = row.split(' ')
            nodes.add(nodeIds[1])
    return rules, nodes


def build_rules(items):
    rulesAdded = {}
    for state, adjacent in items.items():
        for adjacentState in adjacent:
            if adjacentState == '':
                continue
            rule = Rule(state, adjacentState)
            if rule in rulesAdded:
                rulesAdded[rule] += 1
            else:
                rulesAdded[rule] = 1
    for k, v in rulesAdded.items():
        if v != 2:
            print("rule {} is not bidirectional".format(k))
    return rulesAdded.keys()


def get_fitness(genes, rules, stateIndexLookup):
    rulesThatPass = sum(1 for rule in rules
                        if rule.IsValid(genes, stateIndexLookup))
    return rulesThatPass
```

```python
def display(candidate, startTime):
    timeDiff = datetime.datetime.now() - startTime
    print("{}\t{}\t{}".format(
        ''.join(map(str, candidate.Genes)),
        candidate.Fitness,
        timeDiff))


class GraphColoringTests(unittest.TestCase):
    def test_states(self):
        self.color("adjacent_states.col",
                    ["Orange", "Yellow", "Green", "Blue"])

    def test_R100_1gb(self):
        self.color("R100_1gb.col",
                    ["Red", "Orange", "Yellow", "Green", "Blue", "Indigo"])

    def test_benchmark(self):
        genetic.Benchmark.run(lambda: self.test_R100_1gb())

    def color(self, file, colors):
        rules, nodes = load_data(file)
        optimalValue = len(rules)
        colorLookup = {color[0]: color for color in colors}
        geneset = list(colorLookup.keys())
        startTime = datetime.datetime.now()
        nodeIndexLookup = {key: index
                           for index, key in enumerate(sorted(nodes))}

        def fnDisplay(candidate):
            display(candidate, startTime)

        def fnGetFitness(genes):
            return get_fitness(genes, rules, nodeIndexLookup)

        best = genetic.get_best(fnGetFitness, len(nodes), optimalValue,
                                geneset, fnDisplay)
        self.assertTrue(not optimalValue > best.Fitness)

        keys = sorted(nodes)
        for index in range(len(nodes)):
            print(keys[index] + " is " + colorLookup[best.Genes[index]])


class Rule:
    def __init__(self, node, adjacent):
        if node < adjacent:
            node, adjacent = adjacent, node
        self.Node = node
        self.Adjacent = adjacent

    def __eq__(self, other):
```

```
            return self.Node == other.Node and self.Adjacent == other.Adjacent

    def __hash__(self):
        return hash(self.Node) * 397 ^ hash(self.Adjacent)

    def __str__(self):
        return self.Node + " -> " + self.Adjacent

    def IsValid(self, genes, nodeIndexLookup):
        index = nodeIndexLookup[self.Node]
        adjacentNodeIndex = nodeIndexLookup[self.Adjacent]

        return genes[index] != genes[adjacentNodeIndex]


if __name__ == '__main__':
    unittest.main()
```

adjacent_states.csv

```
AK,
AL,FL;GA;MS;TN
AR,LA;MO;MS;OK;TN;TX
AZ,CA;NM;NV;UT
CA,AZ;NV;OR
CO,KS;NE;NM;OK;UT;WY
CT,MA;NY;RI
DC,MD;VA
DE,MD;NJ;PA
FL,AL;GA
GA,AL;FL;NC;SC;TN
HI,
IA,IL;MN;MO;NE;SD;WI
ID,MT;NV;OR;UT;WA;WY
IL,IA;IN;KY;MO;WI
IN,IL;KY;MI;OH
KS,CO;MO;NE;OK
KY,IL;IN;MO;OH;TN;VA;WV
LA,AR;MS;TX
MA,CT;NH;NY;RI;VT
MD,DC;DE;PA;VA;WV
ME,NH
MI,IN;OH;WI
MN,IA;ND;SD;WI
MO,AR;IA;IL;KS;KY;NE;OK;TN
MS,AL;AR;LA;TN
MT,ID;ND;SD;WY
NC,GA;SC;TN;VA
ND,MN;MT;SD
NE,CO;IA;KS;MO;SD;WY
NH,MA;ME;VT
NJ,DE;NY;PA
```

```
NM,AZ;CO;OK;TX
NV,AZ;CA;ID;OR;UT
NY,CT;MA;NJ;PA;VT
OH,IN;KY;MI;PA;WV
OK,AR;CO;KS;MO;NM;TX
OR,CA;ID;NV;WA
PA,DE;MD;NJ;NY;OH;WV
RI,CT;MA
SC,GA;NC
SD,IA;MN;MT;ND;NE;WY
TN,AL;AR;GA;KY;MO;MS;NC;VA
TX,AR;LA;NM;OK
UT,AZ;CO;ID;NV;WY
VA,DC;KY;MD;NC;TN;WV
VT,MA;NH;NY
WA,ID;OR
WI,IA;IL;MI;MN
WV,KY;MD;OH;PA;VA
WY,CO;ID;MT;NE;SD;UT
```

adjacent_states.col

```
p edge 51 214
e AL FL
e AL GA
e AL MS
e AL TN
e AR LA
e AR MO
e AR MS
e AR OK
e AR TN
e AR TX
e AZ CA
e AZ NM
e AZ NV
e AZ UT
e CA AZ
e CA NV
e CA OR
e CO KS
e CO NE
e CO NM
e CO OK
e CO UT
e CO WY
e CT MA
e CT NY
e CT RI
e DC MD
e DC VA
e DE MD
e DE NJ
```

```
e DE PA
e FL AL
e FL GA
e GA AL
e GA FL
e GA NC
e GA SC
e GA TN
e IA IL
e IA MN
e IA MO
e IA NE
e IA SD
e IA WI
e ID MT
e ID NV
e ID OR
e ID UT
e ID WA
e ID WY
e IL IA
e IL IN
e IL KY
e IL MO
e IL WI
e IN IL
e IN KY
e IN MI
e IN OH
e KS CO
e KS MO
e KS NE
e KS OK
e KY IL
e KY IN
e KY MO
e KY OH
e KY TN
e KY VA
e KY WV
e LA AR
e LA MS
e LA TX
e MA CT
e MA NH
e MA NY
e MA RI
e MA VT
e MD DC
e MD DE
e MD PA
e MD VA
e MD WV
```

```
e ME NH
e MI IN
e MI OH
e MI WI
e MN IA
e MN ND
e MN SD
e MN WI
e MO AR
e MO IA
e MO IL
e MO KS
e MO KY
e MO NE
e MO OK
e MO TN
e MS AL
e MS AR
e MS LA
e MS TN
e MT ID
e MT ND
e MT SD
e MT WY
e NC GA
e NC SC
e NC TN
e NC VA
e ND MN
e ND MT
e ND SD
e NE CO
e NE IA
e NE KS
e NE MO
e NE SD
e NE WY
e NH MA
e NH ME
e NH VT
e NJ DE
e NJ NY
e NJ PA
e NM AZ
e NM CO
e NM OK
e NM TX
e NV AZ
e NV CA
e NV ID
e NV OR
e NV UT
e NY CT
```

```
e NY MA
e NY NJ
e NY PA
e NY VT
e OH IN
e OH KY
e OH MI
e OH PA
e OH WV
e OK AR
e OK CO
e OK KS
e OK MO
e OK NM
e OK TX
e OR CA
e OR ID
e OR NV
e OR WA
e PA DE
e PA MD
e PA NJ
e PA NY
e PA OH
e PA WV
e RI CT
e RI MA
e SC GA
e SC NC
e SD IA
e SD MN
e SD MT
e SD ND
e SD NE
e SD WY
e TN AL
e TN AR
e TN GA
e TN KY
e TN MO
e TN MS
e TN NC
e TN VA
e TX AR
e TX LA
e TX NM
e TX OK
e UT AZ
e UT CO
e UT ID
e UT NV
e UT WY
e VA DC
```

```
e VA KY
e VA MD
e VA NC
e VA TN
e VA WV
e VT MA
e VT NH
e VT NY
e WA ID
e WA OR
e WI IA
e WI IL
e WI MI
e WI MN
e WV KY
e WV MD
e WV OH
e WV PA
e WV VA
e WY CO
e WY ID
e WY MT
e WY NE
e WY SD
e WY UT
n AK 0
n HI 0
```

Chapter 6: Card Problem

cardTests.py

```python
# File: cardTests.py
#    from chapter 6 of _Genetic Algorithms with Python_
#
# Author: Clinton Sheppard <fluentcoder@gmail.com>
# Copyright (c) 2016 Clinton Sheppard
#
# Licensed under the Apache License, Version 2.0 (the "License").
# You may not use this file except in compliance with the License.
# You may obtain a copy of the License at
#    http://www.apache.org/licenses/LICENSE-2.0
#
# Unless required by applicable law or agreed to in writing, software
# distributed under the License is distributed on an "AS IS" BASIS,
# WITHOUT WARRANTIES OR CONDITIONS OF ANY KIND, either express or
# implied.  See the License for the specific language governing
# permissions and limitations under the License.

import datetime
import functools
import operator
import random
import unittest

import genetic


def get_fitness(genes):
    group1Sum = sum(genes[0:5])
    group2Product = functools.reduce(operator.mul, genes[5:10])
    duplicateCount = (len(genes) - len(set(genes)))
    return Fitness(group1Sum, group2Product, duplicateCount)


def display(candidate, startTime):
    timeDiff = datetime.datetime.now() - startTime
    print("{} - {}\t{}\t{}".format(
        ', '.join(map(str, candidate.Genes[0:5])),
        ', '.join(map(str, candidate.Genes[5:10])),
        candidate.Fitness,
        timeDiff))


def mutate(genes, geneset):
    if len(genes) == len(set(genes)):
        count = random.randint(1, 4)
        while count > 0:
            count -= 1
            indexA, indexB = random.sample(range(len(genes)), 2)
            genes[indexA], genes[indexB] = genes[indexB], genes[indexA]
```

```python
        else:
            indexA = random.randrange(0, len(genes))
            indexB = random.randrange(0, len(geneset))
            genes[indexA] = geneset[indexB]


class CardTests(unittest.TestCase):
    def test(self):
        geneset = [i + 1 for i in range(10)]
        startTime = datetime.datetime.now()

        def fnDisplay(candidate):
            display(candidate, startTime)

        def fnGetFitness(genes):
            return get_fitness(genes)

        def fnMutate(genes):
            mutate(genes, geneset)

        optimalFitness = Fitness(36, 360, 0)
        best = genetic.get_best(fnGetFitness, 10, optimalFitness, geneset,
                                fnDisplay, custom_mutate=fnMutate)
        self.assertTrue(not optimalFitness > best.Fitness)

    def test_benchmark(self):
        genetic.Benchmark.run(lambda: self.test())


class Fitness:
    def __init__(self, group1Sum, group2Product, duplicateCount):
        self.Group1Sum = group1Sum
        self.Group2Product = group2Product
        sumDifference = abs(36 - group1Sum)
        productDifference = abs(360 - group2Product)
        self.TotalDifference = sumDifference + productDifference
        self.DuplicateCount = duplicateCount

    def __gt__(self, other):
        if self.DuplicateCount != other.DuplicateCount:
            return self.DuplicateCount < other.DuplicateCount
        return self.TotalDifference < other.TotalDifference

    def __str__(self):
        return "sum: {} prod: {} dups: {}".format(
            self.Group1Sum,
            self.Group2Product,
            self.DuplicateCount)


if __name__ == '__main__':
    unittest.main()
```

genetic.py

```
# File: genetic.py
#    from chapter 6 of _Genetic Algorithms with Python_
#
# Author: Clinton Sheppard <fluentcoder@gmail.com>
# Copyright (c) 2016 Clinton Sheppard
#
# Licensed under the Apache License, Version 2.0 (the "License").
# You may not use this file except in compliance with the License.
# You may obtain a copy of the License at
#    http://www.apache.org/licenses/LICENSE-2.0
#
# Unless required by applicable law or agreed to in writing, software
# distributed under the License is distributed on an "AS IS" BASIS,
# WITHOUT WARRANTIES OR CONDITIONS OF ANY KIND, either express or
# implied.  See the License for the specific language governing
# permissions and limitations under the License.

import random
import statistics
import sys
import time


def _generate_parent(length, geneSet, get_fitness):
    genes = []
    while len(genes) < length:
        sampleSize = min(length - len(genes), len(geneSet))
        genes.extend(random.sample(geneSet, sampleSize))
    fitness = get_fitness(genes)
    return Chromosome(genes, fitness)


def _mutate(parent, geneSet, get_fitness):
    childGenes = parent.Genes[:]
    index = random.randrange(0, len(parent.Genes))
    newGene, alternate = random.sample(geneSet, 2)
    childGenes[index] = alternate if newGene == childGenes[index] else newGene
    fitness = get_fitness(childGenes)
    return Chromosome(childGenes, fitness)


def _mutate_custom(parent, custom_mutate, get_fitness):
    childGenes = parent.Genes[:]
    custom_mutate(childGenes)
    fitness = get_fitness(childGenes)
    return Chromosome(childGenes, fitness)


def get_best(get_fitness, targetLen, optimalFitness, geneSet, display,
             custom_mutate=None):
    if custom_mutate is None:
        def fnMutate(parent):
```

```
                return _mutate(parent, geneSet, get_fitness)
        else:
            def fnMutate(parent):
                return _mutate_custom(parent, custom_mutate, get_fitness)

        def fnGenerateParent():
            return _generate_parent(targetLen, geneSet, get_fitness)

        for improvement in _get_improvement(fnMutate, fnGenerateParent):
            display(improvement)
            if not optimalFitness > improvement.Fitness:
                return improvement


def _get_improvement(new_child, generate_parent):
    bestParent = generate_parent()
    yield bestParent
    while True:
        child = new_child(bestParent)
        if bestParent.Fitness > child.Fitness:
            continue
        if not child.Fitness > bestParent.Fitness:
            bestParent = child
            continue
        yield child
        bestParent = child


class Chromosome:
    def __init__(self, genes, fitness):
        self.Genes = genes
        self.Fitness = fitness


class Benchmark:
    @staticmethod
    def run(function):
        timings = []
        stdout = sys.stdout
        for i in range(100):
            sys.stdout = None
            startTime = time.time()
            function()
            seconds = time.time() - startTime
            sys.stdout = stdout
            timings.append(seconds)
            mean = statistics.mean(timings)
            if i < 10 or i % 10 == 9:
                print("{} {:3.2f} {:3.2f}".format(
                    1 + i, mean,
                    statistics.stdev(timings, mean) if i > 1 else 0))
```

Chapter 7: Knights Problem

knightsTests.py

```python
# File: knightsTests.py
#    from chapter 7 of _Genetic Algorithms with Python_
#
# Author: Clinton Sheppard <fluentcoder@gmail.com>
# Copyright (c) 2016 Clinton Sheppard
#
# Licensed under the Apache License, Version 2.0 (the "License").
# You may not use this file except in compliance with the License.
# You may obtain a copy of the License at
#    http://www.apache.org/licenses/LICENSE-2.0
#
# Unless required by applicable law or agreed to in writing, software
# distributed under the License is distributed on an "AS IS" BASIS,
# WITHOUT WARRANTIES OR CONDITIONS OF ANY KIND, either express or
# implied.  See the License for the specific language governing
# permissions and limitations under the License.

import datetime
import random
import unittest

import genetic


def get_fitness(genes, boardWidth, boardHeight):
    attacked = set(pos
                   for kn in genes
                   for pos in get_attacks(kn, boardWidth, boardHeight))
    return len(attacked)


def display(candidate, startTime, boardWidth, boardHeight):
    timeDiff = datetime.datetime.now() - startTime
    board = Board(candidate.Genes, boardWidth, boardHeight)
    board.print()

    print("{}\n\t{}\t{}".format(
        ' '.join(map(str, candidate.Genes)),
        candidate.Fitness,
        timeDiff))


def mutate(genes, boardWidth, boardHeight, allPositions, nonEdgePositions):
    count = 2 if random.randint(0, 10) == 0 else 1
    while count > 0:
        count -= 1
        positionToKnightIndexes = dict((p, []) for p in allPositions)
        for i, knight in enumerate(genes):
            for position in get_attacks(knight, boardWidth, boardHeight):
```

```
                    positionToKnightIndexes[position].append(i)
        knightIndexes = set(i for i in range(len(genes)))
        unattacked = []
        for kvp in positionToKnightIndexes.items():
            if len(kvp[1]) > 1:
                continue
            if len(kvp[1]) == 0:
                unattacked.append(kvp[0])
                continue
            for p in kvp[1]:  # len == 1
                if p in knightIndexes:
                    knightIndexes.remove(p)

        potentialKnightPositions = \
            [p for positions in
              map(lambda x: get_attacks(x, boardWidth, boardHeight),
                 unattacked)
             for p in positions if p in nonEdgePositions] \
                if len(unattacked) > 0 else nonEdgePositions

        geneIndex = random.randrange(0, len(genes)) \
            if len(knightIndexes) == 0 \
            else random.choice([i for i in knightIndexes])

        position = random.choice(potentialKnightPositions)
        genes[geneIndex] = position


def create(fnGetRandomPosition, expectedKnights):
    genes = [fnGetRandomPosition() for _ in range(expectedKnights)]
    return genes


def get_attacks(location, boardWidth, boardHeight):
    return [i for i in set(
        Position(x + location.X, y + location.Y)
        for x in [-2, -1, 1, 2] if 0 <= x + location.X < boardWidth
        for y in [-2, -1, 1, 2] if 0 <= y + location.Y < boardHeight
        and abs(y) != abs(x))]


class KnightsTests(unittest.TestCase):
    def test_3x4(self):
        width = 4
        height = 3
        # 1,0   2,0   3,0
        # 0,2   1,2   2,2
        # 2     N N N .
        # 1     . . . .
        # 0     . N N N
        #       0 1 2 3
        self.find_knight_positions(width, height, 6)
```

```python
    def test_8x8(self):
        width = 8
        height = 8
        self.find_knight_positions(width, height, 14)

    def test_10x10(self):
        width = 10
        height = 10
        self.find_knight_positions(width, height, 22)

    def test_12x12(self):
        width = 12
        height = 12
        self.find_knight_positions(width, height, 28)

    def test_13x13(self):
        width = 13
        height = 13
        self.find_knight_positions(width, height, 32)

    def test_benchmark(self):
        genetic.Benchmark.run(lambda: self.test_10x10())

    def find_knight_positions(self, boardWidth, boardHeight, expectedKnights):
        startTime = datetime.datetime.now()

        def fnDisplay(candidate):
            display(candidate, startTime, boardWidth, boardHeight)

        def fnGetFitness(genes):
            return get_fitness(genes, boardWidth, boardHeight)

        allPositions = [Position(x, y)
                        for y in range(boardHeight)
                        for x in range(boardWidth)]

        if boardWidth < 6 or boardHeight < 6:
            nonEdgePositions = allPositions
        else:
            nonEdgePositions = [i for i in allPositions
                                if 0 < i.X < boardWidth - 1 and
                                0 < i.Y < boardHeight - 1]

        def fnGetRandomPosition():
            return random.choice(nonEdgePositions)

        def fnMutate(genes):
            mutate(genes, boardWidth, boardHeight, allPositions,
                   nonEdgePositions)

        def fnCreate():
            return create(fnGetRandomPosition, expectedKnights)
```

```
            optimalFitness = boardWidth * boardHeight
            best = genetic.get_best(fnGetFitness, None, optimalFitness, None,
                                    fnDisplay, fnMutate, fnCreate)
            self.assertTrue(not optimalFitness > best.Fitness)


class Position:
    def __init__(self, x, y):
        self.X = x
        self.Y = y

    def __str__(self):
        return "{},{}".format(self.X, self.Y)

    def __eq__(self, other):
        return self.X == other.X and self.Y == other.Y

    def __hash__(self):
        return self.X * 1000 + self.Y


class Board:
    def __init__(self, positions, width, height):
        board = [['.'] * width for _ in range(height)]

        for index in range(len(positions)):
            knightPosition = positions[index]
            board[knightPosition.Y][knightPosition.X] = 'N'
        self._board = board
        self._width = width
        self._height = height

    def print(self):
        # 0,0 prints in bottom left corner
        for i in reversed(range(self._height)):
            print(i, "\t", ' '.join(self._board[i]))
        print(" \t", ' '.join(map(str, range(self._width))))


if __name__ == '__main__':
    unittest.main()
```

genetic.py

```
# File: genetic.py
#    from chapter 7 of _Genetic Algorithms with Python_
#
# Author: Clinton Sheppard <fluentcoder@gmail.com>
# Copyright (c) 2016 Clinton Sheppard
#
# Licensed under the Apache License, Version 2.0 (the "License").
# You may not use this file except in compliance with the License.
```

```python
# You may obtain a copy of the License at
#    http://www.apache.org/licenses/LICENSE-2.0
#
# Unless required by applicable law or agreed to in writing, software
# distributed under the License is distributed on an "AS IS" BASIS,
# WITHOUT WARRANTIES OR CONDITIONS OF ANY KIND, either express or
# implied.  See the License for the specific language governing
# permissions and limitations under the License.

import random
import statistics
import sys
import time


def _generate_parent(length, geneSet, get_fitness):
    genes = []
    while len(genes) < length:
        sampleSize = min(length - len(genes), len(geneSet))
        genes.extend(random.sample(geneSet, sampleSize))
    fitness = get_fitness(genes)
    return Chromosome(genes, fitness)


def _mutate(parent, geneSet, get_fitness):
    childGenes = parent.Genes[:]
    index = random.randrange(0, len(parent.Genes))
    newGene, alternate = random.sample(geneSet, 2)
    childGenes[index] = alternate if newGene == childGenes[index] else newGene
    fitness = get_fitness(childGenes)
    return Chromosome(childGenes, fitness)


def _mutate_custom(parent, custom_mutate, get_fitness):
    childGenes = parent.Genes[:]
    custom_mutate(childGenes)
    fitness = get_fitness(childGenes)
    return Chromosome(childGenes, fitness)


def get_best(get_fitness, targetLen, optimalFitness, geneSet, display,
             custom_mutate=None, custom_create=None):
    if custom_mutate is None:
        def fnMutate(parent):
            return _mutate(parent, geneSet, get_fitness)
    else:
        def fnMutate(parent):
            return _mutate_custom(parent, custom_mutate, get_fitness)

    if custom_create is None:
        def fnGenerateParent():
            return _generate_parent(targetLen, geneSet, get_fitness)
    else:
```

```python
    def fnGenerateParent():
        genes = custom_create()
        return Chromosome(genes, get_fitness(genes))

    for improvement in _get_improvement(fnMutate, fnGenerateParent):
        display(improvement)
        if not optimalFitness > improvement.Fitness:
            return improvement


def _get_improvement(new_child, generate_parent):
    bestParent = generate_parent()
    yield bestParent
    while True:
        child = new_child(bestParent)
        if bestParent.Fitness > child.Fitness:
            continue
        if not child.Fitness > bestParent.Fitness:
            bestParent = child
            continue
        yield child
        bestParent = child


class Chromosome:
    def __init__(self, genes, fitness):
        self.Genes = genes
        self.Fitness = fitness


class Benchmark:
    @staticmethod
    def run(function):
        timings = []
        stdout = sys.stdout
        for i in range(100):
            sys.stdout = None
            startTime = time.time()
            function()
            seconds = time.time() - startTime
            sys.stdout = stdout
            timings.append(seconds)
            mean = statistics.mean(timings)
            if i < 10 or i % 10 == 9:
                print("{} {:3.2f} {:3.2f}".format(
                    1 + i, mean,
                    statistics.stdev(timings, mean) if i > 1 else 0))
```

Chapter 8: Magic Squares

magicSquareTests.py

```python
# File: magicSquareTests.py
#    from chapter 8 of _Genetic Algorithms with Python_
#
# Author: Clinton Sheppard <fluentcoder@gmail.com>
# Copyright (c) 2016 Clinton Sheppard
#
# Licensed under the Apache License, Version 2.0 (the "License").
# You may not use this file except in compliance with the License.
# You may obtain a copy of the License at
#   http://www.apache.org/licenses/LICENSE-2.0
#
# Unless required by applicable law or agreed to in writing, software
# distributed under the License is distributed on an "AS IS" BASIS,
# WITHOUT WARRANTIES OR CONDITIONS OF ANY KIND, either express or
# implied.  See the License for the specific language governing
# permissions and limitations under the License.

import datetime
import random
import unittest

import genetic


def get_fitness(genes, diagonalSize, expectedSum):
    rows, columns, northeastDiagonalSum, southeastDiagonalSum = \
        get_sums(genes, diagonalSize)

    sumOfDifferences = sum(int(abs(s - expectedSum))
                           for s in rows + columns +
                           [southeastDiagonalSum, northeastDiagonalSum]
                           if s != expectedSum)

    return Fitness(sumOfDifferences)


def display(candidate, diagonalSize, startTime):
    timeDiff = datetime.datetime.now() - startTime

    rows, columns, northeastDiagonalSum, southeastDiagonalSum = \
        get_sums(candidate.Genes, diagonalSize)

    for rowNumber in range(diagonalSize):
        row = candidate.Genes[
            rowNumber * diagonalSize:(rowNumber + 1) * diagonalSize]
        print("\t ", row, "=", rows[rowNumber])
    print(northeastDiagonalSum, "\t", columns, "\t", southeastDiagonalSum)
    print(" - - - - - - - - - -", candidate.Fitness, timeDiff)
```

```
def get_sums(genes, diagonalSize):
    rows = [0 for _ in range(diagonalSize)]
    columns = [0 for _ in range(diagonalSize)]
    southeastDiagonalSum = 0
    northeastDiagonalSum = 0
    for row in range(diagonalSize):
        for column in range(diagonalSize):
            value = genes[row * diagonalSize + column]
            rows[row] += value
            columns[column] += value
        southeastDiagonalSum += genes[row * diagonalSize + row]
        northeastDiagonalSum += genes[row * diagonalSize +
                                    (diagonalSize - 1 - row)]
    return rows, columns, northeastDiagonalSum, southeastDiagonalSum


def mutate(genes, indexes):
    indexA, indexB = random.sample(indexes, 2)
    genes[indexA], genes[indexB] = genes[indexB], genes[indexA]


class MagicSquareTests(unittest.TestCase):
    def test_size_3(self):
        self.generate(3, 50)

    def test_size_4(self):
        self.generate(4, 50)

    def test_size_5(self):
        self.generate(5, 500)

    def test_size_10(self):
        self.generate(10, 5000)

    def test_benchmark(self):
        genetic.Benchmark.run(self.test_size_4)

    def generate(self, diagonalSize, maxAge):
        nSquared = diagonalSize * diagonalSize
        geneset = [i for i in range(1, nSquared + 1)]
        expectedSum = diagonalSize * (nSquared + 1) / 2

        def fnGetFitness(genes):
            return get_fitness(genes, diagonalSize, expectedSum)

        def fnDisplay(candidate):
            display(candidate, diagonalSize, startTime)

        geneIndexes = [i for i in range(0, len(geneset))]

        def fnMutate(genes):
            mutate(genes, geneIndexes)
```

```python
    def fnCustomCreate():
        return random.sample(geneset, len(geneset))

    optimalValue = Fitness(0)
    startTime = datetime.datetime.now()
    best = genetic.get_best(fnGetFitness, nSquared, optimalValue,
                            geneset, fnDisplay, fnMutate, fnCustomCreate,
                            maxAge)
    self.assertTrue(not optimalValue > best.Fitness)


class Fitness:
    def __init__(self, sumOfDifferences):
        self.SumOfDifferences = sumOfDifferences

    def __gt__(self, other):
        return self.SumOfDifferences < other.SumOfDifferences

    def __str__(self):
        return "{}".format(self.SumOfDifferences)


if __name__ == '__main__':
    unittest.main()
```

genetic.py

```python
# File: genetic.py
#    from chapter 8 of _Genetic Algorithms with Python_
#
# Author: Clinton Sheppard <fluentcoder@gmail.com>
# Copyright (c) 2016 Clinton Sheppard
#
# Licensed under the Apache License, Version 2.0 (the "License").
# You may not use this file except in compliance with the License.
# You may obtain a copy of the License at
#    http://www.apache.org/licenses/LICENSE-2.0
#
# Unless required by applicable law or agreed to in writing, software
# distributed under the License is distributed on an "AS IS" BASIS,
# WITHOUT WARRANTIES OR CONDITIONS OF ANY KIND, either express or
# implied.  See the License for the specific language governing
# permissions and limitations under the License.

import random
import statistics
import sys
import time
from bisect import bisect_left
from math import exp
```

```python
def _generate_parent(length, geneSet, get_fitness):
    genes = []
    while len(genes) < length:
        sampleSize = min(length - len(genes), len(geneSet))
        genes.extend(random.sample(geneSet, sampleSize))
    fitness = get_fitness(genes)
    return Chromosome(genes, fitness)


def _mutate(parent, geneSet, get_fitness):
    childGenes = parent.Genes[:]
    index = random.randrange(0, len(parent.Genes))
    newGene, alternate = random.sample(geneSet, 2)
    childGenes[index] = alternate if newGene == childGenes[index] else newGene
    fitness = get_fitness(childGenes)
    return Chromosome(childGenes, fitness)


def _mutate_custom(parent, custom_mutate, get_fitness):
    childGenes = parent.Genes[:]
    custom_mutate(childGenes)
    fitness = get_fitness(childGenes)
    return Chromosome(childGenes, fitness)


def get_best(get_fitness, targetLen, optimalFitness, geneSet, display,
             custom_mutate=None, custom_create=None, maxAge=None):
    if custom_mutate is None:
        def fnMutate(parent):
            return _mutate(parent, geneSet, get_fitness)
    else:
        def fnMutate(parent):
            return _mutate_custom(parent, custom_mutate, get_fitness)

    if custom_create is None:
        def fnGenerateParent():
            return _generate_parent(targetLen, geneSet, get_fitness)
    else:
        def fnGenerateParent():
            genes = custom_create()
            return Chromosome(genes, get_fitness(genes))

    for improvement in _get_improvement(fnMutate, fnGenerateParent, maxAge):
        display(improvement)
        if not optimalFitness > improvement.Fitness:
            return improvement


def _get_improvement(new_child, generate_parent, maxAge):
    parent = bestParent = generate_parent()
    yield bestParent
    historicalFitnesses = [bestParent.Fitness]
```

```python
    while True:
        child = new_child(parent)
        if parent.Fitness > child.Fitness:
            if maxAge is None:
                continue
            parent.Age += 1
            if maxAge > parent.Age:
                continue
            index = bisect_left(historicalFitnesses, child.Fitness, 0,
                                len(historicalFitnesses))
            proportionSimilar = index / len(historicalFitnesses)
            if random.random() < exp(-proportionSimilar):
                parent = child
                continue
            bestParent.Age = 0
            parent = bestParent
            continue
        if not child.Fitness > parent.Fitness:
            # same fitness
            child.Age = parent.Age + 1
            parent = child
            continue
        child.Age = 0
        parent = child
        if child.Fitness > bestParent.Fitness:
            bestParent = child
            yield bestParent
            historicalFitnesses.append(bestParent.Fitness)


class Chromosome:
    def __init__(self, genes, fitness):
        self.Genes = genes
        self.Fitness = fitness
        self.Age = 0


class Benchmark:
    @staticmethod
    def run(function):
        timings = []
        stdout = sys.stdout
        for i in range(100):
            sys.stdout = None
            startTime = time.time()
            function()
            seconds = time.time() - startTime
            sys.stdout = stdout
            timings.append(seconds)
            mean = statistics.mean(timings)
            if i < 10 or i % 10 == 9:
                print("{} {:3.2f} {:3.2f}".format(
                    1 + i, mean,
```

```
            statistics.stdev(timings, mean) if i > 1 else 0))
```

Chapter 9: Knapsack Problem

knapsackTests.py

```python
# File: knapsackTests.py
#    from chapter 9 of _Genetic Algorithms with Python_
#
# Author: Clinton Sheppard <fluentcoder@gmail.com>
# Copyright (c) 2016 Clinton Sheppard
#
# Licensed under the Apache License, Version 2.0 (the "License").
# You may not use this file except in compliance with the License.
# You may obtain a copy of the License at
#   http://www.apache.org/licenses/LICENSE-2.0
#
# Unless required by applicable law or agreed to in writing, software
# distributed under the License is distributed on an "AS IS" BASIS,
# WITHOUT WARRANTIES OR CONDITIONS OF ANY KIND, either express or
# implied.  See the License for the specific language governing
# permissions and limitations under the License.

import datetime
import random
import sys
import unittest

import genetic


def get_fitness(genes):
    totalWeight = 0
    totalVolume = 0
    totalValue = 0
    for iq in genes:
        count = iq.Quantity
        totalWeight += iq.Item.Weight * count
        totalVolume += iq.Item.Volume * count
        totalValue += iq.Item.Value * count

    return Fitness(totalWeight, totalVolume, totalValue)


def display(candidate, startTime):
    timeDiff = datetime.datetime.now() - startTime
    genes = candidate.Genes[:]
    genes.sort(key=lambda iq: iq.Quantity, reverse=True)

    descriptions = [str(iq.Quantity) + "x" + iq.Item.Name for iq in genes]
    if len(descriptions) == 0:
```

```python
                descriptions.append("Empty")
        print("{}\t{}\t{}".format(
            ', '.join(descriptions),
            candidate.Fitness,
            timeDiff))


def max_quantity(item, maxWeight, maxVolume):
    return min(int(maxWeight / item.Weight)
                if item.Weight > 0 else sys.maxsize,
               int(maxVolume / item.Volume)
                if item.Volume > 0 else sys.maxsize)


def create(items, maxWeight, maxVolume):
    genes = []
    remainingWeight, remainingVolume = maxWeight, maxVolume
    for i in range(random.randrange(1, len(items))):
        newGene = add(genes, items, remainingWeight, remainingVolume)
        if newGene is not None:
            genes.append(newGene)
            remainingWeight -= newGene.Quantity * newGene.Item.Weight
            remainingVolume -= newGene.Quantity * newGene.Item.Volume
    return genes


def add(genes, items, maxWeight, maxVolume):
    usedItems = {iq.Item for iq in genes}
    item = random.choice(items)
    while item in usedItems:
        item = random.choice(items)

    maxQuantity = max_quantity(item, maxWeight, maxVolume)
    return ItemQuantity(item, maxQuantity) if maxQuantity > 0 else None


def mutate(genes, items, maxWeight, maxVolume, window):
    window.slide()
    fitness = get_fitness(genes)
    remainingWeight = maxWeight - fitness.TotalWeight
    remainingVolume = maxVolume - fitness.TotalVolume

    removing = len(genes) > 1 and random.randint(0, 10) == 0
    if removing:
        index = random.randrange(0, len(genes))
        iq = genes[index]
        item = iq.Item
        remainingWeight += item.Weight * iq.Quantity
        remainingVolume += item.Volume * iq.Quantity
        del genes[index]

    adding = (remainingWeight > 0 or remainingVolume > 0) and \
            (len(genes) == 0 or
```

```
                (len(genes) < len(items) and random.randint(0, 100) == 0))
        if adding:
            newGene = add(genes, items, remainingWeight, remainingVolume)
            if newGene is not None:
                genes.append(newGene)
                return

        index = random.randrange(0, len(genes))
        iq = genes[index]
        item = iq.Item
        remainingWeight += item.Weight * iq.Quantity
        remainingVolume += item.Volume * iq.Quantity

        changeItem = len(genes) < len(items) and random.randint(0, 4) == 0
        if changeItem:
            itemIndex = items.index(iq.Item)
            start = max(1, itemIndex - window.Size)
            stop = min(len(items) - 1, itemIndex + window.Size)
            item = items[random.randint(start, stop)]
        maxQuantity = max_quantity(item, remainingWeight, remainingVolume)
        if maxQuantity > 0:
            genes[index] = ItemQuantity(item, maxQuantity
                if window.Size > 1 else random.randint(1, maxQuantity))
        else:
            del genes[index]


class KnapsackTests(unittest.TestCase):
    def test_cookies(self):
        items = [
            Resource("Flour", 1680, 0.265, .41),
            Resource("Butter", 1440, 0.5, .13),
            Resource("Sugar", 1840, 0.441, .29)
        ]
        maxWeight = 10
        maxVolume = 4
        optimal = get_fitness(
            [ItemQuantity(items[0], 1),
             ItemQuantity(items[1], 14),
             ItemQuantity(items[2], 6)])
        self.fill_knapsack(items, maxWeight, maxVolume, optimal)

    def test_exnsd16(self):
        problemInfo = load_data("exnsd16.ukp")
        items = problemInfo.Resources
        maxWeight = problemInfo.MaxWeight
        maxVolume = 0
        optimal = get_fitness(problemInfo.Solution)
        self.fill_knapsack(items, maxWeight, maxVolume, optimal)

    def test_benchmark(self):
        genetic.Benchmark.run(lambda: self.test_exnsd16())
```

```python
    def fill_knapsack(self, items, maxWeight, maxVolume, optimalFitness):
        startTime = datetime.datetime.now()
        window = Window(1,
                        max(1, int(len(items) / 3)),
                        int(len(items) / 2))

        sortedItems = sorted(items, key=lambda item: item.Value)

        def fnDisplay(candidate):
            display(candidate, startTime)

        def fnGetFitness(genes):
            return get_fitness(genes)

        def fnCreate():
            return create(items, maxWeight, maxVolume)

        def fnMutate(genes):
            mutate(genes, sortedItems, maxWeight, maxVolume, window)

        best = genetic.get_best(fnGetFitness, None, optimalFitness, None,
                                fnDisplay, fnMutate, fnCreate, maxAge=50)
        self.assertTrue(not optimalFitness > best.Fitness)


def load_data(localFileName):
    with open(localFileName, mode='r') as infile:
        lines = infile.read().splitlines()
    data = KnapsackProblemData()
    f = find_constraint

    for line in lines:
        f = f(line.strip(), data)
        if f is None:
            break
    return data


def find_constraint(line, data):
    parts = line.split(' ')
    if parts[0] != "c:":
        return find_constraint
    data.MaxWeight = int(parts[1])
    return find_data_start


def find_data_start(line, data):
    if line != "begin data":
        return find_data_start
    return read_resource_or_find_data_end
```

```python
def read_resource_or_find_data_end(line, data):
    if line == "end data":
        return find_solution_start
    parts = line.split('\t')
    resource = Resource("R" + str(1 + len(data.Resources)), int(parts[1]),
                        int(parts[0]), 0)
    data.Resources.append(resource)
    return read_resource_or_find_data_end


def find_solution_start(line, data):
    if line == "sol:":
        return read_solution_resource_or_find_solution_end
    return find_solution_start


def read_solution_resource_or_find_solution_end(line, data):
    if line == "":
        return None
    parts = [p for p in line.split('\t') if p != ""]
    resourceIndex = int(parts[0]) - 1  # make it 0 based
    resourceQuantity = int(parts[1])
    data.Solution.append(
        ItemQuantity(data.Resources[resourceIndex], resourceQuantity))
    return read_solution_resource_or_find_solution_end


class Resource:
    def __init__(self, name, value, weight, volume):
        self.Name = name
        self.Value = value
        self.Weight = weight
        self.Volume = volume


class ItemQuantity:
    def __init__(self, item, quantity):
        self.Item = item
        self.Quantity = quantity

    def __eq__(self, other):
        return self.Item == other.Item and self.Quantity == other.Quantity


class Fitness:
    def __init__(self, totalWeight, totalVolume, totalValue):
        self.TotalWeight = totalWeight
        self.TotalVolume = totalVolume
        self.TotalValue = totalValue

    def __gt__(self, other):
        if self.TotalValue != other.TotalValue:
            return self.TotalValue > other.TotalValue
```

```
        if self.TotalWeight != other.TotalWeight:
            return self.TotalWeight < other.TotalWeight
        return self.TotalVolume < other.TotalVolume

    def __str__(self):
        return "wt: {:0.2f} vol: {:0.2f} value: {}".format(
            self.TotalWeight,
            self.TotalVolume,
            self.TotalValue)


class KnapsackProblemData:
    def __init__(self):
        self.Resources = []
        self.MaxWeight = 0
        self.Solution = []


class Window:
    def __init__(self, minimum, maximum, size):
        self.Min = minimum
        self.Max = maximum
        self.Size = size

    def slide(self):
        self.Size = self.Size - 1 if self.Size > self.Min else self.Max


if __name__ == '__main__':
    unittest.main()
```

Chapter 10: Solving Linear Equations

linearEquationTests.py

```
# File: linearEquationTests.py
#    from chapter 10 of _Genetic Algorithms with Python_
#
# Author: Clinton Sheppard <fluentcoder@gmail.com>
# Copyright (c) 2016 Clinton Sheppard
#
# Licensed under the Apache License, Version 2.0 (the "License").
# You may not use this file except in compliance with the License.
# You may obtain a copy of the License at
#    http://www.apache.org/licenses/LICENSE-2.0
#
# Unless required by applicable law or agreed to in writing, software
# distributed under the License is distributed on an "AS IS" BASIS,
# WITHOUT WARRANTIES OR CONDITIONS OF ANY KIND, either express or
# implied.  See the License for the specific language governing
# permissions and limitations under the License.
```

```python
import datetime
import fractions
import random
import unittest

import genetic


def get_fitness(genes, equations):
    fitness = Fitness(sum(abs(e(genes)) for e in equations))
    return fitness


def display(candidate, startTime, fnGenesToInputs):
    timeDiff = datetime.datetime.now() - startTime
    symbols = "xyza"
    result = ', '.join("{} = {}".format(s, v)
                       for s, v in
                       zip(symbols, fnGenesToInputs(candidate.Genes)))
    print("{}\t{}\t{}".format(
        result,
        candidate.Fitness,
        timeDiff))


def mutate(genes, sortedGeneset, window, geneIndexes):
    indexes = random.sample(geneIndexes, random.randint(1, len(genes))) \
        if random.randint(0, 10) == 0 else [random.choice(geneIndexes)]
    window.slide()
    while len(indexes) > 0:
        index = indexes.pop()
        genesetIndex = sortedGeneset.index(genes[index])
        start = max(0, genesetIndex - window.Size)
        stop = min(len(sortedGeneset) - 1, genesetIndex + window.Size)
        genesetIndex = random.randint(start, stop)
        genes[index] = sortedGeneset[genesetIndex]


class LinearEquationTests(unittest.TestCase):
    def test_2_unknowns(self):
        geneset = [i for i in range(-5, 5) if i != 0]

        def fnGenesToInputs(genes):
            return genes[0], genes[1]

        def e1(genes):
            x, y = fnGenesToInputs(genes)
            return x + 2 * y - 4

        def e2(genes):
            x, y = fnGenesToInputs(genes)
            return 4 * x + 4 * y - 12
```

```
        equations = [e1, e2]
        self.solve_unknowns(2, geneset, equations, fnGenesToInputs)

    def test_3_unknowns(self):
        geneRange = [i for i in range(-5, 5) if i != 0]
        geneset = [i for i in set(
            fractions.Fraction(d, e)
            for d in geneRange
            for e in geneRange if e != 0)]

        def fnGenesToInputs(genes):
            return genes

        def e1(genes):
            x, y, z = genes
            return 6 * x - 2 * y + 8 * z - 20

        def e2(genes):
            x, y, z = genes
            return y + 8 * x * z + 1

        def e3(genes):
            x, y, z = genes
            return 2 * z * fractions.Fraction(6, x) \
                    + 3 * fractions.Fraction(y, 2) - 6

        equations = [e1, e2, e3]
        self.solve_unknowns(3, geneset, equations, fnGenesToInputs)

    def test_4_unknowns(self):
        geneRange = [i for i in range(-13, 13) if i != 0]
        geneset = [i for i in set(
            fractions.Fraction(d, e)
            for d in geneRange
            for e in geneRange if e != 0)]

        def fnGenesToInputs(genes):
            return genes

        def e1(genes):
            x, y, z, a = genes
            return fractions.Fraction(1, 15) * x \
                    - 2 * y \
                    - 15 * z \
                    - fractions.Fraction(4, 5) * a \
                    - 3

        def e2(genes):
            x, y, z, a = genes
            return -fractions.Fraction(5, 2) * x \
                    - fractions.Fraction(9, 4) * y \
                    + 12 * z \
```

```
                            - a \
                            - 17

        def e3(genes):
            x, y, z, a = genes
            return -13 * x \
                    + fractions.Fraction(3, 10) * y \
                    - 6 * z \
                    - fractions.Fraction(2, 5) * a \
                    - 17

        def e4(genes):
            x, y, z, a = genes
            return fractions.Fraction(1, 2) * x \
                    + 2 * y \
                    + fractions.Fraction(7, 4) * z \
                    + fractions.Fraction(4, 3) * a \
                    + 9

        equations = [e1, e2, e3, e4]
        self.solve_unknowns(4, geneset, equations, fnGenesToInputs)

    def test_benchmark(self):
        genetic.Benchmark.run(lambda: self.test_4_unknowns())

    def solve_unknowns(self, numUnknowns, geneset, equations,
                       fnGenesToInputs):
        startTime = datetime.datetime.now()
        maxAge = 50
        window = Window(max(1, int(len(geneset) / (2 * maxAge))),
                        max(1, int(len(geneset) / 3)),
                        int(len(geneset) / 2))
        geneIndexes = [i for i in range(numUnknowns)]
        sortedGeneset = sorted(geneset)

        def fnDisplay(candidate):
            display(candidate, startTime, fnGenesToInputs)

        def fnGetFitness(genes):
            return get_fitness(genes, equations)

        def fnMutate(genes):
            mutate(genes, sortedGeneset, window, geneIndexes)

        optimalFitness = Fitness(0)
        best = genetic.get_best(fnGetFitness, numUnknowns, optimalFitness,
                                geneset, fnDisplay, fnMutate, maxAge=maxAge)
        self.assertTrue(not optimalFitness > best.Fitness)


class Fitness:
    def __init__(self, totalDifference):
        self.TotalDifference = totalDifference
```

```python
    def __gt__(self, other):
        return self.TotalDifference < other.TotalDifference

    def __str__(self):
        return "diff: {:0.2f}".format(float(self.TotalDifference))


class Window:
    def __init__(self, minimum, maximum, size):
        self.Min = minimum
        self.Max = maximum
        self.Size = size

    def slide(self):
        self.Size = self.Size - 1 if self.Size > self.Min else self.Max


if __name__ == '__main__':
    unittest.main()
```

Chapter 11: Generating Sudoku

sudokuTests.py

```python
# File: sudokuTests.py
#    from chapter 11 of _Genetic Algorithms with Python_
#
# Author: Clinton Sheppard <fluentcoder@gmail.com>
# Copyright (c) 2016 Clinton Sheppard
#
# Licensed under the Apache License, Version 2.0 (the "License").
# You may not use this file except in compliance with the License.
# You may obtain a copy of the License at
#    http://www.apache.org/licenses/LICENSE-2.0
#
# Unless required by applicable law or agreed to in writing, software
# distributed under the License is distributed on an "AS IS" BASIS,
# WITHOUT WARRANTIES OR CONDITIONS OF ANY KIND, either express or
# implied.  See the License for the specific language governing
# permissions and limitations under the License.


import datetime
import random
import unittest

import genetic


def get_fitness(genes, validationRules):
    try:
        firstFailingRule = next(rule for rule in validationRules
                                if genes[rule.Index] == genes[rule.OtherIndex])
    except StopIteration:
        fitness = 100
    else:
        fitness = (1 + index_row(firstFailingRule.OtherIndex)) * 10 \
                + (1 + index_column(firstFailingRule.OtherIndex))
    return fitness


def display(candidate, startTime):
    timeDiff = datetime.datetime.now() - startTime

    for row in range(9):
        line = ' | '.join(
            ' '.join(str(i)
                     for i in candidate.Genes[row * 9 + i:row * 9 + i + 3])
            for i in [0, 3, 6])
        print("", line)
        if row < 8 and row % 3 == 2:
            print(" ----- + ----- + -----")
    print(" - = -   - = -   - = - {}\t{}\n"
```

```
                .format(candidate.Fitness, timeDiff))


def mutate(genes, validationRules):
    selectedRule = next(rule for rule in validationRules
                        if genes[rule.Index] == genes[rule.OtherIndex])
    if selectedRule is None:
        return

    if index_row(selectedRule.OtherIndex) % 3 == 2 \
            and random.randint(0, 10) == 0:
        sectionStart = section_start(selectedRule.Index)
        current = selectedRule.OtherIndex
        while selectedRule.OtherIndex == current:
            shuffle_in_place(genes, sectionStart, 80)
            selectedRule = next(rule for rule in validationRules
                                if genes[rule.Index] == genes[rule.OtherIndex])
        return
    row = index_row(selectedRule.OtherIndex)
    start = row * 9
    indexA = selectedRule.OtherIndex
    indexB = random.randrange(start, len(genes))
    genes[indexA], genes[indexB] = genes[indexB], genes[indexA]


def shuffle_in_place(genes, first, last):
    while first < last:
        index = random.randint(first, last)
        genes[first], genes[index] = genes[index], genes[first]
        first += 1


class SudokuTests(unittest.TestCase):
    def test(self):
        geneset = [i for i in range(1, 9 + 1)]
        startTime = datetime.datetime.now()
        optimalValue = 100

        def fnDisplay(candidate):
            display(candidate, startTime)

        validationRules = build_validation_rules()

        def fnGetFitness(genes):
            return get_fitness(genes, validationRules)

        def fnCreate():
            return random.sample(geneset * 9, 81)

        def fnMutate(genes):
            mutate(genes, validationRules)

        best = genetic.get_best(fnGetFitness, None, optimalValue, None,
```

```
                                    fnDisplay, fnMutate, fnCreate, maxAge=50)
        self.assertEqual(best.Fitness, optimalValue)

    def test_benchmark(self):
        genetic.Benchmark.run(lambda: self.test())


def build_validation_rules():
    rules = []
    for index in range(80):
        itsRow = index_row(index)
        itsColumn = index_column(index)
        itsSection = row_column_section(itsRow, itsColumn)

        for index2 in range(index + 1, 81):
            otherRow = index_row(index2)
            otherColumn = index_column(index2)
            otherSection = row_column_section(otherRow, otherColumn)
            if itsRow == otherRow or \
                        itsColumn == otherColumn or \
                        itsSection == otherSection:
                rules.append(Rule(index, index2))

    rules.sort(key=lambda x: x.OtherIndex * 100 + x.Index)
    return rules


def index_row(index):
    return int(index / 9)


def index_column(index):
    return int(index % 9)


def row_column_section(row, column):
    return int(row / 3) * 3 + int(column / 3)


def index_section(index):
    return row_column_section(index_row(index), index_column(index))


def section_start(index):
    return int((index_row(index) % 9) / 3) * 27 + int(
        index_column(index) / 3) * 3


class Rule:
    def __init__(self, it, other):
        if it > other:
            it, other = other, it
        self.Index = it
```

```
        self.OtherIndex = other

    def __eq__(self, other):
        return self.Index == other.Index and \
               self.OtherIndex == other.OtherIndex

    def __hash__(self):
        return self.Index * 100 + self.OtherIndex


if __name__ == '__main__':
    unittest.main()
```

Chapter 12: Traveling Salesman Problem

tspTests.py

```
# File: tspTests.py
#    from chapter 12 of _Genetic Algorithms with Python_
#
# Author: Clinton Sheppard <fluentcoder@gmail.com>
# Copyright (c) 2016 Clinton Sheppard
#
# Licensed under the Apache License, Version 2.0 (the "License").
# You may not use this file except in compliance with the License.
# You may obtain a copy of the License at
#    http://www.apache.org/licenses/LICENSE-2.0
#
# Unless required by applicable law or agreed to in writing, software
# distributed under the License is distributed on an "AS IS" BASIS,
# WITHOUT WARRANTIES OR CONDITIONS OF ANY KIND, either express or
# implied.  See the License for the specific language governing
# permissions and limitations under the License.

import datetime
import math
import random
import unittest
from itertools import chain

import genetic


def get_fitness(genes, idToLocationLookup):
    fitness = get_distance(idToLocationLookup[genes[0]],
                           idToLocationLookup[genes[-1]])

    for i in range(len(genes) - 1):
        start = idToLocationLookup[genes[i]]
        end = idToLocationLookup[genes[i + 1]]
        fitness += get_distance(start, end)
```

Final code from each project   355

```python
        return Fitness(round(fitness, 2))


def display(candidate, startTime):
    timeDiff = datetime.datetime.now() - startTime
    print("{}\t{}\t{}\t{}".format(
        ' '.join(map(str, candidate.Genes)),
        candidate.Fitness,
        candidate.Strategy.name,
        timeDiff))


def get_distance(locationA, locationB):
    sideA = locationA[0] - locationB[0]
    sideB = locationA[1] - locationB[1]
    sideC = math.sqrt(sideA * sideA + sideB * sideB)
    return sideC


def mutate(genes, fnGetFitness):
    count = random.randint(2, len(genes))
    initialFitness = fnGetFitness(genes)
    while count > 0:
        count -= 1
        indexA, indexB = random.sample(range(len(genes)), 2)
        genes[indexA], genes[indexB] = genes[indexB], genes[indexA]
        fitness = fnGetFitness(genes)
        if fitness > initialFitness:
            return


def crossover(parentGenes, donorGenes, fnGetFitness):
    pairs = {Pair(donorGenes[0], donorGenes[-1]): 0}

    for i in range(len(donorGenes) - 1):
        pairs[Pair(donorGenes[i], donorGenes[i + 1])] = 0

    tempGenes = parentGenes[:]
    if Pair(parentGenes[0], parentGenes[-1]) in pairs:
        # find a discontinuity
        found = False
        for i in range(len(parentGenes) - 1):
            if Pair(parentGenes[i], parentGenes[i + 1]) in pairs:
                continue
            tempGenes = parentGenes[i + 1:] + parentGenes[:i + 1]
            found = True
            break
        if not found:
            return None

    runs = [[tempGenes[0]]]
    for i in range(len(tempGenes) - 1):
```

```python
            if Pair(tempGenes[i], tempGenes[i + 1]) in pairs:
                runs[-1].append(tempGenes[i + 1])
                continue
            runs.append([tempGenes[i + 1]])

    initialFitness = fnGetFitness(parentGenes)
    count = random.randint(2, 20)
    runIndexes = range(len(runs))
    while count > 0:
        count -= 1
        for i in runIndexes:
            if len(runs[i]) == 1:
                continue
            if random.randint(0, len(runs)) == 0:
                runs[i] = [n for n in reversed(runs[i])]

        indexA, indexB = random.sample(runIndexes, 2)
        runs[indexA], runs[indexB] = runs[indexB], runs[indexA]
        childGenes = list(chain.from_iterable(runs))
        if fnGetFitness(childGenes) > initialFitness:
            return childGenes
    return childGenes


class TravelingSalesmanTests(unittest.TestCase):
    def test_8_queens(self):
        idToLocationLookup = {
            'A': [4, 7],
            'B': [2, 6],
            'C': [0, 5],
            'D': [1, 3],
            'E': [3, 0],
            'F': [5, 1],
            'G': [7, 2],
            'H': [6, 4]
        }
        optimalSequence = ['A', 'B', 'C', 'D', 'E', 'F', 'G', 'H']
        self.solve(idToLocationLookup, optimalSequence)

    def test_ulysses16(self):
        idToLocationLookup = load_data("ulysses16.tsp")
        optimalSequence = [14, 13, 12, 16, 1, 3, 2, 4,
                           8, 15, 5, 11, 9, 10, 7, 6]
        self.solve(idToLocationLookup, optimalSequence)

    def test_benchmark(self):
        genetic.Benchmark.run(lambda: self.test_ulysses16())

    def solve(self, idToLocationLookup, optimalSequence):
        geneset = [i for i in idToLocationLookup.keys()]

        def fnCreate():
            return random.sample(geneset, len(geneset))
```

```
            def fnDisplay(candidate):
                display(candidate, startTime)

            def fnGetFitness(genes):
                return get_fitness(genes, idToLocationLookup)

            def fnMutate(genes):
                mutate(genes, fnGetFitness)

            def fnCrossover(parent, donor):
                return crossover(parent, donor, fnGetFitness)

            optimalFitness = fnGetFitness(optimalSequence)
            startTime = datetime.datetime.now()
            best = genetic.get_best(fnGetFitness, None, optimalFitness, None,
                                    fnDisplay, fnMutate, fnCreate, maxAge=500,
                                    poolSize=25, crossover=fnCrossover)
            self.assertTrue(not optimalFitness > best.Fitness)


def load_data(localFileName):
    """ expects:
        HEADER section before DATA section, all lines start in column 0
        DATA section element all have space in column  0
            <space>1 23.45 67.89
        last line of file is: " EOF"
    """
    with open(localFileName, mode='r') as infile:
        content = infile.read().splitlines()
    idToLocationLookup = {}
    for row in content:
        if row[0] != ' ':  # HEADERS
            continue
        if row == " EOF":
            break

        id, x, y = row.split(' ')[1:4]
        idToLocationLookup[int(id)] = [float(x), float(y)]
    return idToLocationLookup


class Fitness:
    def __init__(self, totalDistance):
        self.TotalDistance = totalDistance

    def __gt__(self, other):
        return self.TotalDistance < other.TotalDistance

    def __str__(self):
        return "{:0.2f}".format(self.TotalDistance)
```

```python
class Pair:
    def __init__(self, node, adjacent):
        if node < adjacent:
            node, adjacent = adjacent, node
        self.Node = node
        self.Adjacent = adjacent

    def __eq__(self, other):
        return self.Node == other.Node and self.Adjacent == other.Adjacent

    def __hash__(self):
        return hash(self.Node) * 397 ^ hash(self.Adjacent)


if __name__ == '__main__':
    unittest.main()
```

genetic.py

```python
# File: genetic.py
#    from chapter 12 of _Genetic Algorithms with Python_
#
# Author: Clinton Sheppard <fluentcoder@gmail.com>
# Copyright (c) 2016 Clinton Sheppard
#
# Licensed under the Apache License, Version 2.0 (the "License").
# You may not use this file except in compliance with the License.
# You may obtain a copy of the License at
#    http://www.apache.org/licenses/LICENSE-2.0
#
# Unless required by applicable law or agreed to in writing, software
# distributed under the License is distributed on an "AS IS" BASIS,
# WITHOUT WARRANTIES OR CONDITIONS OF ANY KIND, either express or
# implied.  See the License for the specific language governing
# permissions and limitations under the License.

import random
import statistics
import sys
import time
from bisect import bisect_left
from enum import Enum
from math import exp


def _generate_parent(length, geneSet, get_fitness):
    genes = []
    while len(genes) < length:
        sampleSize = min(length - len(genes), len(geneSet))
        genes.extend(random.sample(geneSet, sampleSize))
    fitness = get_fitness(genes)
    return Chromosome(genes, fitness, Strategies.Create)
```

```python
def _mutate(parent, geneSet, get_fitness):
    childGenes = parent.Genes[:]
    index = random.randrange(0, len(parent.Genes))
    newGene, alternate = random.sample(geneSet, 2)
    childGenes[index] = alternate if newGene == childGenes[index] else newGene
    fitness = get_fitness(childGenes)
    return Chromosome(childGenes, fitness, Strategies.Mutate)


def _mutate_custom(parent, custom_mutate, get_fitness):
    childGenes = parent.Genes[:]
    custom_mutate(childGenes)
    fitness = get_fitness(childGenes)
    return Chromosome(childGenes, fitness, Strategies.Mutate)


def _crossover(parentGenes, index, parents, get_fitness, crossover, mutate,
               generate_parent):
    donorIndex = random.randrange(0, len(parents))
    if donorIndex == index:
        donorIndex = (donorIndex + 1) % len(parents)
    childGenes = crossover(parentGenes, parents[donorIndex].Genes)
    if childGenes is None:
        # parent and donor are indistinguishable
        parents[donorIndex] = generate_parent()
        return mutate(parents[index])
    fitness = get_fitness(childGenes)
    return Chromosome(childGenes, fitness, Strategies.Crossover)


def get_best(get_fitness, targetLen, optimalFitness, geneSet, display,
             custom_mutate=None, custom_create=None, maxAge=None,
             poolSize=1, crossover=None):
    if custom_mutate is None:
        def fnMutate(parent):
            return _mutate(parent, geneSet, get_fitness)
    else:
        def fnMutate(parent):
            return _mutate_custom(parent, custom_mutate, get_fitness)

    if custom_create is None:
        def fnGenerateParent():
            return _generate_parent(targetLen, geneSet, get_fitness)
    else:
        def fnGenerateParent():
            genes = custom_create()
            return Chromosome(genes, get_fitness(genes), Strategies.Create)

    strategyLookup = {
        Strategies.Create: lambda p, i, o: fnGenerateParent(),
        Strategies.Mutate: lambda p, i, o: fnMutate(p),
```

```
            Strategies.Crossover: lambda p, i, o:_
            crossover(p.Genes, i, o, get_fitness, crossover, fnMutate,
                    fnGenerateParent)
    }

    usedStrategies = [strategyLookup[Strategies.Mutate]]
    if crossover is not None:
        usedStrategies.append(strategyLookup[Strategies.Crossover])

        def fnNewChild(parent, index, parents):
            return random.choice(usedStrategies)(parent, index, parents)
    else:
        def fnNewChild(parent, index, parents):
            return fnMutate(parent)

    for improvement in _get_improvement(fnNewChild, fnGenerateParent,
                                        maxAge, poolSize):
        display(improvement)
        f = strategyLookup[improvement.Strategy]
        usedStrategies.append(f)
        if not optimalFitness > improvement.Fitness:
            return improvement


def _get_improvement(new_child, generate_parent, maxAge, poolSize):
    bestParent = generate_parent()
    yield bestParent
    parents = [bestParent]
    historicalFitnesses = [bestParent.Fitness]
    for _ in range(poolSize - 1):
        parent = generate_parent()
        if parent.Fitness > bestParent.Fitness:
            yield parent
            bestParent = parent
            historicalFitnesses.append(parent.Fitness)
        parents.append(parent)
    lastParentIndex = poolSize - 1
    pindex = 1
    while True:
        pindex = pindex - 1 if pindex > 0 else lastParentIndex
        parent = parents[pindex]
        child = new_child(parent, pindex, parents)
        if parent.Fitness > child.Fitness:
            if maxAge is None:
                continue
            parent.Age += 1
            if maxAge > parent.Age:
                continue
            index = bisect_left(historicalFitnesses, child.Fitness, 0,
                                len(historicalFitnesses))
            proportionSimilar = index / len(historicalFitnesses)
            if random.random() < exp(-proportionSimilar):
                parents[pindex] = child
```

```
                continue
            bestParent.Age = 0
            parents[pindex] = bestParent
            continue
        if not child.Fitness > parent.Fitness:
            # same fitness
            child.Age = parent.Age + 1
            parents[pindex] = child
            continue
        child.Age = 0
        parents[pindex] = child
        if child.Fitness > bestParent.Fitness:
            bestParent = child
            yield bestParent
            historicalFitnesses.append(bestParent.Fitness)


class Chromosome:
    def __init__(self, genes, fitness, strategy):
        self.Genes = genes
        self.Fitness = fitness
        self.Strategy = strategy
        self.Age = 0


class Strategies(Enum):
    Create = 0,
    Mutate = 1,
    Crossover = 2


class Benchmark:
    @staticmethod
    def run(function):
        timings = []
        stdout = sys.stdout
        for i in range(100):
            sys.stdout = None
            startTime = time.time()
            function()
            seconds = time.time() - startTime
            sys.stdout = stdout
            timings.append(seconds)
            mean = statistics.mean(timings)
            if i < 10 or i % 10 == 9:
                print("{} {:3.2f} {:3.2f}".format(
                    1 + i, mean,
                    statistics.stdev(timings, mean) if i > 1 else 0))
```

Chapter 13: Approximating Pi

approximatePiTests.py

```python
# File: approximatePiTests.py
#    from chapter 13 of _Genetic Algorithms with Python_
#
# Author: Clinton Sheppard <fluentcoder@gmail.com>
# Copyright (c) 2016 Clinton Sheppard
#
# Licensed under the Apache License, Version 2.0 (the "License").
# You may not use this file except in compliance with the License.
# You may obtain a copy of the License at
#    http://www.apache.org/licenses/LICENSE-2.0
#
# Unless required by applicable law or agreed to in writing, software
# distributed under the License is distributed on an "AS IS" BASIS,
# WITHOUT WARRANTIES OR CONDITIONS OF ANY KIND, either express or
# implied.  See the License for the specific language governing
# permissions and limitations under the License.


import datetime
import math
import random
import sys
import time
import unittest

import genetic


def get_fitness(genes, bitValues):
    denominator = get_denominator(genes, bitValues)
    if denominator == 0:
        return 0

    ratio = get_numerator(genes, bitValues) / denominator
    return math.pi - math.fabs(math.pi - ratio)


def display(candidate, startTime, bitValues):
    timeDiff = datetime.datetime.now() - startTime
    numerator = get_numerator(candidate.Genes, bitValues)
    denominator = get_denominator(candidate.Genes, bitValues)
    print("{}/{}\t{}\t{}".format(
        numerator,
        denominator,
        candidate.Fitness, timeDiff))


def bits_to_int(bits, bitValues):
    result = 0
    for i, bit in enumerate(bits):
```

```python
            if bit == 0:
                continue
            result += bitValues[i]
        return result


def get_numerator(genes, bitValues):
    return 1 + bits_to_int(genes[:len(bitValues)], bitValues)


def get_denominator(genes, bitValues):
    return bits_to_int(genes[len(bitValues):], bitValues)


def mutate(genes, numBits):
    numeratorIndex, denominatorIndex \
        = random.randrange(0, numBits), random.randrange(numBits,
                                                         len(genes))
    genes[numeratorIndex] = 1 - genes[numeratorIndex]
    genes[denominatorIndex] = 1 - genes[denominatorIndex]


class ApproximatePiTests(unittest.TestCase):
    def test(self, bitValues=[512, 256, 128, 64, 32, 16, 8, 4, 2, 1],
             maxSeconds=None):
        geneset = [i for i in range(2)]
        startTime = datetime.datetime.now()

        def fnDisplay(candidate):
            display(candidate, startTime, bitValues)

        def fnGetFitness(genes):
            return get_fitness(genes, bitValues)

        optimalFitness = 3.14159

        def fnMutate(genes):
            mutate(genes, len(bitValues))

        length = 2 * len(bitValues)
        best = genetic.get_best(fnGetFitness, length, optimalFitness,
                                geneset, fnDisplay, fnMutate, maxAge=250,
                                maxSeconds=maxSeconds)
        return optimalFitness <= best.Fitness

    def test_optimize(self):
        geneset = [i for i in range(1, 512 + 1)]
        length = 10
        maxSeconds = 2

        def fnGetFitness(genes):
            startTime = time.time()
            count = 0
```

```python
                stdout = sys.stdout
                sys.stdout = None
                while time.time() - startTime < maxSeconds:
                    if self.test(genes, maxSeconds):
                        count += 1
                sys.stdout = stdout
                distance = abs(sum(genes) - 1023)
                fraction = 1 / distance if distance > 0 else distance
                count += round(fraction, 4)
                return count

            def fnDisplay(chromosome):
                print("{}\t{}".format(chromosome.Genes, chromosome.Fitness))

            initial = [512, 256, 128, 64, 32, 16, 8, 4, 2, 1]
            print("initial:", initial, fnGetFitness(initial))

            optimalFitness = 10 * maxSeconds
            genetic.get_best(fnGetFitness, length, optimalFitness, geneset,
                             fnDisplay, maxSeconds=600)

        def test_benchmark(self):
            genetic.Benchmark.run(
                lambda: self.test([98, 334, 38, 339, 117,
                                   39, 145, 123, 40, 129]))

        def test_find_top_10_approximations(self):
            best = {}
            for numerator in range(1, 1024):
                for denominator in range(1, 1024):
                    ratio = numerator / denominator
                    piDist = math.pi - abs(math.pi - ratio)
                    if piDist not in best or best[piDist][0] > numerator:
                        best[piDist] = [numerator, denominator]

            bestApproximations = list(reversed(sorted(best.keys())))
            for i in range(10):
                ratio = bestApproximations[i]
                nd = best[ratio]
                print("%i / %i\t%f" % (nd[0], nd[1], ratio))


if __name__ == '__main__':
    unittest.main()
```

genetic.py

```
# File: genetic.py
#     from chapter 13 of _Genetic Algorithms with Python_
#
# Author: Clinton Sheppard <fluentcoder@gmail.com>
# Copyright (c) 2016 Clinton Sheppard
#
# Licensed under the Apache License, Version 2.0 (the "License").
# You may not use this file except in compliance with the License.
# You may obtain a copy of the License at
#     http://www.apache.org/licenses/LICENSE-2.0
#
# Unless required by applicable law or agreed to in writing, software
# distributed under the License is distributed on an "AS IS" BASIS,
# WITHOUT WARRANTIES OR CONDITIONS OF ANY KIND, either express or
# implied.  See the License for the specific language governing
# permissions and limitations under the License.

import random
import statistics
import sys
import time
from bisect import bisect_left
from enum import Enum
from math import exp


def _generate_parent(length, geneSet, get_fitness):
    genes = []
    while len(genes) < length:
        sampleSize = min(length - len(genes), len(geneSet))
        genes.extend(random.sample(geneSet, sampleSize))
    fitness = get_fitness(genes)
    return Chromosome(genes, fitness, Strategies.Create)


def _mutate(parent, geneSet, get_fitness):
    childGenes = parent.Genes[:]
    index = random.randrange(0, len(parent.Genes))
    newGene, alternate = random.sample(geneSet, 2)
    childGenes[index] = alternate if newGene == childGenes[index] else newGene
    fitness = get_fitness(childGenes)
    return Chromosome(childGenes, fitness, Strategies.Mutate)


def _mutate_custom(parent, custom_mutate, get_fitness):
    childGenes = parent.Genes[:]
    custom_mutate(childGenes)
    fitness = get_fitness(childGenes)
    return Chromosome(childGenes, fitness, Strategies.Mutate)


def _crossover(parentGenes, index, parents, get_fitness, crossover, mutate,
```

```python
        generate_parent):
    donorIndex = random.randrange(0, len(parents))
    if donorIndex == index:
        donorIndex = (donorIndex + 1) % len(parents)
    childGenes = crossover(parentGenes, parents[donorIndex].Genes)
    if childGenes is None:
        # parent and donor are indistinguishable
        parents[donorIndex] = generate_parent()
        return mutate(parents[index])
    fitness = get_fitness(childGenes)
    return Chromosome(childGenes, fitness, Strategies.Crossover)


def get_best(get_fitness, targetLen, optimalFitness, geneSet, display,
             custom_mutate=None, custom_create=None, maxAge=None, poolSize=1,
             crossover=None, maxSeconds=None):
    if custom_mutate is None:
        def fnMutate(parent):
            return _mutate(parent, geneSet, get_fitness)
    else:
        def fnMutate(parent):
            return _mutate_custom(parent, custom_mutate, get_fitness)

    if custom_create is None:
        def fnGenerateParent():
            return _generate_parent(targetLen, geneSet, get_fitness)
    else:
        def fnGenerateParent():
            genes = custom_create()
            return Chromosome(genes, get_fitness(genes), Strategies.Create)

    strategyLookup = {
        Strategies.Create: lambda p, i, o: fnGenerateParent(),
        Strategies.Mutate: lambda p, i, o: fnMutate(p),
        Strategies.Crossover: lambda p, i, o:_
        crossover(p.Genes, i, o, get_fitness, crossover, fnMutate,
                  fnGenerateParent)
    }

    usedStrategies = [strategyLookup[Strategies.Mutate]]
    if crossover is not None:
        usedStrategies.append(strategyLookup[Strategies.Crossover])

        def fnNewChild(parent, index, parents):
            return random.choice(usedStrategies)(parent, index, parents)
    else:
        def fnNewChild(parent, index, parents):
            return fnMutate(parent)

    for timedOut, improvement in \
            get_improvement(fnNewChild, fnGenerateParent, maxAge, poolSize,
                            maxSeconds):
        if timedOut:
```

```
            return improvement
        display(improvement)
        f = strategyLookup[improvement.Strategy]
        usedStrategies.append(f)
        if not optimalFitness > improvement.Fitness:
            return improvement


def _get_improvement(new_child, generate_parent, maxAge, poolSize, maxSeconds):
    startTime = time.time()
    bestParent = generate_parent()
    yield maxSeconds is not None and time.time() \
            - startTime > maxSeconds, bestParent
    parents = [bestParent]
    historicalFitnesses = [bestParent.Fitness]
    for _ in range(poolSize - 1):
        parent = generate_parent()
        if maxSeconds is not None and time.time() - startTime > maxSeconds:
            yield True, parent
        if parent.Fitness > bestParent.Fitness:
            yield False, parent
            bestParent = parent
            historicalFitnesses.append(parent.Fitness)
        parents.append(parent)
    lastParentIndex = poolSize - 1
    pindex = 1
    while True:
        if maxSeconds is not None and time.time() - startTime > maxSeconds:
            yield True, bestParent
        pindex = pindex - 1 if pindex > 0 else lastParentIndex
        parent = parents[pindex]
        child = new_child(parent, pindex, parents)
        if parent.Fitness > child.Fitness:
            if maxAge is None:
                continue
            parent.Age += 1
            if maxAge > parent.Age:
                continue
            index = bisect_left(historicalFitnesses, child.Fitness, 0,
                                len(historicalFitnesses))
            proportionSimilar = index / len(historicalFitnesses)
            if random.random() < exp(-proportionSimilar):
                parents[pindex] = child
                continue
            bestParent.Age = 0
            parents[pindex] = bestParent
            continue
        if not child.Fitness > parent.Fitness:
            # same fitness
            child.Age = parent.Age + 1
            parents[pindex] = child
            continue
        child.Age = 0
```

```
            parents[pindex] = child
            if child.Fitness > bestParent.Fitness:
                bestParent = child
                yield False, bestParent
                historicalFitnesses.append(bestParent.Fitness)


class Chromosome:
    def __init__(self, genes, fitness, strategy):
        self.Genes = genes
        self.Fitness = fitness
        self.Strategy = strategy
        self.Age = 0


class Strategies(Enum):
    Create = 0,
    Mutate = 1,
    Crossover = 2


class Benchmark:
    @staticmethod
    def run(function):
        timings = []
        stdout = sys.stdout
        for i in range(100):
            sys.stdout = None
            startTime = time.time()
            function()
            seconds = time.time() - startTime
            sys.stdout = stdout
            timings.append(seconds)
            mean = statistics.mean(timings)
            if i < 10 or i % 10 == 9:
                print("{} {:3.2f} {:3.2f}".format(
                    1 + i, mean,
                    statistics.stdev(timings, mean) if i > 1 else 0))
```

Chapter 14: Equation Generation

equationGenerationTests.py

```python
# File: equationGenerationTests.py
#    from chapter 14 of _Genetic Algorithms with Python_
#
# Author: Clinton Sheppard <fluentcoder@gmail.com>
# Copyright (c) 2016 Clinton Sheppard
#
# Licensed under the Apache License, Version 2.0 (the "License").
# You may not use this file except in compliance with the License.
# You may obtain a copy of the License at
#    http://www.apache.org/licenses/LICENSE-2.0
#
# Unless required by applicable law or agreed to in writing, software
# distributed under the License is distributed on an "AS IS" BASIS,
# WITHOUT WARRANTIES OR CONDITIONS OF ANY KIND, either express or
# implied.  See the License for the specific language governing
# permissions and limitations under the License.

import datetime
import random
import unittest

import genetic


def evaluate(genes, prioritizedOperations):
    equation = genes[:]
    for operationSet in prioritizedOperations:
        iOffset = 0
        for i in range(1, len(equation), 2):
            i += iOffset
            opToken = equation[i]
            if opToken in operationSet:
                leftOperand = equation[i - 1]
                rightOperand = equation[i + 1]
                equation[i - 1] = operationSet[opToken](leftOperand,
                                                        rightOperand)
                del equation[i + 1]
                del equation[i]
                iOffset += -2
    return equation[0]


def add(a, b):
    return a + b


def subtract(a, b):
    return a - b
```

```python
def multiply(a, b):
    return a * b


def get_fitness(genes, expectedTotal, fnEvaluate):
    result = fnEvaluate(genes)

    if result != expectedTotal:
        fitness = expectedTotal - abs(result - expectedTotal)
    else:
        fitness = 1000 - len(genes)

    return fitness


def display(candidate, startTime):
    timeDiff = datetime.datetime.now() - startTime
    print("{}\t{}\t{}".format(
        (' '.join(map(str, [i for i in candidate.Genes]))),
        candidate.Fitness,
        timeDiff))


def create(numbers, operations, minNumbers, maxNumbers):
    genes = [random.choice(numbers)]
    count = random.randint(minNumbers, 1 + maxNumbers)
    while count > 1:
        count -= 1
        genes.append(random.choice(operations))
        genes.append(random.choice(numbers))
    return genes


def mutate(genes, numbers, operations, minNumbers, maxNumbers,
           fnGetFitness):
    count = random.randint(1, 10)
    initialFitness = fnGetFitness(genes)
    while count > 0:
        count -= 1
        if fnGetFitness(genes) > initialFitness:
            return
        numberCount = (1 + len(genes)) / 2
        adding = numberCount < maxNumbers and random.randint(0, 100) == 0
        if adding:
            genes.append(random.choice(operations))
            genes.append(random.choice(numbers))
            continue

        removing = numberCount > minNumbers and random.randint(0, 20) == 0
        if removing:
            index = random.randrange(0, len(genes) - 1)
            del genes[index]
```

```
            del genes[index]
            continue

        index = random.randrange(0, len(genes))
        genes[index] = random.choice(operations) \
            if (index & 1) == 1 else random.choice(numbers)


class EquationGenerationTests(unittest.TestCase):
    def test_addition(self):
        operations = ['+', '-']
        prioritizedOperations = [{'+': add,
                                  '-': subtract}]
        optimalLengthSolution = [7, '+', 7, '+', 7, '+', 7, '+', 7, '-', 6]
        self.solve(operations, prioritizedOperations, optimalLengthSolution)

    def test_multiplication(self):
        operations = ['+', '-', '*']
        prioritizedOperations = [{'*': multiply},
                                 {'+': add,
                                  '-': subtract}]
        optimalLengthSolution = [6, '*', 3, '*', 3, '*', 6, '-', 7]
        self.solve(operations, prioritizedOperations, optimalLengthSolution)

    def test_exponent(self):
        operations = ['^', '+', '-', '*']
        prioritizedOperations = [{'^': lambda a, b: a ** b},
                                 {'*': multiply},
                                 {'+': add,
                                  '-': subtract}]
        optimalLengthSolution = [6, '^', 3, '*', 2, '-', 5]
        self.solve(operations, prioritizedOperations, optimalLengthSolution)

    def solve(self, operations, prioritizedOperations,
              optimalLengthSolution):
        numbers = [1, 2, 3, 4, 5, 6, 7]
        expectedTotal = evaluate(optimalLengthSolution,
                                 prioritizedOperations)
        minNumbers = (1 + len(optimalLengthSolution)) / 2
        maxNumbers = 6 * minNumbers
        startTime = datetime.datetime.now()

        def fnDisplay(candidate):
            display(candidate, startTime)

        def fnEvaluate(genes):
            return evaluate(genes, prioritizedOperations)

        def fnGetFitness(genes):
            return get_fitness(genes, expectedTotal, fnEvaluate)

        def fnCreate():
            return create(numbers, operations, minNumbers, maxNumbers)
```

```python
    def fnMutate(child):
        mutate(child, numbers, operations, minNumbers, maxNumbers,
               fnGetFitness)

    optimalFitness = fnGetFitness(optimalLengthSolution)
    best = genetic.get_best(fnGetFitness, None, optimalFitness, None,
                            fnDisplay, fnMutate, fnCreate, maxAge=50)
    self.assertTrue(not optimalFitness > best.Fitness)

    def test_benchmark(self):
        genetic.Benchmark.run(self.test_exponent)


if __name__ == '__main__':
    unittest.main()
```

Chapter 15: The Lawnmower Problem

lawnmowerTests.py

```python
# File: lawnmowerTests.py
#    from chapter 15 of _Genetic Algorithms with Python_
#
# Author: Clinton Sheppard <fluentcoder@gmail.com>
# Copyright (c) 2016 Clinton Sheppard
#
# Licensed under the Apache License, Version 2.0 (the "License").
# You may not use this file except in compliance with the License.
# You may obtain a copy of the License at
#    http://www.apache.org/licenses/LICENSE-2.0
#
# Unless required by applicable law or agreed to in writing, software
# distributed under the License is distributed on an "AS IS" BASIS,
# WITHOUT WARRANTIES OR CONDITIONS OF ANY KIND, either express or
# implied.  See the License for the specific language governing
# permissions and limitations under the License.

import datetime
import random
import unittest

import genetic
import lawnmower


def get_fitness(genes, fnEvaluate):
    field, mower, _ = fnEvaluate(genes)
    return Fitness(field.count_mowed(), len(genes), mower.StepCount)
```

```python
def display(candidate, startTime, fnEvaluate):
    field, mower, program = fnEvaluate(candidate.Genes)
    timeDiff = datetime.datetime.now() - startTime
    field.display(mower)
    print("{}\t{}".format(
        candidate.Fitness,
        timeDiff))
    program.print()


def mutate(genes, geneSet, minGenes, maxGenes, fnGetFitness, maxRounds):
    count = random.randint(1, maxRounds)
    initialFitness = fnGetFitness(genes)
    while count > 0:
        count -= 1
        if fnGetFitness(genes) > initialFitness:
            return
        adding = len(genes) == 0 or \
                 (len(genes) < maxGenes and random.randint(0, 5) == 0)
        if adding:
            genes.append(random.choice(geneSet)())
            continue

        removing = len(genes) > minGenes and random.randint(0, 50) == 0
        if removing:
            index = random.randrange(0, len(genes))
            del genes[index]
            continue

        index = random.randrange(0, len(genes))
        genes[index] = random.choice(geneSet)()


def create(geneSet, minGenes, maxGenes):
    numGenes = random.randint(minGenes, maxGenes)
    genes = [random.choice(geneSet)() for _ in range(1, numGenes)]
    return genes


def crossover(parent, otherParent):
    childGenes = parent[:]
    if len(parent) <= 2 or len(otherParent) < 2:
        return childGenes
    length = random.randint(1, len(parent) - 2)
    start = random.randrange(0, len(parent) - length)
    childGenes[start:start + length] = otherParent[start:start + length]
    return childGenes


class LawnmowerTests(unittest.TestCase):
    def test_mow_turn(self):
        width = height = 8
        geneSet = [lambda: Mow(),
```

```
                                    lambda: Turn()]
        minGenes = width * height
        maxGenes = int(1.5 * minGenes)
        maxMutationRounds = 3
        expectedNumberOfInstructions = 78

        def fnCreateField():
            return lawnmower.ToroidField(width, height,
                                         lawnmower.FieldContents.Grass)

        self.run_with(geneSet, width, height, minGenes, maxGenes,
                      expectedNumberOfInstructions, maxMutationRounds,
                      fnCreateField, expectedNumberOfInstructions)

    def test_mow_turn_jump(self):
        width = height = 8
        geneSet = [lambda: Mow(),
                   lambda: Turn(),
                   lambda: Jump(random.randint(0, min(width, height)),
                               random.randint(0, min(width, height)))]
        minGenes = width * height
        maxGenes = int(1.5 * minGenes)
        maxMutationRounds = 1
        expectedNumberOfInstructions = 64

        def fnCreateField():
            return lawnmower.ToroidField(width, height,
                                         lawnmower.FieldContents.Grass)

        self.run_with(geneSet, width, height, minGenes, maxGenes,
                      expectedNumberOfInstructions, maxMutationRounds,
                      fnCreateField, expectedNumberOfInstructions)

    def test_mow_turn_jump_validating(self):
        width = height = 8
        geneSet = [lambda: Mow(),
                   lambda: Turn(),
                   lambda: Jump(random.randint(0, min(width, height)),
                               random.randint(0, min(width, height)))]
        minGenes = width * height
        maxGenes = int(1.5 * minGenes)
        maxMutationRounds = 3
        expectedNumberOfInstructions = 79

        def fnCreateField():
            return lawnmower.ValidatingField(width, height,
                                             lawnmower.FieldContents.Grass)

        self.run_with(geneSet, width, height, minGenes, maxGenes,
                      expectedNumberOfInstructions, maxMutationRounds,
                      fnCreateField, expectedNumberOfInstructions)

    def test_mow_turn_repeat(self):
```

Final code from each project   375

```
            width = height = 8
            geneSet = [lambda: Mow(),
                       lambda: Turn(),
                       lambda: Repeat(random.randint(0, 8),
                                      random.randint(0, 8))]
        minGenes = 3
        maxGenes = 20
        maxMutationRounds = 3
        expectedNumberOfInstructions = 9
        expectedNumberOfSteps = 88

        def fnCreateField():
            return lawnmower.ToroidField(width, height,
                                         lawnmower.FieldContents.Grass)

        self.run_with(geneSet, width, height, minGenes, maxGenes,
                      expectedNumberOfInstructions, maxMutationRounds,
                      fnCreateField, expectedNumberOfSteps)

    def test_mow_turn_jump_func(self):
        width = height = 8
        geneSet = [lambda: Mow(),
                   lambda: Turn(),
                   lambda: Jump(random.randint(0, min(width, height)),
                                random.randint(0, min(width, height))),
                   lambda: Func()]
        minGenes = 3
        maxGenes = 20
        maxMutationRounds = 3
        expectedNumberOfInstructions = 18
        expectedNumberOfSteps = 65

        def fnCreateField():
            return lawnmower.ToroidField(width, height,
                                         lawnmower.FieldContents.Grass)

        self.run_with(geneSet, width, height, minGenes, maxGenes,
                      expectedNumberOfInstructions, maxMutationRounds,
                      fnCreateField, expectedNumberOfSteps)

    def test_mow_turn_jump_call(self):
        width = height = 8
        geneSet = [lambda: Mow(),
                   lambda: Turn(),
                   lambda: Jump(random.randint(0, min(width, height)),
                                random.randint(0, min(width, height))),
                   lambda: Func(expectCall=True),
                   lambda: Call(random.randint(0, 5))]
        minGenes = 3
        maxGenes = 20
        maxMutationRounds = 3
        expectedNumberOfInstructions = 18
        expectedNumberOfSteps = 65
```

```python
        def fnCreateField():
            return lawnmower.ToroidField(width, height,
                                         lawnmower.FieldContents.Grass)

        self.run_with(geneSet, width, height, minGenes, maxGenes,
                      expectedNumberOfInstructions, maxMutationRounds,
                      fnCreateField, expectedNumberOfSteps)

    def run_with(self, geneSet, width, height, minGenes, maxGenes,
                 expectedNumberOfInstructions, maxMutationRounds,
                 fnCreateField, expectedNumberOfSteps):
        mowerStartLocation = lawnmower.Location(int(width / 2),
                                                int(height / 2))
        mowerStartDirection = lawnmower.Directions.South.value

        def fnCreate():
            return create(geneSet, 1, height)

        def fnEvaluate(instructions):
            program = Program(instructions)
            mower = lawnmower.Mower(mowerStartLocation, mowerStartDirection)
            field = fnCreateField()
            try:
                program.evaluate(mower, field)
            except RecursionError:
                pass
            return field, mower, program

        def fnGetFitness(genes):
            return get_fitness(genes, fnEvaluate)

        startTime = datetime.datetime.now()

        def fnDisplay(candidate):
            display(candidate, startTime, fnEvaluate)

        def fnMutate(child):
            mutate(child, geneSet, minGenes, maxGenes, fnGetFitness,
                   maxMutationRounds)

        optimalFitness = Fitness(width * height,
                                 expectedNumberOfInstructions,
                                 expectedNumberOfSteps)

        best = genetic.get_best(fnGetFitness, None, optimalFitness, None,
                                fnDisplay, fnMutate, fnCreate, maxAge=None,
                                poolSize=10, crossover=crossover)

        self.assertTrue(not optimalFitness > best.Fitness)


class Mow:
```

```python
    def __init__(self):
        pass

    @staticmethod
    def execute(mower, field):
        mower.mow(field)

    def __str__(self):
        return "mow"


class Turn:
    def __init__(self):
        pass

    @staticmethod
    def execute(mower, field):
        mower.turn_left()

    def __str__(self):
        return "turn"


class Jump:
    def __init__(self, forward, right):
        self.Forward = forward
        self.Right = right

    def execute(self, mower, field):
        mower.jump(field, self.Forward, self.Right)

    def __str__(self):
        return "jump({},{})".format(self.Forward, self.Right)


class Repeat:
    def __init__(self, opCount, times):
        self.OpCount = opCount
        self.Times = times
        self.Ops = []

    def execute(self, mower, field):
        for i in range(self.Times):
            for op in self.Ops:
                op.execute(mower, field)

    def __str__(self):
        return "repeat({},{})".format(
            ' '.join(map(str, self.Ops))
            if len(self.Ops) > 0
            else self.OpCount,
            self.Times)
```

```python
class Func:
    def __init__(self, expectCall=False):
        self.Ops = []
        self.ExpectCall = expectCall
        self.Id = None

    def execute(self, mower, field):
        for op in self.Ops:
            op.execute(mower, field)

    def __str__(self):
        return "func{1}: {0}".format(
            ' '.join(map(str, self.Ops)),
            self.Id if self.Id is not None else '')


class Call:
    def __init__(self, funcId=None):
        self.FuncId = funcId
        self.Funcs = None

    def execute(self, mower, field):
        funcId = 0 if self.FuncId is None else self.FuncId
        if len(self.Funcs) > funcId:
            self.Funcs[funcId].execute(mower, field)

    def __str__(self):
        return "call-{}".format(
            self.FuncId
            if self.FuncId is not None
            else 'func')


class Program:
    def __init__(self, genes):
        temp = genes[:]
        funcs = []

        for index in reversed(range(len(temp))):
            if type(temp[index]) is Repeat:
                start = index + 1
                end = min(index + temp[index].OpCount + 1, len(temp))
                temp[index].Ops = [i for i in temp[start:end]
                                   if type(i) is not Repeat or
                                   type(i) is Repeat and len(i.Ops) > 0
                                   ]
                del temp[start:end]
                continue

            if type(temp[index]) is Call:
                temp[index].Funcs = funcs
            if type(temp[index]) is Func:
```

```python
                    if len(funcs) > 0 and not temp[index].ExpectCall:
                        temp[index] = Call()
                        temp[index].Funcs = funcs
                        continue
                    start = index + 1
                    end = len(temp)
                    func = Func()
                    if temp[index].ExpectCall:
                        func.Id = len(funcs)
                    func.Ops = [i for i in temp[start:end]
                                if type(i) is not Repeat or
                                type(i) is Repeat and len(i.Ops) > 0
                                ]
                    funcs.append(func)
                    del temp[index:end]

            for func in funcs:
                for index in reversed(range(len(func.Ops))):
                    if type(func.Ops[index]) is Call:
                        func_id = func.Ops[index].FuncId
                        if func_id is None:
                            continue
                        if func_id >= len(funcs) or \
                                      len(funcs[func_id].Ops) == 0:
                            del func.Ops[index]

            for index in reversed(range(len(temp))):
                if type(temp[index]) is Call:
                    func_id = temp[index].FuncId
                    if func_id is None:
                        continue
                    if func_id >= len(funcs) or \
                                  len(funcs[func_id].Ops) == 0:
                        del temp[index]
            self.Main = temp
            self.Funcs = funcs

    def evaluate(self, mower, field):
        for i, instruction in enumerate(self.Main):
            instruction.execute(mower, field)

    def print(self):
        if self.Funcs is not None:
            for func in self.Funcs:
                if func.Id is not None and len(func.Ops) == 0:
                    continue
                print(func)
        print(' '.join(map(str, self.Main)))


class Fitness:
    def __init__(self, totalMowed, totalInstructions, stepCount):
        self.TotalMowed = totalMowed
```

```python
        self.TotalInstructions = totalInstructions
        self.StepCount = stepCount

    def __gt__(self, other):
        if self.TotalMowed != other.TotalMowed:
            return self.TotalMowed > other.TotalMowed
        if self.StepCount != other.StepCount:
            return self.StepCount < other.StepCount
        return self.TotalInstructions < other.TotalInstructions

    def __str__(self):
        return "{} mowed with {} instructions and {} steps".format(
            self.TotalMowed, self.TotalInstructions, self.StepCount)


if __name__ == '__main__':
    unittest.main()
```

lawnmower.py

```python
# File: lawnmower.py
#    from chapter 15 of _Genetic Algorithms with Python_
#
# Author: Clinton Sheppard <fluentcoder@gmail.com>
# Copyright (c) 2016 Clinton Sheppard
#
# Licensed under the Apache License, Version 2.0 (the "License").
# You may not use this file except in compliance with the License.
# You may obtain a copy of the License at
#    http://www.apache.org/licenses/LICENSE-2.0
#
# Unless required by applicable law or agreed to in writing, software
# distributed under the License is distributed on an "AS IS" BASIS,
# WITHOUT WARRANTIES OR CONDITIONS OF ANY KIND, either express or
# implied.  See the License for the specific language governing
# permissions and limitations under the License.

from enum import Enum


class FieldContents(Enum):
    Grass = ' #'
    Mowed = ' .'
    Mower = 'M'

    def __str__(self):
        return self.value


class Direction:
    def __init__(self, index, xOffset, yOffset, symbol):
        self.Index = index
```

```python
        self.XOffset = xOffset
        self.YOffset = yOffset
        self.Symbol = symbol

    def move_from(self, location, distance=1):
        return Location(location.X + distance * self.XOffset,
                        location.Y + distance * self.YOffset)


class Directions(Enum):
    North = Direction(0, 0, -1, '^')
    East = Direction(1, 1, 0, '>')
    South = Direction(2, 0, 1, 'v')
    West = Direction(3, -1, 0, '<')

    @staticmethod
    def get_direction_after_turn_left_90_degrees(direction):
        newIndex = direction.Index - 1 \
            if direction.Index > 0 \
            else len(Directions) - 1
        newDirection = next(i for i in Directions
                            if i.value.Index == newIndex)
        return newDirection.value

    @staticmethod
    def get_direction_after_turn_right_90_degrees(direction):
        newIndex = direction.Index + 1 \
            if direction.Index < len(Directions) - 1 \
            else 0
        newDirection = next(i for i in Directions
                            if i.value.Index == newIndex)
        return newDirection.value


class Location:
    def __init__(self, x, y):
        self.X, self.Y = x, y

    def move(self, xOffset, yOffset):
        return Location(self.X + xOffset,
                        self.Y + yOffset)


class Mower:
    def __init__(self, location, direction):
        self.Location = location
        self.Direction = direction
        self.StepCount = 0

    def turn_left(self):
        self.StepCount += 1
        self.Direction = Directions\
            .get_direction_after_turn_left_90_degrees(self.Direction)
```

```python
    def mow(self, field):
        newLocation = self.Direction.move_from(self.Location)
        newLocation, isValid = field.fix_location(newLocation)
        if isValid:
            self.Location = newLocation
            self.StepCount += 1
            field.set(self.Location, self.StepCount
                if self.StepCount > 9
                else " {}".format(self.StepCount))

    def jump(self, field, forward, right):
        newLocation = self.Direction.move_from(self.Location, forward)
        rightDirection = Directions\
            .get_direction_after_turn_right_90_degrees(self.Direction)
        newLocation = rightDirection.move_from(newLocation, right)
        newLocation, isValid = field.fix_location(newLocation)
        if isValid:
            self.Location = newLocation
            self.StepCount += 1
            field.set(self.Location, self.StepCount
                if self.StepCount > 9
                else " {}".format(self.StepCount))


class Field:
    def __init__(self, width, height, initialContent):
        self.Field = [[initialContent] * width for _ in range(height)]
        self.Width = width
        self.Height = height

    def set(self, location, symbol):
        self.Field[location.Y][location.X] = symbol

    def count_mowed(self):
        return sum(1 for row in range(self.Height)
                   for column in range(self.Width)
                   if self.Field[row][column] != FieldContents.Grass)

    def display(self, mower):
        for rowIndex in range(self.Height):
            if rowIndex != mower.Location.Y:
                row = ' '.join(map(str, self.Field[rowIndex]))
            else:
                r = self.Field[rowIndex][:]
                r[mower.Location.X] = "{}{}".format(
                    FieldContents.Mower, mower.Direction.Symbol)
                row = ' '.join(map(str, r))
            print(row)


class ValidatingField(Field):
    def __init__(self, width, height, initialContent):
```

```
                super().__init__(width, height, initialContent)

        def fix_location(self, location):
            if location.X >= self.Width or \
                         location.X < 0 or \
                         location.Y >= self.Height or \
                         location.Y < 0:
                return None, False
            return location, True


class ToroidField(Field):
    def __init__(self, width, height, initialContent):
        super().__init__(width, height, initialContent)

    def fix_location(self, location):
        newLocation = Location(location.X, location.Y)
        if newLocation.X < 0:
            newLocation.X += self.Width
        elif newLocation.X >= self.Width:
            newLocation.X %= self.Width

        if newLocation.Y < 0:
            newLocation.Y += self.Height
        elif newLocation.Y >= self.Height:
            newLocation.Y %= self.Height

        return newLocation, True
```

Chapter 16: Logic Circuits

circuitTests.py

```
# File: circuitTests.py
#    from chapter 16 of _Genetic Algorithms with Python_
#
# Author: Clinton Sheppard <fluentcoder@gmail.com>
# Copyright (c) 2016 Clinton Sheppard
#
# Licensed under the Apache License, Version 2.0 (the "License").
# You may not use this file except in compliance with the License.
# You may obtain a copy of the License at
#   http://www.apache.org/licenses/LICENSE-2.0
#
# Unless required by applicable law or agreed to in writing, software
# distributed under the License is distributed on an "AS IS" BASIS,
# WITHOUT WARRANTIES OR CONDITIONS OF ANY KIND, either express or
# implied.  See the License for the specific language governing
# permissions and limitations under the License.

import datetime
```

```python
import random
import unittest

import circuits
import genetic


def get_fitness(genes, rules, inputs):
    circuit = nodes_to_circuit(genes)[0]
    sourceLabels = "ABCD"
    rulesPassed = 0
    for rule in rules:
        inputs.clear()
        inputs.update(zip(sourceLabels, rule[0]))
        if circuit.get_output() == rule[1]:
            rulesPassed += 1
    return rulesPassed


def display(candidate, startTime):
    circuit = nodes_to_circuit(candidate.Genes)[0]
    timeDiff = datetime.datetime.now() - startTime
    print("{}\t{}\t{}".format(
        circuit,
        candidate.Fitness,
        timeDiff))


def create_gene(index, gates, sources):
    if index < len(sources):
        gateType = sources[index]
    else:
        gateType = random.choice(gates)
    indexA = indexB = None
    if gateType[1].input_count() > 0:
        indexA = random.randint(0, index)
    if gateType[1].input_count() > 1:
        indexB = random.randint(0, index) \
            if index > 1 and index >= len(sources) else 0
        if indexB == indexA:
            indexB = random.randint(0, index)
    return Node(gateType[0], indexA, indexB)


def mutate(childGenes, fnCreateGene, fnGetFitness, sourceCount):
    count = random.randint(1, 5)
    initialFitness = fnGetFitness(childGenes)
    while count > 0:
        count -= 1
        indexesUsed = [i for i in nodes_to_circuit(childGenes)[1]
                       if i >= sourceCount]
        if len(indexesUsed) == 0:
            return
```

```
                index = random.choice(indexesUsed)
                childGenes[index] = fnCreateGene(index)
                if fnGetFitness(childGenes) > initialFitness:
                    return


class CircuitTests(unittest.TestCase):
    @classmethod
    def setUpClass(cls):
        cls.inputs = dict()
        cls.gates = [[circuits.And, circuits.And],
                     [lambda i1, i2: circuits.Not(i1), circuits.Not]]
        cls.sources = [
            [lambda i1, i2: circuits.Source('A', cls.inputs),
             circuits.Source],
            [lambda i1, i2: circuits.Source('B', cls.inputs),
             circuits.Source]]

    def test_generate_OR(self):
        rules = [[[False, False], False],
                 [[False, True], True],
                 [[True, False], True],
                 [[True, True], True]]

        optimalLength = 6
        self.find_circuit(rules, optimalLength)

    def test_generate_XOR(self):
        rules = [[[False, False], False],
                 [[False, True], True],
                 [[True, False], True],
                 [[True, True], False]]
        self.find_circuit(rules, 9)

    def test_generate_AxBxC(self):
        rules = [[[False, False, False], False],
                 [[False, False, True], True],
                 [[False, True, False], True],
                 [[False, True, True], False],
                 [[True, False, False], True],
                 [[True, False, True], False],
                 [[True, True, False], False],
                 [[True, True, True], True]]
        self.sources.append(
            [lambda l, r: circuits.Source('C', self.inputs),
             circuits.Source])
        self.gates.append([circuits.Or, circuits.Or])
        self.find_circuit(rules, 12)

    def get_2_bit_adder_rules_for_bit(self, bit):
        rules = [[[0, 0, 0, 0], [0, 0, 0]],    # 0 + 0 = 0
                 [[0, 0, 0, 1], [0, 0, 1]],    # 0 + 1 = 1
                 [[0, 0, 1, 0], [0, 1, 0]],    # 0 + 2 = 2
```

```
                    [[0, 0, 1, 1], [0, 1, 1]],  # 0 + 3 = 3
                    [[0, 1, 0, 0], [0, 0, 1]],  # 1 + 0 = 1
                    [[0, 1, 0, 1], [0, 1, 0]],  # 1 + 1 = 2
                    [[0, 1, 1, 0], [0, 1, 1]],  # 1 + 2 = 3
                    [[0, 1, 1, 1], [1, 0, 0]],  # 1 + 3 = 4
                    [[1, 0, 0, 0], [0, 1, 0]],  # 2 + 0 = 2
                    [[1, 0, 0, 1], [0, 1, 1]],  # 2 + 1 = 3
                    [[1, 0, 1, 0], [1, 0, 0]],  # 2 + 2 = 4
                    [[1, 0, 1, 1], [1, 0, 1]],  # 2 + 3 = 5
                    [[1, 1, 0, 0], [0, 1, 1]],  # 3 + 0 = 3
                    [[1, 1, 0, 1], [1, 0, 0]],  # 3 + 1 = 4
                    [[1, 1, 1, 0], [1, 0, 1]],  # 3 + 2 = 5
                    [[1, 1, 1, 1], [1, 1, 0]]]  # 3 + 3 = 6
        bitNRules = [[rule[0], rule[1][2 - bit]] for rule in rules]
        self.gates.append([circuits.Or, circuits.Or])
        self.gates.append([circuits.Xor, circuits.Xor])
        self.sources.append(
            [lambda l, r: circuits.Source('C', self.inputs),
             circuits.Source])
        self.sources.append(
            [lambda l, r: circuits.Source('D', self.inputs),
             circuits.Source])
        return bitNRules

    def test_2_bit_adder_1s_bit(self):
        rules = self.get_2_bit_adder_rules_for_bit(0)
        self.find_circuit(rules, 3)

    def test_2_bit_adder_2s_bit(self):
        rules = self.get_2_bit_adder_rules_for_bit(1)
        self.find_circuit(rules, 7)

    def test_2_bit_adder_4s_bit(self):
        rules = self.get_2_bit_adder_rules_for_bit(2)
        self.find_circuit(rules, 9)

    def find_circuit(self, rules, expectedLength):
        startTime = datetime.datetime.now()

        def fnDisplay(candidate, length=None):
            if length is not None:
                print("-- distinct nodes in circuit:",
                      len(nodes_to_circuit(candidate.Genes)[1]))
            display(candidate, startTime)

        def fnGetFitness(genes):
            return get_fitness(genes, rules, self.inputs)

        def fnCreateGene(index):
            return create_gene(index, self.gates, self.sources)

        def fnMutate(genes):
            mutate(genes, fnCreateGene, fnGetFitness, len(self.sources))
```

```
            maxLength = 50

        def fnCreate():
            return [fnCreateGene(i) for i in range(maxLength)]

        def fnOptimizationFunction(variableLength):
            nonlocal maxLength
            maxLength = variableLength
            return genetic.get_best(fnGetFitness, None, len(rules), None,
                                    fnDisplay, fnMutate, fnCreate,
                                    poolSize=3, maxSeconds=30)

        def fnIsImprovement(currentBest, child):
            return child.Fitness == len(rules) and \
                len(nodes_to_circuit(child.Genes)[1]) < \
                len(nodes_to_circuit(currentBest.Genes)[1])

        def fnIsOptimal(child):
            return child.Fitness == len(rules) and \
                len(nodes_to_circuit(child.Genes)[1]) <= expectedLength

        def fnGetNextFeatureValue(currentBest):
            return len(nodes_to_circuit(currentBest.Genes)[1])

        best = genetic.hill_climbing(fnOptimizationFunction,
                                     fnIsImprovement, fnIsOptimal,
                                     fnGetNextFeatureValue, fnDisplay,
                                     maxLength)
        self.assertTrue(best.Fitness == len(rules))
        self.assertFalse(len(nodes_to_circuit(best.Genes)[1])
                         > expectedLength)


def nodes_to_circuit(genes):
    circuit = []
    usedIndexes = []
    for i, node in enumerate(genes):
        used = {i}
        inputA = inputB = None
        if node.IndexA is not None and i > node.IndexA:
            inputA = circuit[node.IndexA]
            used.update(usedIndexes[node.IndexA])
            if node.IndexB is not None and i > node.IndexB:
                inputB = circuit[node.IndexB]
                used.update(usedIndexes[node.IndexB])
        circuit.append(node.CreateGate(inputA, inputB))
        usedIndexes.append(used)
    return circuit[-1], usedIndexes[-1]


class Node:
    def __init__(self, createGate, indexA=None, indexB=None):
```

```
                self.CreateGate = createGate
                self.IndexA = indexA
                self.IndexB = indexB


if __name__ == '__main__':
    unittest.main()
```

circuits.py

```
# File: circuits.py
#    from chapter 16 of _Genetic Algorithms with Python_
#
# Author: Clinton Sheppard <fluentcoder@gmail.com>
# Copyright (c) 2016 Clinton Sheppard
#
# Licensed under the Apache License, Version 2.0 (the "License").
# You may not use this file except in compliance with the License.
# You may obtain a copy of the License at
#   http://www.apache.org/licenses/LICENSE-2.0
#
# Unless required by applicable law or agreed to in writing, software
# distributed under the License is distributed on an "AS IS" BASIS,
# WITHOUT WARRANTIES OR CONDITIONS OF ANY KIND, either express or
# implied.  See the License for the specific language governing
# permissions and limitations under the License.

class Not:
    def __init__(self, input):
        self._input = input

    def get_output(self):
        if self._input is None:
            return None
        value = self._input.get_output()
        if value is None:
            return None
        return not value

    def __str__(self):
        if self._input is None:
            return "Not(?)"
        return "Not({})".format(self._input)

    @staticmethod
    def input_count():
        return 1


class GateWith2Inputs:
    def __init__(self, inputA, inputB, label, fnTest):
        self._inputA = inputA
```

```python
        self._inputB = inputB
        self._label = label
        self._fnTest = fnTest

    def get_output(self):
        if self._inputA is None or self._inputB is None:
            return None
        aValue = self._inputA.get_output()
        if aValue is None:
            return None
        bValue = self._inputB.get_output()
        if bValue is None:
            return None
        return self._fnTest(aValue, bValue)

    def __str__(self):
        if self._inputA is None or self._inputB is None:
            return "{}(?)".format(self._label)
        return "{}({} {})".format(self._label, self._inputA, self._inputB)

    @staticmethod
    def input_count():
        return 2


class And(GateWith2Inputs):
    def __init__(self, inputA, inputB):
        super().__init__(inputA, inputB, type(self).__name__,
                         lambda a, b: a and b)


class Or(GateWith2Inputs):
    def __init__(self, inputA, inputB):
        super().__init__(inputA, inputB, type(self).__name__,
                         lambda a, b: a or b)


class Xor(GateWith2Inputs):
    def __init__(self, inputA, inputB):
        super().__init__(inputA, inputB, type(self).__name__,
                         lambda a, b: a != b)


class Source:
    def __init__(self, sourceId, sourceContainer):
        self._sourceId = sourceId
        self._sourceContainer = sourceContainer

    def get_output(self):
        return self._sourceContainer[self._sourceId]

    def __str__(self):
        return self._sourceId
```

```
    @staticmethod
    def input_count():
        return 0
```

genetic.py

```python
# File: genetic.py
#    from chapter 16 of _Genetic Algorithms with Python_
#
# Author: Clinton Sheppard <fluentcoder@gmail.com>
# Copyright (c) 2016 Clinton Sheppard
#
# Licensed under the Apache License, Version 2.0 (the "License").
# You may not use this file except in compliance with the License.
# You may obtain a copy of the License at
#    http://www.apache.org/licenses/LICENSE-2.0
#
# Unless required by applicable law or agreed to in writing, software
# distributed under the License is distributed on an "AS IS" BASIS,
# WITHOUT WARRANTIES OR CONDITIONS OF ANY KIND, either express or
# implied.  See the License for the specific language governing
# permissions and limitations under the License.

import random
import statistics
import sys
import time
from bisect import bisect_left
from enum import Enum
from math import exp


def _generate_parent(length, geneSet, get_fitness):
    genes = []
    while len(genes) < length:
        sampleSize = min(length - len(genes), len(geneSet))
        genes.extend(random.sample(geneSet, sampleSize))
    fitness = get_fitness(genes)
    return Chromosome(genes, fitness, Strategies.Create)


def _mutate(parent, geneSet, get_fitness):
    childGenes = parent.Genes[:]
    index = random.randrange(0, len(parent.Genes))
    newGene, alternate = random.sample(geneSet, 2)
    childGenes[index] = alternate if newGene == childGenes[index] else newGene
    fitness = get_fitness(childGenes)
    return Chromosome(childGenes, fitness, Strategies.Mutate)


def _mutate_custom(parent, custom_mutate, get_fitness):
```

```python
        childGenes = parent.Genes[:]
    custom_mutate(childGenes)
    fitness = get_fitness(childGenes)
    return Chromosome(childGenes, fitness, Strategies.Mutate)


def _crossover(parentGenes, index, parents, get_fitness, crossover, mutate,
               generate_parent):
    donorIndex = random.randrange(0, len(parents))
    if donorIndex == index:
        donorIndex = (donorIndex + 1) % len(parents)
    childGenes = crossover(parentGenes, parents[donorIndex].Genes)
    if childGenes is None:
        # parent and donor are indistinguishable
        parents[donorIndex] = generate_parent()
        return mutate(parents[index])
    fitness = get_fitness(childGenes)
    return Chromosome(childGenes, fitness, Strategies.Crossover)


def get_best(get_fitness, targetLen, optimalFitness, geneSet, display,
             custom_mutate=None, custom_create=None, maxAge=None,
             poolSize=1, crossover=None, maxSeconds=None):
    if custom_mutate is None:
        def fnMutate(parent):
            return _mutate(parent, geneSet, get_fitness)
    else:
        def fnMutate(parent):
            return _mutate_custom(parent, custom_mutate, get_fitness)

    if custom_create is None:
        def fnGenerateParent():
            return _generate_parent(targetLen, geneSet, get_fitness)
    else:
        def fnGenerateParent():
            genes = custom_create()
            return Chromosome(genes, get_fitness(genes), Strategies.Create)

    strategyLookup = {
        Strategies.Create: lambda p, i, o: fnGenerateParent(),
        Strategies.Mutate: lambda p, i, o: fnMutate(p),
        Strategies.Crossover: lambda p, i, o:_
        crossover(p.Genes, i, o, get_fitness, crossover, fnMutate,
                  fnGenerateParent)
    }

    usedStrategies = [strategyLookup[Strategies.Mutate]]
    if crossover is not None:
        usedStrategies.append(strategyLookup[Strategies.Crossover])

        def fnNewChild(parent, index, parents):
            return random.choice(usedStrategies)(parent, index, parents)
    else:
```

```python
        def fnNewChild(parent, index, parents):
            return fnMutate(parent)

    for timedOut, improvement in _get_improvement(fnNewChild,
                                                  fnGenerateParent, maxAge,
                                                  poolSize, maxSeconds):
        if timedOut:
            return improvement
        display(improvement)
        f = strategyLookup[improvement.Strategy]
        usedStrategies.append(f)
        if not optimalFitness > improvement.Fitness:
            return improvement


def _get_improvement(new_child, generate_parent, maxAge, poolSize,
                     maxSeconds):
    startTime = time.time()
    bestParent = generate_parent()
    yield maxSeconds is not None and time.time() \
        - startTime > maxSeconds, bestParent
    parents = [bestParent]
    historicalFitnesses = [bestParent.Fitness]
    for _ in range(poolSize - 1):
        parent = generate_parent()
        if maxSeconds is not None and time.time() - startTime > maxSeconds:
            yield True, parent
        if parent.Fitness > bestParent.Fitness:
            yield False, parent
            bestParent = parent
            historicalFitnesses.append(parent.Fitness)
        parents.append(parent)
    lastParentIndex = poolSize - 1
    pindex = 1
    while True:
        if maxSeconds is not None and time.time() - startTime > maxSeconds:
            yield True, bestParent
        pindex = pindex - 1 if pindex > 0 else lastParentIndex
        parent = parents[pindex]
        child = new_child(parent, pindex, parents)
        if parent.Fitness > child.Fitness:
            if maxAge is None:
                continue
            parent.Age += 1
            if maxAge > parent.Age:
                continue
            index = bisect_left(historicalFitnesses, child.Fitness, 0,
                                len(historicalFitnesses))
            proportionSimilar = index / len(historicalFitnesses)
            if random.random() < exp(-proportionSimilar):
                parents[pindex] = child
                continue
            bestParent.Age = 0
```

Final code from each project   393

```
            parents[pindex] = bestParent
            continue
        if not child.Fitness > parent.Fitness:
            # same fitness
            child.Age = parent.Age + 1
            parents[pindex] = child
            continue
        child.Age = 0
        parents[pindex] = child
        if child.Fitness > bestParent.Fitness:
            bestParent = child
            yield False, bestParent
            historicalFitnesses.append(bestParent.Fitness)


def hill_climbing(optimizationFunction, is_improvement, is_optimal,
                  get_next_feature_value, display, initialFeatureValue):
    best = optimizationFunction(initialFeatureValue)
    stdout = sys.stdout
    sys.stdout = None
    while not is_optimal(best):
        featureValue = get_next_feature_value(best)
        child = optimizationFunction(featureValue)
        if is_improvement(best, child):
            best = child
            sys.stdout = stdout
            display(best, featureValue)
            sys.stdout = None
    sys.stdout = stdout
    return best


class Chromosome:
    def __init__(self, genes, fitness, strategy):
        self.Genes = genes
        self.Fitness = fitness
        self.Strategy = strategy
        self.Age = 0


class Strategies(Enum):
    Create = 0,
    Mutate = 1,
    Crossover = 2


class Benchmark:
    @staticmethod
    def run(function):
        timings = []
        stdout = sys.stdout
        for i in range(100):
            sys.stdout = None
```

```
            startTime = time.time()
            function()
            seconds = time.time() - startTime
            sys.stdout = stdout
            timings.append(seconds)
            mean = statistics.mean(timings)
            if i < 10 or i % 10 == 9:
                print("{} {:3.2f} {:3.2f}".format(
                    1 + i, mean,
                    statistics.stdev(timings, mean) if i > 1 else 0))
```

Chapter 17: Regular Expressions

regexTests.py

```
# File: regexTests.py
#    from chapter 17 of _Genetic Algorithms with Python_
#
# Author: Clinton Sheppard <fluentcoder@gmail.com>
# Copyright (c) 2016 Clinton Sheppard
#
# Licensed under the Apache License, Version 2.0 (the "License").
# You may not use this file except in compliance with the License.
# You may obtain a copy of the License at
#    http://www.apache.org/licenses/LICENSE-2.0
#
# Unless required by applicable law or agreed to in writing, software
# distributed under the License is distributed on an "AS IS" BASIS,
# WITHOUT WARRANTIES OR CONDITIONS OF ANY KIND, either express or
# implied.  See the License for the specific language governing
# permissions and limitations under the License.

import datetime
import random
import re
import unittest
from functools import partial

import genetic

repeatMetas = {'?', '*', '+', '{2}', '{2,}'}
startMetas = {'|', '(', '['}
endMetas = {')', ']'}
allMetas = repeatMetas | startMetas | endMetas

regexErrorsSeen = {}


def repair_regex(genes):
    result = []
    finals = []
```

```
        f = repair_ignore_repeat_metas
        for token in genes:
            f = f(token, result, finals)
        if ']' in finals and result[-1] == '[':
            del result[-1]
        result.extend(reversed(finals))
        return ''.join(result)


def repair_ignore_repeat_metas(token, result, finals):
    if token in repeatMetas or token in endMetas:
        return repair_ignore_repeat_metas
    if token == '(':
        finals.append(')')
    result.append(token)
    if token == '[':
        finals.append(']')
        return repair_in_character_set
    return repair_ignore_repeat_metas_following_repeat_or_start_metas


def repair_ignore_repeat_metas_following_repeat_or_start_metas(token,
                                                               result,
                                                               finals):
    last = result[-1]
    if token not in repeatMetas:
        if token == '[':
            result.append(token)
            finals.append(']')
            return repair_in_character_set
        if token == '(':
            finals.append(')')
        elif token == ')':
            match = ''.join(finals).rfind(')')
            if match != -1:
                del finals[match]
            else:
                result[0:0] = ['(']
        result.append(token)
    elif last in startMetas:
        pass
    elif token == '?' and last == '?' and len(result) > 2 and \
                    result[-2] in repeatMetas:
        pass
    elif last in repeatMetas:
        pass
    else:
        result.append(token)
    return repair_ignore_repeat_metas_following_repeat_or_start_metas


def repair_in_character_set(token, result, finals):
    if token == ']':
```

```
            if result[-1] == '[':
                del result[-1]
            result.append(token)
            match = ''.join(finals).rfind(']')
            if match != -1:
                del finals[match]
            return repair_ignore_repeat_metas_following_repeat_or_start_metas
        elif token == '[':
            pass
        elif token == '|' and result[-1] == '|':
            pass  # suppresses FutureWarning about ||
        else:
            result.append(token)
    return repair_in_character_set


def get_fitness(genes, wanted, unwanted):
    pattern = repair_regex(genes)
    length = len(pattern)

    try:
        re.compile(pattern)
    except re.error as e:
        key = str(e)
        key = key[:key.index("at position")]
        info = [str(e),
                "genes = ['{}']".format("', '".join(genes)),
                "regex: " + pattern]
        if key not in regexErrorsSeen or len(info[1]) < len(
                regexErrorsSeen[key][1]):
            regexErrorsSeen[key] = info
        return Fitness(0, len(wanted), len(unwanted), length)

    numWantedMatched = sum(1 for i in wanted if re.fullmatch(pattern, i))
    numUnwantedMatched = sum(1 for i in unwanted if re.fullmatch(pattern, i))
    return Fitness(numWantedMatched, len(wanted), numUnwantedMatched,
                   length)


def display(candidate, startTime):
    timeDiff = datetime.datetime.now() - startTime
    print("{}\t{}\t{}".format(
        repair_regex(candidate.Genes), candidate.Fitness, timeDiff))


def mutate_add(genes, geneset):
    index = random.randrange(0, len(genes) + 1) if len(genes) > 0 else 0
    genes[index:index] = [random.choice(geneset)]
    return True


def mutate_remove(genes):
    if len(genes) < 1:
```

```
                return False
        del genes[random.randrange(0, len(genes))]
        if len(genes) > 1 and random.randint(0, 1) == 1:
            del genes[random.randrange(0, len(genes))]
        return True


def mutate_replace(genes, geneset):
    if len(genes) < 1:
        return False
    index = random.randrange(0, len(genes))
    genes[index] = random.choice(geneset)
    return True


def mutate_swap(genes):
    if len(genes) < 2:
        return False
    indexA, indexB = random.sample(range(len(genes)), 2)
    genes[indexA], genes[indexB] = genes[indexB], genes[indexA]
    return True


def mutate_move(genes):
    if len(genes) < 3:
        return False
    start = random.choice(range(len(genes)))
    stop = start + random.randint(1, 2)
    toMove = genes[start:stop]
    genes[start:stop] = []
    index = random.choice(range(len(genes)))
    if index >= start:
        index += 1
    genes[index:index] = toMove
    return True


def mutate_to_character_set(genes):
    if len(genes) < 3:
        return False
    ors = [i for i in range(1, len(genes) - 1)
           if genes[i] == '|' and
           genes[i - 1] not in allMetas and
           genes[i + 1] not in allMetas]
    if len(ors) == 0:
        return False
    shorter = [i for i in ors
               if sum(len(w) for w in genes[i - 1:i + 2:2]) >
               len(set(c for w in genes[i - 1:i + 2:2] for c in w))]
    if len(shorter) == 0:
        return False
    index = random.choice(ors)
    distinct = set(c for w in genes[index - 1:index + 2:2] for c in w)
```

```
        sequence = ['['] + [i for i in distinct] + [']']
        genes[index - 1:index + 2] = sequence
        return True


def mutate_to_character_set_left(genes, wanted):
    if len(genes) < 4:
        return False
    ors = [i for i in range(-1, len(genes) - 3)
              if (i == -1 or genes[i] in startMetas) and
              len(genes[i + 1]) == 2 and
              genes[i + 1] in wanted and
              (len(genes) == i + 1 or genes[i + 2] == '|' or
               genes[i + 2] in endMetas)]
    if len(ors) == 0:
        return False
    lookup = {}
    for i in ors:
        lookup.setdefault(genes[i + 1][0], []).append(i)
    min2 = [i for i in lookup.values() if len(i) > 1]
    if len(min2) == 0:
        return False
    choice = random.choice(min2)
    characterSet = ['|', genes[choice[0] + 1][0], '[']
    characterSet.extend([genes[i + 1][1] for i in choice])
    characterSet.append(']')
    for i in reversed(choice):
        if i >= 0:
            genes[i:i + 2] = []
    genes.extend(characterSet)
    return True


def mutate_add_wanted(genes, wanted):
    index = random.randrange(0, len(genes) + 1) if len(genes) > 0 else 0
    genes[index:index] = ['|'] + [random.choice(wanted)]
    return True


def mutate(genes, fnGetFitness, mutationOperators, mutationRoundCounts):
    initialFitness = fnGetFitness(genes)
    count = random.choice(mutationRoundCounts)
    for i in range(1, count + 2):
        copy = mutationOperators[:]
        func = random.choice(copy)
        while not func(genes):
            copy.remove(func)
            func = random.choice(copy)
        if fnGetFitness(genes) > initialFitness:
            mutationRoundCounts.append(i)
            return
```

```python
class RegexTests(unittest.TestCase):
    def test_two_digits(self):
        wanted = {"01", "11", "10"}
        unwanted = {"00", ""}
        self.find_regex(wanted, unwanted, 7)

    def test_grouping(self):
        wanted = {"01", "0101", "010101"}
        unwanted = {"0011", ""}
        self.find_regex(wanted, unwanted, 5)

    def test_state_codes(self):
        Fitness.UseRegexLength = True
        wanted = {"NE", "NV", "NH", "NJ", "NM", "NY", "NC", "ND"}
        unwanted = {"N" + l for l in "ABCDEFGHIJKLMNOPQRSTUVWXYZ"
                    if "N" + l not in wanted}
        customOperators = [
            partial(mutate_to_character_set_left, wanted=wanted),
        ]
        self.find_regex(wanted, unwanted, 11, customOperators)

    def test_even_length(self):
        wanted = {"00", "01", "10", "11", "0000", "0001", "0010", "0011",
                  "0100", "0101", "0110", "0111", "1000", "1001", "1010",
                  "1011", "1100", "1101", "1110", "1111"}
        unwanted = {"0", "1", "000", "001", "010", "011", "100", "101",
                    "110", "111", ""}
        customOperators = [
            mutate_to_character_set,
        ]
        self.find_regex(wanted, unwanted, 10, customOperators)

    def test_50_state_codes(self):
        Fitness.UseRegexLength = True
        wanted = {"AL", "AK", "AZ", "AR", "CA",
                  "CO", "CT", "DE", "FL", "GA",
                  "HI", "ID", "IL", "IN", "IA",
                  "KS", "KY", "LA", "ME", "MD",
                  "MA", "MI", "MN", "MS", "MO",
                  "MT", "NE", "NV", "NH", "NJ",
                  "NM", "NY", "NC", "ND", "OH",
                  "OK", "OR", "PA", "RI", "SC",
                  "SD", "TN", "TX", "UT", "VT",
                  "VA", "WA", "WV", "WI", "WY"}
        unwanted = {a + b for a in "ABCDEFGHIJKLMNOPQRSTUVWXYZ"
                    for b in "ABCDEFGHIJKLMNOPQRSTUVWXYZ"
                    if a + b not in wanted} | \
                    set(i for i in "ABCDEFGHIJKLMNOPQRSTUVWXYZ")
        customOperators = [
            partial(mutate_to_character_set_left, wanted=wanted),
            mutate_to_character_set,
            partial(mutate_add_wanted, wanted=[i for i in wanted]),
        ]
```

```python
        self.find_regex(wanted, unwanted, 120, customOperators)

    def find_regex(self, wanted, unwanted, expectedLength,
                   customOperators=None):
        startTime = datetime.datetime.now()
        textGenes = wanted | set(c for w in wanted for c in w)
        fullGeneset = [i for i in allMetas | textGenes]

        def fnDisplay(candidate):
            display(candidate, startTime)

        def fnGetFitness(genes):
            return get_fitness(genes, wanted, unwanted)

        mutationRoundCounts = [1]

        mutationOperators = [
            partial(mutate_add, geneset=fullGeneset),
            partial(mutate_replace, geneset=fullGeneset),
            mutate_remove,
            mutate_swap,
            mutate_move,
        ]
        if customOperators is not None:
            mutationOperators.extend(customOperators)

        def fnMutate(genes):
            mutate(genes, fnGetFitness, mutationOperators,
                   mutationRoundCounts)

        optimalFitness = Fitness(len(wanted), len(wanted), 0,
                                 expectedLength)

        best = genetic.get_best(fnGetFitness,
                                max(len(i) for i in textGenes),
                                optimalFitness, fullGeneset, fnDisplay,
                                fnMutate, poolSize=10)
        self.assertTrue(not optimalFitness > best.Fitness)

        for info in regexErrorsSeen.values():
            print("")
            print(info[0])
            print(info[1])
            print(info[2])

    def test_benchmark(self):
        genetic.Benchmark.run(self.test_two_digits)


class Fitness:
    UseRegexLength = False

    def __init__(self, numWantedMatched, totalWanted, numUnwantedMatched,
```

```
            length):
        self.NumWantedMatched = numWantedMatched
        self._totalWanted = totalWanted
        self.NumUnwantedMatched = numUnwantedMatched
        self.Length = length

    def __gt__(self, other):
        combined = (self._totalWanted - self.NumWantedMatched) \
                    + self.NumUnwantedMatched
        otherCombined = (other._totalWanted - other.NumWantedMatched) \
                    + other.NumUnwantedMatched
        if combined != otherCombined:
            return combined < otherCombined
        success = combined == 0
        otherSuccess = otherCombined == 0
        if success != otherSuccess:
            return success
        if not success:
            return self.Length <= other.Length if Fitness.UseRegexLength else False
        return self.Length < other.Length

    def __str__(self):
        return "matches: {} wanted, {} unwanted, len {}".format(
            "all" if self._totalWanted == self.NumWantedMatched else self.
                NumWantedMatched,
            self.NumUnwantedMatched,
            self.Length)


if __name__ == '__main__':
    unittest.main()
```

Chapter 18: Tic-tac-toe

ticTacToeTests.py

```
# File: ticTacToeTests.py
#    from chapter 18 of _Genetic Algorithms with Python_
#
# Author: Clinton Sheppard <fluentcoder@gmail.com>
# Copyright (c) 2016 Clinton Sheppard
#
# Licensed under the Apache License, Version 2.0 (the "License").
# You may not use this file except in compliance with the License.
# You may obtain a copy of the License at
#    http://www.apache.org/licenses/LICENSE-2.0
#
# Unless required by applicable law or agreed to in writing, software
# distributed under the License is distributed on an "AS IS" BASIS,
# WITHOUT WARRANTIES OR CONDITIONS OF ANY KIND, either express or
# implied.  See the License for the specific language governing
```

```
# permissions and limitations under the License.

import datetime
import random
import unittest
from functools import partial

import genetic


def get_fitness(genes):
    localCopy = genes[:]
    fitness = get_fitness_for_games(localCopy)
    fitness.GeneCount = len(genes)
    return fitness


squareIndexes = [1, 2, 3, 4, 5, 6, 7, 8, 9]


def play1on1(xGenes, oGenes):
    board = dict((i, Square(i, ContentType.Empty)) for i in range(1, 9 + 1))
    empties = [v for v in board.values() if v.Content == ContentType.Empty]
    roundData = [[xGenes, ContentType.Mine, genetic.CompetitionResult.Loss,
                    genetic.CompetitionResult.Win],
                 [oGenes, ContentType.Opponent, genetic.CompetitionResult.Win,
                    genetic.CompetitionResult.Loss]]
    playerIndex = 0

    while len(empties) > 0:
        playerData = roundData[playerIndex]
        playerIndex = 1 - playerIndex
        genes, piece, lossResult, winResult = playerData

        moveAndRuleIndex = get_move(genes, board, empties)
        if moveAndRuleIndex is None:   # could not find a move
            return lossResult

        index = moveAndRuleIndex[0]
        board[index] = Square(index, piece)

        mostRecentMoveOnly = [board[index]]
        if len(RowContentFilter(piece, 3).get_matches(board, mostRecentMoveOnly)) > 0 \
            or \
            len(ColumnContentFilter(piece, 3).get_matches(board, mostRecentMoveOnly)) \
                > 0 or \
            len(DiagonalContentFilter(piece, 3).get_matches(board, mostRecentMoveOnly)
                ) > 0:
            return winResult
        empties = [v for v in board.values() if v.Content == ContentType.Empty]
    return genetic.CompetitionResult.Tie
```

```python
def get_fitness_for_games(genes):
    def getBoardString(b):
        return ''.join(map(lambda i:
                           '.' if b[i].Content == ContentType.Empty
                           else 'x' if b[i].Content == ContentType.Mine
                           else 'o', squareIndexes))

    board = dict((i, Square(i, ContentType.Empty)) for i in range(1, 9 + 1))

    queue = [board]
    for square in board.values():
        candiateCopy = board.copy()
        candiateCopy[square.Index] = Square(square.Index, ContentType.Opponent)
        queue.append(candiateCopy)

    winningRules = {}
    wins = ties = losses = 0

    while len(queue) > 0:
        board = queue.pop()
        boardString = getBoardString(board)
        empties = [v for v in board.values() if v.Content == ContentType.Empty]

        if len(empties) == 0:
            ties += 1
            continue

        candidateIndexAndRuleIndex = get_move(genes, board, empties)

        if candidateIndexAndRuleIndex is None:  # could not find a move
            # there are empties but didn't find a move
            losses += 1
            # go to next board
            continue

        # found at least one move
        index = candidateIndexAndRuleIndex[0]
        board[index] = Square(index, ContentType.Mine)
        # newBoardString = getBoardString(board)

        # if we now have three MINE in any ROW, COLUMN or DIAGONAL, we won
        mostRecentMoveOnly = [board[index]]
        if len(iHaveThreeInRow.get_matches(board, mostRecentMoveOnly)) > 0 or \
           len(iHaveThreeInColumn.get_matches(board, mostRecentMoveOnly)) > 0 or \
           len(iHaveThreeInDiagonal.get_matches(board, mostRecentMoveOnly)) > 0:
            ruleId = candidateIndexAndRuleIndex[1]
            if ruleId not in winningRules:
                winningRules[ruleId] = list()
            winningRules[ruleId].append(boardString)
            wins += 1
            # go to next board
            continue
```

```python
        # we lose if any empties have two OPPONENT pieces in ROW, COL or DIAG
        empties = [v for v in board.values() if v.Content == ContentType.Empty]
        if len(opponentHasTwoInARow.get_matches(board, empties)) > 0:
            losses += 1
            # go to next board
            continue

        # queue all possible OPPONENT responses
        for square in empties:
            candiateCopy = board.copy()
            candiateCopy[square.Index] = Square(square.Index,
                                        ContentType.Opponent)
            queue.append(candiateCopy)

    return Fitness(wins, ties, losses, len(genes))


def get_move(ruleSet, board, empties, startingRuleIndex=0):
    ruleSetCopy = ruleSet[:]

    for ruleIndex in range(startingRuleIndex, len(ruleSetCopy)):
        gene = ruleSetCopy[ruleIndex]
        matches = gene.get_matches(board, empties)
        if len(matches) == 0:
            continue
        if len(matches) == 1:
            return [list(matches)[0], ruleIndex]
        if len(empties) > len(matches):
            empties = [e for e in empties if e.Index in matches]

    return None


def display(candidate, startTime):
    timeDiff = datetime.datetime.now() - startTime
    localCopy = candidate.Genes[:]
    for i in reversed(range(len(localCopy))):
        localCopy[i] = str(localCopy[i])

    print("\t{}\n{}\n{}".format(
        '\n\t'.join([d for d in localCopy]),
        candidate.Fitness,
        timeDiff))


def mutate_add(genes, geneset):
    index = random.randrange(0, len(genes) + 1) if len(genes) > 0 else 0
    genes[index:index] = [random.choice(geneset)]
    return True


def mutate_remove(genes):
    if len(genes) < 1:
```

```
            return False
        del genes[random.randrange(0, len(genes))]
        if len(genes) > 1 and random.randint(0, 1) == 1:
            del genes[random.randrange(0, len(genes))]
        return True


def mutate_replace(genes, geneset):
    if len(genes) < 1:
        return False
    index = random.randrange(0, len(genes))
    genes[index] = random.choice(geneset)
    return True


def mutate_swap_adjacent(genes):
    if len(genes) < 2:
        return False
    index = random.choice(range(len(genes) - 1))
    genes[index], genes[index + 1] = genes[index + 1], genes[index]
    return True


def mutate_move(genes):
    if len(genes) < 3:
        return False
    start = random.choice(range(len(genes)))
    stop = start + random.randint(1, 2)
    toMove = genes[start:stop]
    genes[start:stop] = []
    index = random.choice(range(len(genes)))
    if index >= start:
        index += 1
    genes[index:index] = toMove
    return True


def mutate(genes, fnGetFitness, mutationOperators, mutationRoundCounts):
    initialFitness = fnGetFitness(genes)
    count = random.choice(mutationRoundCounts)
    for i in range(1, count + 2):
        copy = mutationOperators[:]
        func = random.choice(copy)
        while not func(genes):
            copy.remove(func)
            func = random.choice(copy)
        if fnGetFitness(genes) > initialFitness:
            mutationRoundCounts.append(i)
            return


def create_geneset():
    options = [[ContentType.Opponent, [0, 1, 2]],
```

```
                    [ContentType.Mine, [0, 1, 2]]]
    geneset = [
        RuleMetadata(RowContentFilter, options),
        RuleMetadata(lambda expectedContent, count: TopRowFilter(), options),
        RuleMetadata(lambda expectedContent, count: MiddleRowFilter(),
                     options),
        RuleMetadata(lambda expectedContent, count: BottomRowFilter(),
                     options),
        RuleMetadata(ColumnContentFilter, options),
        RuleMetadata(lambda expectedContent, count: LeftColumnFilter(),
                     options),
        RuleMetadata(lambda expectedContent, count: MiddleColumnFilter(),
                     options),
        RuleMetadata(lambda expectedContent, count: RightColumnFilter(),
                     options),
        RuleMetadata(DiagonalContentFilter, options),
        RuleMetadata(lambda expectedContent, count: DiagonalLocationFilter(),
                     options),
        RuleMetadata(lambda expectedContent, count: CornerFilter()),
        RuleMetadata(lambda expectedContent, count: SideFilter()),
        RuleMetadata(lambda expectedContent, count: CenterFilter()),
        RuleMetadata(lambda expectedContent, count:
                     RowOppositeFilter(expectedContent), options,
                     needsSpecificContent=True),
        RuleMetadata(lambda expectedContent, count: ColumnOppositeFilter(
            expectedContent), options, needsSpecificContent=True),
        RuleMetadata(lambda expectedContent, count: DiagonalOppositeFilter(
            expectedContent), options, needsSpecificContent=True),
    ]

    genes = list()
    for gene in geneset:
        genes.extend(gene.create_rules())

    print("created " + str(len(genes)) + " genes")
    return genes


class TicTacToeTests(unittest.TestCase):
    def test_perfect_knowledge(self):
        minGenes = 10
        maxGenes = 20
        geneset = create_geneset()
        startTime = datetime.datetime.now()

        def fnDisplay(candidate):
            display(candidate, startTime)

        def fnGetFitness(genes):
            return get_fitness(genes)

        mutationRoundCounts = [1]
```

```
            mutationOperators = [
                partial(mutate_add, geneset=geneset),
                partial(mutate_replace, geneset=geneset),
                mutate_remove,
                mutate_swap_adjacent,
                mutate_move,
            ]

            def fnMutate(genes):
                mutate(genes, fnGetFitness, mutationOperators, mutationRoundCounts)

            def fnCrossover(parent, donor):
                child = parent[0:int(len(parent) / 2)] + \
                        donor[int(len(donor) / 2):]
                fnMutate(child)
                return child

            def fnCreate():
                return random.sample(geneset, random.randrange(minGenes, maxGenes))

        optimalFitness = Fitness(620, 120, 0, 11)
        best = genetic.get_best(fnGetFitness, minGenes, optimalFitness, None,
                                fnDisplay, fnMutate, fnCreate, maxAge=500,
                                poolSize=20, crossover=fnCrossover)
        self.assertTrue(not optimalFitness > best.Fitness)

    def test_tornament(self):
        minGenes = 10
        maxGenes = 20
        geneset = create_geneset()
        startTime = datetime.datetime.now()

        def fnDisplay(genes, wins, ties, losses, generation):
            print("-- generation {} --".format(generation))
            display(genetic.Chromosome(genes,
                                       Fitness(wins, ties, losses, len(genes)),
                                       None), startTime)

        mutationRoundCounts = [1]

        mutationOperators = [
            partial(mutate_add, geneset=geneset),
            partial(mutate_replace, geneset=geneset),
            mutate_remove,
            mutate_swap_adjacent,
            mutate_move,
        ]

        def fnMutate(genes):
            mutate(genes, lambda x: 0, mutationOperators, mutationRoundCounts)

        def fnCrossover(parent, donor):
            child = parent[0:int(len(parent) / 2)] + \
```

```
                        donor[int(len(donor) / 2):]
                fnMutate(child)
                return child

        def fnCreate():
            return random.sample(geneset, random.randrange(minGenes, maxGenes))

        def fnSortKey(genes, wins, ties, losses):
            return -1000 * losses - ties + 1 / len(genes)

        genetic.tournament(fnCreate, fnCrossover, play1on1, fnDisplay,
                            fnSortKey, 13)


class ContentType:
    Empty = 'EMPTY'
    Mine = 'MINE'
    Opponent = 'OPPONENT'


class Square:
    def __init__(self, index, content=ContentType.Empty):
        self.Content = content
        self.Index = index
        self.Diagonals = []
        # board layout is
        #   1  2  3
        #   4  5  6
        #   7  8  9
        self.IsCenter = False
        self.IsCorner = False
        self.IsSide = False
        self.IsTopRow = False
        self.IsMiddleRow = False
        self.IsBottomRow = False
        self.IsLeftColumn = False
        self.IsMiddleColumn = False
        self.IsRightColumn = False
        self.Row = None
        self.Column = None
        self.DiagonalOpposite = None
        self.RowOpposite = None
        self.ColumnOpposite = None

        if index == 1 or index == 2 or index == 3:
            self.IsTopRow = True
            self.Row = [1, 2, 3]
        elif index == 4 or index == 5 or index == 6:
            self.IsMiddleRow = True
            self.Row = [4, 5, 6]
        elif index == 7 or index == 8 or index == 9:
            self.IsBottomRow = True
            self.Row = [7, 8, 9]
```

```
        if index % 3 == 1:
            self.Column = [1, 4, 7]
            self.IsLeftColumn = True
        elif index % 3 == 2:
            self.Column = [2, 5, 8]
            self.IsMiddleColumn = True
        elif index % 3 == 0:
            self.Column = [3, 6, 9]
            self.IsRightColumn = True

        if index == 5:
            self.IsCenter = True
        else:
            if index == 1 or index == 3 or index == 7 or index == 9:
                self.IsCorner = True
            elif index == 2 or index == 4 or index == 6 or index == 8:
                self.IsSide = True

            if index == 1:
                self.RowOpposite = 3
                self.ColumnOpposite = 7
                self.DiagonalOpposite = 9
            elif index == 2:
                self.ColumnOpposite = 8
            elif index == 3:
                self.RowOpposite = 1
                self.ColumnOpposite = 9
                self.DiagonalOpposite = 7
            elif index == 4:
                self.RowOpposite = 6
            elif index == 6:
                self.RowOpposite = 4
            elif index == 7:
                self.RowOpposite = 9
                self.ColumnOpposite = 1
                self.DiagonalOpposite = 3
            elif index == 8:
                self.ColumnOpposite = 2
            else:  # index == 9
                self.RowOpposite = 7
                self.ColumnOpposite = 3
                self.DiagonalOpposite = 1

        if index == 1 or self.DiagonalOpposite == 1 or self.IsCenter:
            self.Diagonals.append([1, 5, 9])
        if index == 3 or self.DiagonalOpposite == 3 or self.IsCenter:
            self.Diagonals.append([7, 5, 3])


class Rule:
    def __init__(self, descriptionPrefix, expectedContent=None, count=None):
        self.DescriptionPrefix = descriptionPrefix
```

```python
        self.ExpectedContent = expectedContent
        self.Count = count

    def __str__(self):
        result = self.DescriptionPrefix + " "
        if self.Count is not None:
            result += str(self.Count) + " "
        if self.ExpectedContent is not None:
            result += self.ExpectedContent + " "
        return result


class RuleMetadata:
    def __init__(self, create, options=None, needsSpecificContent=True,
                 needsSpecificCount=True):
        if options is None:
            needsSpecificContent = False
            needsSpecificCount = False
        if needsSpecificCount and not needsSpecificContent:
            raise ValueError('needsSpecificCount is only valid if '
                'needsSpecificContent is true')
        self.create = create
        self.options = options
        self.needsSpecificContent = needsSpecificContent
        self.needsSpecificCount = needsSpecificCount

    def create_rules(self):
        option = None
        count = None

        seen = set()
        if self.needsSpecificContent:
            rules = list()

            for optionInfo in self.options:
                option = optionInfo[0]
                if self.needsSpecificCount:
                    optionCounts = optionInfo[1]

                    for count in optionCounts:
                        gene = self.create(option, count)
                        if str(gene) not in seen:
                            seen.add(str(gene))
                            rules.append(gene)
                else:
                    gene = self.create(option, None)
                    if str(gene) not in seen:
                        seen.add(str(gene))
                        rules.append(gene)
            return rules
        else:
            return [self.create(option, count)]
```

```python
class ContentFilter(Rule):
    def __init__(self, description, expectedContent, expectedCount,
                 getValueFromSquare):
        super().__init__(description, expectedContent, expectedCount)
        self.getValueFromSquare = getValueFromSquare

    def get_matches(self, board, squares):
        result = set()
        for square in squares:
            m = list(map(lambda i: board[i].Content,
                         self.getValueFromSquare(square)))
            if m.count(self.ExpectedContent) == self.Count:
                result.add(square.Index)
        return result


class RowContentFilter(ContentFilter):
    def __init__(self, expectedContent, expectedCount):
        super().__init__("its ROW has", expectedContent, expectedCount,
                         lambda s: s.Row)


class ColumnContentFilter(ContentFilter):
    def __init__(self, expectedContent, expectedCount):
        super().__init__("its COLUMN has", expectedContent, expectedCount,
                         lambda s: s.Column)


class LocationFilter(Rule):
    def __init__(self, expectedLocation, containerDescription, func):
        super().__init__(
            "is in " + expectedLocation + " " + containerDescription)
        self.func = func

    def get_matches(self, board, squares):
        result = set()
        for square in squares:
            if self.func(square):
                result.add(square.Index)
        return result


class RowLocationFilter(LocationFilter):
    def __init__(self, expectedLocation, func):
        super().__init__(expectedLocation, "ROW", func)


class ColumnLocationFilter(LocationFilter):
    def __init__(self, expectedLocation, func):
        super().__init__(expectedLocation, "COLUMN", func)
```

```python
class TopRowFilter(RowLocationFilter):
    def __init__(self):
        super().__init__("TOP", lambda square: square.IsTopRow)


class MiddleRowFilter(RowLocationFilter):
    def __init__(self):
        super().__init__("MIDDLE", lambda square: square.IsMiddleRow)


class BottomRowFilter(RowLocationFilter):
    def __init__(self):
        super().__init__("BOTTOM", lambda square: square.IsBottomRow)


class LeftColumnFilter(ColumnLocationFilter):
    def __init__(self):
        super().__init__("LEFT", lambda square: square.IsLeftColumn)


class MiddleColumnFilter(ColumnLocationFilter):
    def __init__(self):
        super().__init__("MIDDLE", lambda square: square.IsMiddleColumn)


class RightColumnFilter(ColumnLocationFilter):
    def __init__(self):
        super().__init__("RIGHT", lambda square: square.IsRightColumn)


class DiagonalLocationFilter(LocationFilter):
    def __init__(self):
        super().__init__("DIAGONAL", "",
                         lambda square: not (square.IsMiddleRow or
                                             square.IsMiddleColumn) or
                         square.IsCenter)


class DiagonalContentFilter(Rule):
    def __init__(self, expectedContent, count):
        super().__init__("its DIAGONAL has", expectedContent, count)

    def get_matches(self, board, squares):
        result = set()
        for square in squares:
            for diagonal in square.Diagonals:
                m = list(map(lambda i: board[i].Content, diagonal))
                if m.count(self.ExpectedContent) == self.Count:
                    result.add(square.Index)
                    break
        return result
```

```python
class WinFilter(Rule):
    def __init__(self, content):
        super().__init__("WIN" if content == ContentType
                               .Mine else "block OPPONENT WIN")
        self.rowRule = RowContentFilter(content, 2)
        self.columnRule = ColumnContentFilter(content, 2)
        self.diagonalRule = DiagonalContentFilter(content, 2)

    def get_matches(self, board, squares):
        inDiagonal = self.diagonalRule.get_matches(board, squares)
        if len(inDiagonal) > 0:
            return inDiagonal
        inRow = self.rowRule.get_matches(board, squares)
        if len(inRow) > 0:
            return inRow
        inColumn = self.columnRule.get_matches(board, squares)
        return inColumn


class DiagonalOppositeFilter(Rule):
    def __init__(self, expectedContent):
        super().__init__("DIAGONAL-OPPOSITE is", expectedContent)

    def get_matches(self, board, squares):
        result = set()
        for square in squares:
            if square.DiagonalOpposite is None:
                continue
            if board[square.DiagonalOpposite].Content == self.ExpectedContent:
                result.add(square.Index)
        return result


class RowOppositeFilter(Rule):
    def __init__(self, expectedContent):
        super().__init__("ROW-OPPOSITE is", expectedContent)

    def get_matches(self, board, squares):
        result = set()
        for square in squares:
            if square.RowOpposite is None:
                continue
            if board[square.RowOpposite].Content == self.ExpectedContent:
                result.add(square.Index)
        return result


class ColumnOppositeFilter(Rule):
    def __init__(self, expectedContent):
        super().__init__("COLUMN-OPPOSITE is", expectedContent)

    def get_matches(self, board, squares):
        result = set()
```

```python
        for square in squares:
            if square.ColumnOpposite is None:
                continue
            if board[square.ColumnOpposite].Content == self.ExpectedContent:
                result.add(square.Index)
        return result


class CenterFilter(Rule):
    def __init__(self):
        super().__init__("is in CENTER")

    @staticmethod
    def get_matches(board, squares):
        result = set()
        for square in squares:
            if square.IsCenter:
                result.add(square.Index)
        return result


class CornerFilter(Rule):
    def __init__(self):
        super().__init__("is a CORNER")

    @staticmethod
    def get_matches(board, squares):
        result = set()
        for square in squares:
            if square.IsCorner:
                result.add(square.Index)
        return result


class SideFilter(Rule):
    def __init__(self):
        super().__init__("is SIDE")

    @staticmethod
    def get_matches(board, squares):
        result = set()
        for square in squares:
            if square.IsSide:
                result.add(square.Index)
        return result


iHaveThreeInRow = RowContentFilter(ContentType.Mine, 3)
iHaveThreeInColumn = ColumnContentFilter(ContentType.Mine, 3)
iHaveThreeInDiagonal = DiagonalContentFilter(ContentType.Mine, 3)
opponentHasTwoInARow = WinFilter(ContentType.Opponent)
```

```python
class Fitness:
    def __init__(self, wins, ties, losses, geneCount):
        self.Wins = wins
        self.Ties = ties
        self.Losses = losses
        totalGames = wins + ties + losses
        percentWins = 100 * round(wins / totalGames, 3)
        percentLosses = 100 * round(losses / totalGames, 3)
        percentTies = 100 * round(ties / totalGames, 3)
        self.PercentTies = percentTies
        self.PercentWins = percentWins
        self.PercentLosses = percentLosses
        self.GeneCount = geneCount

    def __gt__(self, other):
        if self.PercentLosses != other.PercentLosses:
            return self.PercentLosses < other.PercentLosses

        if self.Losses > 0:
            return False

        if self.Ties != other.Ties:
            return self.Ties < other.Ties
        return self.GeneCount < other.GeneCount

    def __str__(self):
        return "{:.1f}% Losses ({}), {:.1f}% Ties ({}), {:.1f}% Wins ({}), {} rules".\
            format(
            self.PercentLosses,
            self.Losses,
            self.PercentTies,
            self.Ties,
            self.PercentWins,
            self.Wins,
            self.GeneCount)


if __name__ == '__main__':
    unittest.main()
```

genetic.py

```python
# File: genetic.py
#     from chapter 18 of _Genetic Algorithms with Python_
#
# Author: Clinton Sheppard <fluentcoder@gmail.com>
# Copyright (c) 2016 Clinton Sheppard
#
# Licensed under the Apache License, Version 2.0 (the "License").
# You may not use this file except in compliance with the License.
# You may obtain a copy of the License at
#    http://www.apache.org/licenses/LICENSE-2.0
```

```
#
# Unless required by applicable law or agreed to in writing, software
# distributed under the License is distributed on an "AS IS" BASIS,
# WITHOUT WARRANTIES OR CONDITIONS OF ANY KIND, either express or
# implied.  See the License for the specific language governing
# permissions and limitations under the License.

import random
import statistics
import sys
import time
from bisect import bisect_left
from enum import Enum
from enum import IntEnum
from math import exp


def _generate_parent(length, geneSet, get_fitness):
    genes = []
    while len(genes) < length:
        sampleSize = min(length - len(genes), len(geneSet))
        genes.extend(random.sample(geneSet, sampleSize))
    fitness = get_fitness(genes)
    return Chromosome(genes, fitness, Strategies.Create)


def _mutate(parent, geneSet, get_fitness):
    childGenes = parent.Genes[:]
    index = random.randrange(0, len(parent.Genes))
    newGene, alternate = random.sample(geneSet, 2)
    childGenes[index] = alternate if newGene == childGenes[index] else newGene
    fitness = get_fitness(childGenes)
    return Chromosome(childGenes, fitness, Strategies.Mutate)


def _mutate_custom(parent, custom_mutate, get_fitness):
    childGenes = parent.Genes[:]
    custom_mutate(childGenes)
    fitness = get_fitness(childGenes)
    return Chromosome(childGenes, fitness, Strategies.Mutate)


def _crossover(parentGenes, index, parents, get_fitness, crossover, mutate,
               generate_parent):
    donorIndex = random.randrange(0, len(parents))
    if donorIndex == index:
        donorIndex = (donorIndex + 1) % len(parents)
    childGenes = crossover(parentGenes, parents[donorIndex].Genes)
    if childGenes is None:
        # parent and donor are indistinguishable
        parents[donorIndex] = generate_parent()
        return mutate(parents[index])
    fitness = get_fitness(childGenes)
```

```
        return Chromosome(childGenes, fitness, Strategies.Crossover)


def get_best(get_fitness, targetLen, optimalFitness, geneSet, display,
             custom_mutate=None, custom_create=None, maxAge=None,
             poolSize=1, crossover=None, maxSeconds=None):
    if custom_mutate is None:
        def fnMutate(parent):
            return _mutate(parent, geneSet, get_fitness)
    else:
        def fnMutate(parent):
            return _mutate_custom(parent, custom_mutate, get_fitness)

    if custom_create is None:
        def fnGenerateParent():
            return _generate_parent(targetLen, geneSet, get_fitness)
    else:
        def fnGenerateParent():
            genes = custom_create()
            return Chromosome(genes, get_fitness(genes), Strategies.Create)

    strategyLookup = {
        Strategies.Create: lambda p, i, o: fnGenerateParent(),
        Strategies.Mutate: lambda p, i, o: fnMutate(p),
        Strategies.Crossover: lambda p, i, o:_
        crossover(p.Genes, i, o, get_fitness, crossover, fnMutate,
                  fnGenerateParent)
    }

    usedStrategies = [strategyLookup[Strategies.Mutate]]
    if crossover is not None:
        usedStrategies.append(strategyLookup[Strategies.Crossover])

        def fnNewChild(parent, index, parents):
            return random.choice(usedStrategies)(parent, index, parents)
    else:
        def fnNewChild(parent, index, parents):
            return fnMutate(parent)

    for timedOut, improvement in _get_improvement(fnNewChild,
                                                  fnGenerateParent, maxAge,
                                                  poolSize, maxSeconds):
        if timedOut:
            return improvement
        display(improvement)
        f = strategyLookup[improvement.Strategy]
        usedStrategies.append(f)
        if not optimalFitness > improvement.Fitness:
            return improvement


def _get_improvement(new_child, generate_parent, maxAge, poolSize,
                     maxSeconds):
```

```
    startTime = time.time()
    bestParent = generate_parent()
    yield maxSeconds is not None and time.time() - \
        startTime > maxSeconds, bestParent
    parents = [bestParent]
    historicalFitnesses = [bestParent.Fitness]
    for _ in range(poolSize - 1):
        parent = generate_parent()
        if maxSeconds is not None and time.time() - startTime > maxSeconds:
            yield True, parent
        if parent.Fitness > bestParent.Fitness:
            yield False, parent
            bestParent = parent
            historicalFitnesses.append(parent.Fitness)
        parents.append(parent)
    lastParentIndex = poolSize - 1
    pindex = 1
    while True:
        if maxSeconds is not None and time.time() - startTime > maxSeconds:
            yield True, bestParent
        pindex = pindex - 1 if pindex > 0 else lastParentIndex
        parent = parents[pindex]
        child = new_child(parent, pindex, parents)
        if parent.Fitness > child.Fitness:
            if maxAge is None:
                continue
            parent.Age += 1
            if maxAge > parent.Age:
                continue
            index = bisect_left(historicalFitnesses, child.Fitness, 0,
                                len(historicalFitnesses))
            proportionSimilar = index / len(historicalFitnesses)
            if random.random() < exp(-proportionSimilar):
                parents[pindex] = child
                continue
            bestParent.Age = 0
            parents[pindex] = bestParent
            continue
        if not child.Fitness > parent.Fitness:
            # same fitness
            child.Age = parent.Age + 1
            parents[pindex] = child
            continue
        child.Age = 0
        parents[pindex] = child
        if child.Fitness > bestParent.Fitness:
            bestParent = child
            yield False, bestParent
            historicalFitnesses.append(bestParent.Fitness)


def hill_climbing(optimizationFunction, is_improvement, is_optimal,
                  get_next_feature_value, display, initialFeatureValue):
```

```
    best = optimizationFunction(initialFeatureValue)
    stdout = sys.stdout
    sys.stdout = None
    while not is_optimal(best):
        featureValue = get_next_feature_value(best)
        child = optimizationFunction(featureValue)
        if is_improvement(best, child):
            best = child
            sys.stdout = stdout
            display(best, featureValue)
            sys.stdout = None
    sys.stdout = stdout
    return best


def tournament(generate_parent, crossover, compete, display, sort_key,
               numParents=10, max_generations=100):
    pool = [[generate_parent(), [0, 0, 0]] for _ in
            range(1 + numParents * numParents)]
    best, bestScore = pool[0]

    def getSortKey(x):
        return sort_key(x[0], x[1][CompetitionResult.Win],
                        x[1][CompetitionResult.Tie],
                        x[1][CompetitionResult.Loss])

    generation = 0
    while generation < max_generations:
        generation += 1
        for i in range(0, len(pool)):
            for j in range(0, len(pool)):
                if i == j:
                    continue
                playera, scorea = pool[i]
                playerb, scoreb = pool[j]
                result = compete(playera, playerb)
                scorea[result] += 1
                scoreb[2 - result] += 1

        pool.sort(key=getSortKey, reverse=True)
        if getSortKey(pool[0]) > getSortKey([best, bestScore]):
            best, bestScore = pool[0]
            display(best, bestScore[CompetitionResult.Win],
                    bestScore[CompetitionResult.Tie],
                    bestScore[CompetitionResult.Loss], generation)

        parents = [pool[i][0] for i in range(numParents)]
        pool = [[crossover(parents[i], parents[j]), [0, 0, 0]]
                for i in range(len(parents))
                for j in range(len(parents))
                if i != j]
        pool.extend([parent, [0, 0, 0]] for parent in parents)
        pool.append([generate_parent(), [0, 0, 0]])
```

```python
        return best


class CompetitionResult(IntEnum):
    Loss = 0,
    Tie = 1,
    Win = 2,


class Chromosome:
    def __init__(self, genes, fitness, strategy):
        self.Genes = genes
        self.Fitness = fitness
        self.Strategy = strategy
        self.Age = 0


class Strategies(Enum):
    Create = 0,
    Mutate = 1,
    Crossover = 2


class Benchmark:
    @staticmethod
    def run(function):
        timings = []
        stdout = sys.stdout
        for i in range(100):
            sys.stdout = None
            startTime = time.time()
            function()
            seconds = time.time() - startTime
            sys.stdout = stdout
            timings.append(seconds)
            mean = statistics.mean(timings)
            if i < 10 or i % 10 == 9:
                print("{} {:3.2f} {:3.2f}".format(
                    1 + i, mean,
                    statistics.stdev(timings, mean) if i > 1 else 0))
```

Made in the USA
Las Vegas, NV
17 April 2021